COACHING THE
YOUNG SWIMMER

COACHING THE YOUNG SWIMMER

Kurt Wilke

and

Ørjan Madsen

Translated from the German by Paul Perkins

PELHAM BOOKS

English edition first published in Great Britain by
Pelham Books Ltd
27 Wrights Lane
Kensington
London W8
1986

First published in the Federal Republic
of Germany as *Das Training des Jugendlichen
Schwimmers* by
Verlag Karl Hofmann
7060 Schorndorf
Steinwasenstrasse 6–8
1983

Drawings: Karlheinz Grindler
Graphs: Ursula Düse
Photographs: the authors

British Library Cataloguing in Publication Data
Wilke, Kurt
  Coaching the young swimmer.
  1. Swimming—Training
  I. Title   II. Madsen, Ørjan   III. Das
  Training des jugendlichen Schwimmers.
  English
  797.2′1   GV837.7

ISBN 0 7207 1676 4

Typeset by Cambrian Typesetters
Frimley, Camberley, Surrey.
Printed in Great Britain by
Butler & Tanner, Frome, Somerset

Contents

PREFACE   vii

FOREWORD   ix

INTRODUCTION   xi

1 The theoretical basis of a training schedule for an age-group
  swimmer   1

2 Planning a long-term training programme   13

3 Hints on mental development and mental-attitude
  coaching   19

4 Composition and emphases of a long-term training
  programme   23

5 Skills essential to competitive swimming and their
  importance in planning the training programme   28

6 The four strokes, starts and turns   34

7 Swimming technique exercises   48

8 Flexibility training   104

9 Endurance in relation to swimming   118

10 Control of training using load norms   123

11 Training for basic swimming endurance   125

12 Training for basic swimming speed   138

13 Strength training and swimming   149

14 Training for swimming speed endurance   188

15 The element of competition in the training schedule   195

16 Dividing up the training year   200

17 Hints on training methods for the individual training years,
   distances and composition of training   211

18 Criteria for classification into different training groups   237

19 Organisation of swimming training   243

20 Examples of training sessions   246

21 Methods of determining the level of physical condition –
   swimming-related tests   262
22 Tapering   271
23 Overtraining   278
24 Recovery measures   282
25 Technical terms   283
   REFERENCES   295
   INDEX   300

Preface

Swimming experts, training supervisers, teachers and coaches have long awaited this book.

How should the young swimmer begin exercising and training? How should he develop his capabilities and achieve mastery? What training content should most appropriately constitute the emphasis in his or her work, and when? And what does a comprehensible development schedule related to serious pedagogical categories look like?

All these are questions which have just been touched on *en passant* in other works: here they are at the very centre of things.

The two authors, Kurt Wilke and Ørjan Madsen, have graduated from the hard school of competitive sport. As successful coaches and university lecturers, they have now written a book which combines years of practical experience and scientific know-how with critical reflection.

May this book find its way into the hands of all those interested in or making a contribution to swimming and may it prove helpful in their activities.

W. GÜNTHER LINGENAU
Vice-president of the German Swimming Association

Foreword

When one looks through the literature on swimming, one is struck by the fact that there are a number of publications providing an introduction for the beginner and instruction on the various swimming strokes. Coaching literature for swimming relates in the main to the trained competitive swimmer or even the top-class swimmer, particularly the books of James E. Counsilman. There is virtually no theory or systematic instruction on how a swimming-loving talented boy or girl, having learned a few strokes, can be set on a promising path towards competitive swimming, and how this path can be made to lead to national level. We trust that *Coaching the Young Swimmer* may help to fill this void.

The content and structure of a long-term training programme for a young swimmer (or 'age-group' swimmer) naturally proceed from particular concepts or theories. The basis of this book is a review of the results of scientific coaching literature, of swimming training practices, chiefly in the USA, USSR, East Germany and Australia, of contributions from sports educationalists and of personal experience as active swimmers, coaches, sports officials and teachers.

A review and synthesis of such varied sources must, on the one hand, not neglect a profound consideration of individual points-of-view, and, on the other, ought to mediate between absolute demands. We have consequently had to do some pruning when imparting information on strength training in order to arrive at an acceptable compromise with demands made by endurance training in the water.

In our view, the greatest contradictions occur between the considerable time demands which have to be met in accordance with the tenets of training theory and the overall pedagogic/human responsibility towards the young swimmer.

The fact that the authors, in full awareness of this difficulty, have made an attempt with this book to offer the age-group swimmer and his coach an aid to planning and implementing his training schedule, and to offer the parents involved and association and club officials an aid which will provide information and assist in decision making, could be adjudged to be a confession: a confession on the part of the authors that they are, even today, convinced that it is still worthwhile for young people to devote several years of their lives to competitive swimming, and that this commitment need in no way conflict with the serious interests of their later life or of our society.

When we have talked up to now and will, for convenience, speak in the book as a whole of the young swimmer or the age-group swimmer as 'he', we intend these expressions to cover swimmers of both sexes.

We are particularly grateful to our colleagues Armin Lang and Wolfgang Kremer, who, after a critical read-through of the first draft, encouraged us in the preparation of the text and offered a great deal of expert advice.

KURT WILKE AND ØRJAN MADSEN

Introduction

Competitive swimming can be an enriching and exciting episode in the life of a young person: a continuous battle with the water, but also enjoyment of the water; training efforts; the excitement of races; the joy of success; disappointment over defeats; travel and new impressions; meeting people and making new friends. Sooner or later, however, other priorities in life assert themselves: training and races decline and eventually peter out completely. The swimmer is left with the memories of an eventful sporting interlude.

Competitive swimming can, however, also represent a life-long enrichment, providing more than just memories. It can in addition influence relationships with other areas of human existence and with later periods in the swimmer's life. These areas include enjoyment of water; conditioning to regular stress; voluntary acceptance of commitments; integration into a group of people with different roles; the development of realistic but increasingly demanding targets; the steadfast pursuance of these targets; early planning of one's life, making allowance for those around one; the essential integration of the centre of activity of swimming into the other demands of life; early absolute commitment with occasional disappointments; coming to terms with failures and defeats, but with overall confirmation of one's own abilities.

Even this brief inventory of the human possibilities which a swimming career can offer makes it obvious that each particular opportunity also carries with it the danger of its adverse or detrimental development. The responsibility of all those concerned with the young person's upbringing is consequently considerable. The responsibility is particularly onerous since boys and girls are involved in this development from such an early age. Their appreciation of its significance therefore lags behind that of the adults around them. For this reason, coaches, parents, swimming club supervisors and teachers should be continuously aware of this educational responsibility when planning a long-term swimming career, and in their service to the sport in general.

Let us illustrate the difficulties associated with such a responsibility by two problems, the possible solutions to which are the essence of this book.

1   A number of biological advantages in childhood, such as a low body-weight in relation to body surface, or the high trainability of the cardio-circulatory system, favour an early start on high-pressure training related to this system. These factors also favour early specialisation on particular swimming strokes or competitive disciplines. The frequently observed steep rise in performance resulting from early heavy stress and specialisation appears to confirm the appropriateness of this form of training.

In spite of this, if a multi-year development-oriented training schedule, with comprehensive basic swimming instruction during the childhood years and comparatively late specialisation, is subsequently recommended, this is because as a result of early training and early specialisation, one can indeed expect an early and/or steeper rise in performance, but also a 'short high-performance phase, rapid fall-off in performance and a premature end to the swimmer's career' (Feige 1973).

A swimming career which is years longer and a peak period which occurs later, but is maintained longer, fully justify the input of all those involved, in time, energy and money. This relationship between input and sporting return applies in the first instance to the young swimmer himself. It is vital that *he* is aware that his personal peak will occur later, but that in absolute terms it will be somewhat superior to that of an 'early starter'.

Up to this point the planning of the training schedule is less a matter of pedagogics than of down-to-earth sporting and economic consider-ations, extending even as far as international top-level swimming.

A more evident educational responsibility is the consideration that the young athlete should, assuming a protracted career, reach the age of physical and mental stability in order to practise his competitive sport knowledgeably and to fit it in sensibly with his later life.

2   Even a carefully planned training programme, approved by all those concerned, will, when the age-group swimmer progresses to high-pressure training, come up against the competing demands of schooling. The day simply does not seem long enough to fit in school time, doing one's homework thoroughly, one or two workouts, and periodic time-consuming preparation for examinations.

The existence of these difficulties is inevitable. But teachers and coaches should not attempt to avoid them by moving peak training forward into childhood, for the reasons given earlier, especially since an early improvement in performance conceals the danger of later stagnation and an early end to the swimmer's career. Neither should a swimming career be terminated permaturely in favour of essential schooling demands and equally – and this could even be a fundamental objection – school development towards professional training should not be completely neglected on the grounds of a highly uncertain assessment of sporting success. This is a difficulty which has to be acknowledged and faced up to.

It must be borne in mind that, in the emotionally strong attachment of a young person to the sport, the swimmer may see a great opportunity to organise himself from an early age and to arrange his life around an aim of his own choosing. This is particularly true when the young person refuses to accept other targets set by the adult world or is not capable of appreciating them.

The above-mentioned conflict between time demands of schooling and those of training can only be overcome by long-term integration of the two fields of activity. The basis of this is formed by a gradually progressive planning and regulation of the daily timetable and also gradually increasing periods of up to a year. The young athlete should be aware of how he is making use of the time available. Naturally, to start with he needs the help of parents and coach. As time passes he can tackle longer periods and greater sporting challenges with an awareness of 'achievability'. He has to learn, however, that the only way to train is by fulfilling school obligations properly. The guardianship of the responsible adults around should prevent any imbalances occurring between pretensions to sporting success and an unsatisfactory performance at school. Such imbalances almost inevitably lead to insuperable conflicts, to stress initiating failure and to emotional perplexity. They can never be the basis for sustained performance or for a positive sporting experience.

How tedious and painstaking the road to becoming a top-flight swimmer is has to be spelled out in detail. It is not aimed at brilliant early successes, but has as its goal sound swimming and human development up to participation in regional and national competitions. It covers a period of six to eight years. This book is designed to help swimmers achieve this goal as surely as possible and without unnecessary detours.

One thing, of course, has to be stressed. If the above goal is to be achieved with the help of the recommendations and proposals made here, and if inclination, success and a kind of sporting philosophy constitute a stimulus to facing great international challenges in top-level sport, then the athlete must ask himself again, and with a far greater degree of seriousness, whether he is to give preference in his life to concentrating on competitive swimming or to his professional development.

On the basis of past experience, the path of parallel development of the two fields of activity is hardly an option any longer. This is the point at which a decision has to be taken over where the emphasis is to lie in the next few years.

In cases where the decision goes in favour of swimming, it also implies that the success of a school year or of a term will be sacrificed to the great international championships.

Whatever the swimmer decides, to go for a multi-year international swimming career or for steady, careful schooling and professional training, one thing should have been ensured by the educationally responsible path followed up to that point. That is that the decision is taken for the right reasons: not because a swimming career has been described enthusiastically and in rosy tones, nor as a result of bitterness over an unpromising school career. He or she should be in a position to choose between the two specialisations deliberately and in complete freedom.

An essential constituent of a development-related training programme, which serves at the same time as an impetus to reorientation, is a comparatively late start in competition. Strictly speaking, it is not the timing of the first races that is shifted, but the nature and manner of the stress from the races which changes. This is based on the principle that competitiveness is not simply a result of training but that races too have to be studied. The stresses involved in competition are appropriately graded for the age-group swimmer. The graduation relates both to the physical stress and to the associated mental stress.

Like the planning of a training programme, the pre-planning of a competition schedule starts by assuming ideal conditions. Naturally no swimmer and no coach encounters such ideal conditions, which means that the programme has to be adjusted again and again and alternative solutions found. In many instances in the chapters of this book, alternative solutions found. In many instances in the chapters of this book, alternative solutions and possible methods of training are given for restricted conditions. The frequently expressed desire of tailoring the entire training of the age-group swimmer to a minimum demand for training time, water area and equipment, cannot be entertained for three reasons:

a) With such a policy, the main features of the training programme would be watered down out of all recognition. It would no longer be possible to recognise the fundamental features of the concept.

b) The constant striving for improved training conditions would disappear: satisfaction with restricted conditions and continuous improvisation could fundamentally affect attitudes towards the sport.

c) In relation to international swimming, even with talented and willing young people, it would neither be possible to reach their potential personal performance, nor to achieve the competitiveness of which they are potentially capable.

It therefore seems appropriate to base the basic representation of the training schedule on favourable conditions in order to demonstrate clearly to all concerned the direction in which essential improvements in training conditions should be aimed.

This endeavour should not, of course, prevent optimum use being made of existing modest facilities.

The reader may be surprised at times to come across numerous references and indications of sources, while in other chapters there are no such references. The explanation is that, in view of the practical nature of the book as a coaching manual, references have been limited to pronouncements and recommendations which will be new to most readers and which may differ to some extent from previous coaching practices.

1 The theoretical basis of a training schedule for an age-group swimmer

SPORTS COACHING AS A MULTI-DIMENSIONAL FORM OF HUMAN EDUCATION

Physical activities such as the learning and drilling of sporting movements are associated with intellectual and emotional processes in the participant.

In sports coaching, for this reason, despite the predominantly physical nature of the activity, attention also has to be paid to effects in intellectual and emotional areas. In addition, any long-term training schedule should include 'training' of intellectual, emotional and attitude-related components as an essential prerequisite for performance. Accordingly, both in the overall plan for a long-term (multi-year) swimming training schedule (TABLE 1) and in the hints for the individual training years (pp. 211–36), details have been given of important mental-attitude objectives (see p. 19 ff).

In some cases this is a matter of acquiring simple knowledge, such as competition rules or movement patterns. It can now be regarded as definite that mental analysis of the essential features of a particular stroke assists in its correct and deliberate execution. 'The qualitatively better instruction of a sporting technique in the initial coaching of children demands at the same time that this instruction process be intellectually more strictly controlled. In extensive experiments conducted using various scientific disciplines, we have found that there is a reliable correlation between intellectual performance and stress and aspiration levels and the physical sporting area' (Thiess/Gropler 1978, 200).

What is more, the long-term collaboration between age-group swimmer and coach calls for the development of a common under-

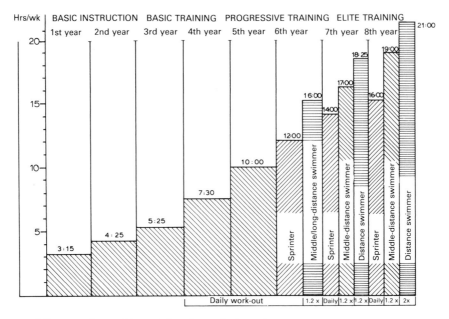

FIG. 1 Increase in weekly training times (in hours)

standing of diagrams and sports terminology. This eventually gives the athlete an understanding of the relationship between energy expenditure on a movement and the result, between systematic training and the success of that training, and also an understanding of an appropriate attitude. This is based on the conviction that a child is more likely to be prepared to devote himself to swimming through the critical period of puberty if he or she derives intellectual satisfaction from swimming. 'The mental age peculiarities of this stage of individual development permit to a considerable extent the development of lasting positive attitudes to regular sporting activities. It should also be mentioned that reasonable physical activity constitutes a "stimulus" for intellectual functions' (Israel/Buhl 1980, 199).

VARIETY IN TRAINING FOR SWIMMING

'Training based on only a few factors can admittedly result in a temporary improvement in performance in relation to a particular discipline or event, but it prevents systematic performance development and the achievement of best performances at peak performance age, because favourable development phases can only be used in an unsatisfactory manner to bring out the essential prerequisites for performance. It has been found, for example, that age-group swimmers who have spent up to 70 per cent of general training on dry land will attain the same levels of achievement in swimming events as those swimmers who have had the opposite proportions in training and were exposed to a one-sided training programme for the development of specific basic endurance' (Rahn/Räsch 1978, 684/685).

During the long-term programme, the total volume of training increases from year to year. According to Matveyev/Moltsinikolov (1979), specialised training for a particular sport increases by up to 100 per cent from the first to the third year. Such an increase in the volume of training can hardly be achieved if a limited number of methods and forms of training are used. Because of the comparatively narrow range of movements possible in water, this limitation is particularly evident in the case of swimming.

Swimming training based on only a limited number of methods and forms inevitably results in special training measures being employed at a very early age. Admittedly, the use of special training measures during the early years can produce considerable successes, since the demands of the exercise apply an unusual stimulus to the child's or young person's organism and stimulate great adaptations. However, 'when the training method* and forms of loading are narrow and specific, reserves of psycho-physical potential are prematurely exhausted. This retards the further development of subsequent sporting performances, because athletic ability and the quality of swimming technique cannot keep up with the work load if the child is forced to undertake specific preparation' (Rahn/Räsch 1978, 685). Stiehler too (1974) warns of unbalanced sporting stresses in childhood producing early stagnation or deterioration of performance.

It is therefore a question, at least for the period from childhood to puberty, of avoiding frequently repeated stresses which exclusively involve individual parts of the body, organs or functions (Israel/Buhl 1980).

'Varied basic physical exercise and sports instruction is required as a basis for the development of good performances in a sport or discipline, because the young organism needs varied growth stimuli, whereby the maximum development of the various physical factors determining performance is possible. Since this task cannot be performed by a particular sport or discipline on its own, other training methods*, so-called "general training methods", should be used in

---

*The term 'training method' is used by the authors here in the sense of forms of training, i.e. of sports and movement sequences used in training.

training, in addition to the training methods specific to the sport or discipline' (Schroeder 1978, 173).

During this period (between childhood and puberty) swimming training is not necessarily synonymous with training in the water.

Although the general training methods using sports other than swimming decrease throughout the training years in favour of training methods specific to swimming, their use with children and young people should never be allowed to fall below a lower limit of 30 per cent (Schroeder 1978, Tschiene 1977).

The variety of methods and forms of training used, particularly for young swimmers up to puberty, is necessary because children, and in most cases teenagers too, have generally not yet acquired the ability to strive persistently after a goal, or the conscious staying power necessary to achieve long-term goals. They need intermediate targets which are not too far off and which can be reached. They look for immediate objectives which they think they can achieve and for which they are prepared to make the effort.

Thereafter, what they want above all is a return for their efforts in order to be able to tackle the next section (in later years known as a training cycle) with as many changes and new stimuli as possible, and remaining a challenge that is within their sights. If, however, there is too great a similarity between the intermediate targets and their contents (methods and forms of training), the novelty stimulus is lacking. The known and anticipated sequence of too many similar training sections produces a feeling of discouragement in having to cope with excessively long and monotonous periods.

A further drawback of unbalanced training and early specialization has proved to be increased susceptibility to injury and illness.

After the general strength of the whole organism has been raised to a high level by varied loading of as many organs as possible, then specific training can be applied without harm to individual organs (Rahn 1977, Matveyev 1977).

In this way the general athletic condition of the young swimmer can be considerably improved. This is in most cases manifested in reduced susceptibility to illness or injury.

Susceptibility to illness is particularly relevant in the case of competitive swimmers. Training for several hours a day in a uniformly air-conditioned swimming pool, in uniformly heated and chlorinated water, conditions the body exclusively to those conditions to such an extent that sudden environmental changes, e.g. a trip to a swimming competition or to a training camp, can cause a drop in performance and even illness.

As the amount of training in the water increases, intermittent stressing on dry land is necessary, particularly in fresh air and sun.

Running in the woods, cycling, cross-country skiing, rowing or canoeing contribute considerably to maintaining or improving the desired vitality of the swimmer.

PRIORITY OF SWIMMING TECHNIQUE INSTRUCTION AND DEVELOPMENT OF COORDINATION AT THE BASIC INSTRUCTION STAGE

'The younger the child the more uniform the motor talent appears' (Filippovich/Turevskii 1977, 506). This finding is the result of research on talented children and youngsters selected from various sports, including swimming. The basic motor skill of a child can be established before his twelfth year; it presents no problem in most sports or main movements. It is not possible, however, using reliable scientific methods, to forecast the child's specific aptitude for one sport, for one swimming stroke or even for a particular swimming distance. An experiment on 45 fourteen-year-old male swimmers, who, on the grounds of their assumed talent, had been successfully trained for three years in a Czech sports school, revealed that swimming performance was up to 62 per cent determined by physical development. The body weight and body size of the swimmers were above the average for untrained lads of the same age (Komadel 1975). Accelerated growth, combined with regular training, influenced swimming performances far more than the assumed talent.

It is easier to understand this finding if one bears in mind the changes in growth and maturation a young person goes through during puberty and in the period up to adolescence (roughly the thirteenth to seventeenth year in the case of girls and fifteenth to nineteenth in boys). Above-average increases in body length and weight of 12 to 15 cm and 12 to 15 kg a year occur in puberty (Winter 1979). Despite the temporary upset to coordination, this only has an adverse effect on swimming technique if the different movement patterns have not been carefully learned and practised before and after the surges in growth.

If, for example, a child has learned the technique of the crawl with quite specific positional and time-related movement patterns of arms and legs, the same patterns will in all probability no longer apply, because the length of his or her limbs, the associated lever ratios and the weight and force conditions will have changed appreciably.

The centre of gravity of a child's body differs considerably from that of an adult up to the twelfth year, after which it gradually becomes the same (Komadel 1975).

It is during puberty that the legs reach their final length, although arm length and especially shoulder width often follow considerably later. This phenomenon frequently leads to the false conclusion that a child who is talented at sport in general or is even a talented swimmer has an exceptional gift as a breaststroke swimmer. There have been instances where the apparently outstanding breaststroke talent has levelled out after the physical changes described above. Despite his talent as a swimmer, the age-group swimmer concerned did not achieve any particular competition successes, since, given the false evaluation, he only mastered breaststroke swimming and not the full range of strokes.

It should consequently be the main concern of basic sports motor coaching and a large part of the basic swimming training to learn all four competitive strokes and to consolidate them by frequent and correct grooving. In addition to this fixed store of movement patterns which are to be practised very precisely (Demeter 1981), there are a great many movements in the water which occasionally crop up in coaching and which are only performed from time to time. These include the variations, e.g. early breathing and late breathing, six-beat and two-beat kicks, different starts and turns, as well as a multiplicity of swimming technique exercises (cf. p. 48). Despite their infrequent use, all participants in a training group should be able to swim all the variations.

Besides the multiplicity of different movement patterns, in view of the varying anatomical relationships of the body during puberty and adolescence, the coordinative skills too should be continually put to the test.

This involves learning at least one new movement pattern in every instructional session.

What is more important, however, is to undertake and practise growth-conditioned adaptation of coordination patterns learned earlier. 'The control of movement must be tuned to the varying characteristics of the body. This situation, together with the necessity for the further development of speed and coordination, renders it necessary to maintain continuously appropriate coordination adjustments in the programme of controlled physical development. This means that the mastery of new movement patterns (in the form of swimming strokes, say), should have a permanent place in the sports coaching programme' (Israel/Buhl 1980, 196).

The first years of training are dominated by the learning and practising of numerous movement patterns (so-called technique training), occupying up to 60 or 70 per cent of training time (Thiess/ Gropler 1978). Periodic practising of other sports, such as athletics, gymnastics and games, increases the number of movement patterns which can be learned. In addition to contributing to general athletic development, this helps the coordinative flexibility referred to above.

According to recent motor learning theories, chiefly the 'schema' or 'pattern' learning theory (Schmidt 1975, Pew 1974, Kerr 1977), the quality of the adaptation of movement patterns already learned depends on the altered external and internal conditions. This in turn depends essentially on how many different movement patterns have actually been learned and on how often they have been performed in modified form (variants).

The necessity for the widest and most flexible possible motor development is also derived from the experience that all swimming takes place in a comparatively uniform and unstimulating environment. There are few sports in which the entire exercising, drilling and training take place in such constant ambient conditions (water, swimming pool, training lanes, equipment).

The demand for movement patterns, variants and game-disguised exercises is limited compared with almost all land sports.

For precisely this reason, the coaching of children and young swimmers calls for the greatest possible variation in movement patterns and training methods in order to avoid monotony, boredom and an inward aversion to swimming.

An injury or a strain can be overcome without a break in training if the swimmer can swim a different stroke which does not aggravate the injury. Since a 'specialist' in a particular stroke can swim only a part of his programme in his stroke and because the training lanes are usually crowded out by a large number of swimmers, every swimmer in a training group should be capable of swimming for long sessions without disturbing the others. These sessions consist of movement patterns and swimming technique exercises not associated with the individual's special stroke.

The most important argument in support of variety in swimming coaching has been around for a while: that complete stagnation of performance in one stroke and the associated loss of motivation in the age-group swimmer can be brought under control, provided the other strokes are being swum well. Briefly stepping up training in the weaker stroke can often improve performance and restore the swimmer's confidence. Finally, one has to consider the possibility that a swimmer with only average motor skills may have an above-average chance of success in medley swimming if he can call on a basis of comprehensive coaching. This includes not only mastery of all four strokes, but also the ability to switch from one movement pattern to another, to use arms and legs with different degrees of intensity, etc.

DEVELOPMENT-RELATED NATURE OF SWIMMING TRAINING

It can be regarded as scientifically certain that, in phases of rapid natural development-determined changes in bodily organs, the exercising and training of certain motor skills can produce a particularly good adaptation of the organs concerned (Koinzer 1979).

A training programme which is planned in the interests of the age-group swimmer and with a view to his greatest possible success must be designed to make optimum use of these surges in natural growth. Such a training programme will therefore choose the most appropriate time-periods for encouraging those motor skills whose development is chiefly dependent on the growth spurts. In this way the coaching of the age-group swimmer will follow his development, which seems desirable in three respects:

1 The demands on the young person occur in the order provided by nature in the form of growth. Such loads should result in a solid long-term improvement in performance and avoid adverse developments in relation to physical or mental health.

2 In view of the rapid effectiveness of measures for learning, practising and training motor skills, no more time should be spent on them than is absolutely necessary. The other areas of the young swimmer's life, such as schooling and professional training, family life, relationships, dealings with people outside the sport, satisfying intellectual and musical needs, are then not fully sacrificed to the shortage of time.

3 The demonstrable success of training efforts enables the age-group swimmer to feel for himself that a well-planned and committed approach reaches the goal. His self-confidence increases as does his belief in his own capabilities.

Feige (1973), John (1980) and Bley (1977) also give prominence to the natural development-related training programme. Feige, in particular, investigated the performance development and competitive careers of swimmers and runners after maximum training loads in childhood and early youth, as well as after a long-term development-related training programme. He arrived at the result that heavy training loads at a very early age appreciably accelerate improvement in performance and lead to rapid competition successes.

'The improved performances in childhood and youth and the shorter build-up to personal best performance are offset however by a failure to reach full potential as an adult and a shorter duration both of the high-performance phase and of the sporting career as a whole.

Finally, the average values of the best performances of those athletes who specialized early are generally below those of the top-class athlete whose performance has been built up in accordance with natural development' (Feige 1973, 70).

Besides the pure sporting-performance benefit from the investment in training time, trouble, effort and actual material cost on the part of all those involved, it is to be hoped that the young person can derive long-term advantage in later life from this input. The longer his or her swimming career lasts, the more time there will be to harvest the results of the efforts, to experience the ups and downs of competition and training, to reflect on them and benefit from them. It is not until the transition from youth to maturity that the athlete develops the ability to appreciate and to use not just the direct experience of the sport but its attendant circumstances, physical and social effects, and personal and cultural possibilities.

Experience has shown that the age-group swimmer who has gone through the maximum training and competition stresses at an early age is not capable, even on trips to swimming competitions in faraway countries, of achieving a deep and lasting impression of his surroundings. He is not in a position to take in and store such impressions because he is too preoccupied with apprehension before the event and with the experience of success or failure afterwards. It takes the experience and conditioning of several years of training and competition with progressive performance demands and stresses – in the emotional and attitude-related areas – for the young person to be consciously aware of the sport of swimming itself and of its environment as a whole and to be able to enjoy it to the full.

What does a development-related training programme look like then? With normal development, the greatest structural change in the motor skills occurs at the ages of 10 to 11 and 15 to 16 (Filippovich/ Turevskii 1977). At these ages there is also a change in the athletic movements. This means that the periods prior to these phases of rapid movement-changes should be used for systematic preparatory instruction.

As far as emphasis is concerned, this applies to the entire area of swimming technique and coordination training (i.e. the coordinative motor skills) up to the eleventh year, and to general training or training specific to swimming, particularly basic swimming endurance, flexibility and stamina (i.e. the conditional motor skills) before the fifteenth/sixteenth year (cf. FIG. 5).

If these periods are omitted from the training schedule, it is unlikely that personal best swimming performance will be developed.

The omission can best be rectified by putting in a considerably greater amount of time and effort. We can take as the starting point the fact that the body-construction prerequisites have been largely established by the time of the second pubic phase (roughly from the thirteenth to seventeenth year in the case of girls, and fifteenth to nineteenth for boys) (Winter 1979).

It is certainly too late then for basic training.

In contrast to accepted swimming-training practice, it is recommended that short-term basic speed should be emphasised early in the framework of the young person's training schedule, i.e. from the first year of training.

In addition to general and basic swimming endurance, it should be the conditional motor skill that is systematically trained (cf. TABLE 1). The reason for this is the knowledge that the nervous system is on average fully developed by the eleventh/thirteenth year. The greatest growth spurts in terms of reactions ability and speed occur up to this age (Joch 1976, Meinel 1976, Stemmler 1977). These include, in particular, improved reactions and movement frequency as the neuro-coordinative side of speed of movement, and not of the muscular component, i.e. of power. The greatest increase in this is experienced by 12 to 13-year-olds (Hollmann/Hettinger 1976).

Because of the importance of the coordinative side of basic speed, it is appropriate to not always choose the same old exercises and situations for training. Rather different tasks and movement patterns in the water and on dry land, with different frequencies and changes in frequency, should open up and extend the possibility of flexible speeds of movement. 'A basis of multiple variation is of particular importance to the development of motor skills, combined with the creation of a wide motor experience. For the coaching of motor reaction capability this means: "Variation of the signals, conditions, reaction exercises and organizational forms in which the exercises are performed." ' (Vilkner 1978, 400) (cf. Chapter 12: The training of basic swimming speed).

The young swimmer's training up to the eleventh year includes primarily: teaching of technique, improvement of basic swimming endurance and of reaction time, short-term acceleration, all-round coordination and flexibility. It must not be forgotten that at this age the muscular strength of all parts of the body should be uniformly promoted by general strengthening exercises and other sports. The increase in strength at this age is based mainly on improved coordination within the individual muscles and between the various muscles. The flexibility of the muscles should also be increased by regularly performed stretching exercises. Only with very good neuro-muscular coordination and excellent flexibility is the transition between tensing and relaxing the driving muscles guaranteed, which is crucial for the economical execution of the swimming movements which have to be continuously repeated over long distances. 'Command of the transition between tension and relaxation of the skeletal muscles is an important consideration at each phase of coaching' (Israel/Buhl 1980, 198).

With regard to elasticity and flexibility of the muscles, this is, incidentally, the only sex-associated difference between boys and girls up to that age (Koinzer 1977). The advantage enjoyed by the girls means that boys need to do more swimming-related stretching exercises.

Since the elasticity of the capsular and ligament tissue of the joints declines from about the tenth year (Weiss 1980), there is really a place for regular flexibility exercises in the age-group swimmer's programme from the outset.

Relating training to development also requires that the volume and intensity of training be systematically increased and distributed differently. FIG. 2 shows, for the example of strength, how the time

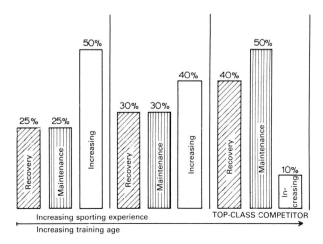

FIG. 2 Time expenditure on recovery, increase and maintenance of strength with experience (as training progresses (after Kuznetsov 1975))

spent on the recovery, maintenance and increasing of strength changes as training progresses.

Even for beginners it is important to train regularly and all the year round, because at this stage it is only possible to train for short periods and with the sessions well spaced out. Since only increasing loads exert a sufficient stimulus on the organism to develop increasing strength, the volume and intensity of training have to be stepped up during the course of the years of training (see FIG. 1). This is best done at set intervals. The periods produced are gradually transformed into repeated short 'cycles'. The increase in the amount of time spent training should first be implemented by increasing the number of workouts; only after that is training time increased by making the daily workouts longer (Rahn 1979).

In this way the volume of activities can be systematically increased over three or four years, i.e. during basic sport-motor coaching and basic training (cf. FIG. 1). Progressive training is the stage at which two workouts a day are sometimes introduced. The reason for twice-a-day training is to distribute the requisite increased training over the time available by measured and varied loads. A favourable ratio between loading and recovery can thus be created.

The increase in intensity is simply effected by making the age-group swimmer achieve high average speeds in training from year to year as a result of coaching stimuli and the effect of training. As the years of training pass, he will thus cover greater distances in the water than before in the same training period. One thing ought to be borne in mind, however:

'Quality comes before quantity, i.e. the greater volume must not be achieved with poor execution of the movements' (Rahn 1977, 679).

2 Planning a long-term training programme

Any training schedule covering a short period should be integrated into the framework of a multi-year training programme. Ideally, the complete long-term training programme (cf. TABLE 1) should cover a period of eight to 10 years and be divided into four stages:

1 basic swimming and sports instruction;
2 basic training;
3 progressive (build-up) training;
4 elite training.

The tolerance in dictating the duration of each of these stages takes account of the acceleration or retardation of development which frequently occurs. It is attributable in the first place to the fundamentally different rate of development of girls and boys, and secondly to individual variation in development.

The speed of development varying from person to person is manifested in the fact that, compared with the actual age of the young swimmer, the typical maturation characteristics (cf. FIGS. 3 and 4) are not yet exhibited or only to a slight extent. He or she is lagging in development behind the average for that age (retardation). In sport we more often come across young people whose growth and maturation characteristics are ahead of their age (acceleration).

The fact that such differences in development have to be taken into account in all coaching plans is expressed in the first instance in an earlier or later start to a training stage, e.g. by high-pressure training starting at an age of 14 to 15½. This figure may itself be shifted up or down by about one year if the child has taken up swimming very early or very late.

Basically, girls and 'accelerated' boys should aim at an early start, whereas for normal male developers and retarded girls the upper time limit is suitable for transfer to the next stage. The varying state of development of infant and young swimmers is also taken into consideration by varying the intervals of rest within the individual stages.

A period of two years has thus been set for the progressive or "build-up" training, which may be extended to three years for a retarded youth or an early starter.

A rough assessment of the state of biological development of a young swimmer can be made on the basis of FIGS. 3 and 4. Firstly, the diagrams show the major outward biological maturation characteristics, which are apparent even to the layman, plotted against time. They also give the times of greatest growth of attributes significant to swimming, which are dependent on biological development, and conclusions are drawn for the programming of the points of emphasis.

Since the start of sports and swimming instruction often depends on chance external organization, the transition to the particular stages may be a year earlier or later depending on whether the first stage was begun at seven or nine (8±1). The age of eight has proved favourable for starting sports instruction. It is recommended that on no account should a start be made earlier than seven, since it is not until 'the age of seven to eight years that the higher nervous system reaches an advanced stage of development' (Fomin/Filin 1975, 32). From that age onwards complicated sports movement techniques can be learned with comparative ease.

It would appear from the actual situation in the world of swimming that girls and boys who are willing and who have shown an aptitude for swimming often join a training group at ten or eleven. Children of that age, and even young persons of 13 or 14, naturally have prospects of success in swimming, despite their late start on a systematic but rather compressed training programme.

We would warn against one or more stages of swimming coaching simply being missed out or jumped: the omission will later cause a limitation of performance.

In such instances of a late start on a long-term training programme the coach should check which stage or which aims have been completely omitted or curtailed, and how they can be made good. The swimmer can catch up either by time-wise compression or by overlapping two training stages. Thus, for example, a normally developed eleven-year-old girl will receive her basic swimming motor coaching in a group twice a week in her first year of training and will participate twice weekly in the lowest degree of load in the basic training.

In the second year of training the ratio of basic coaching to basic

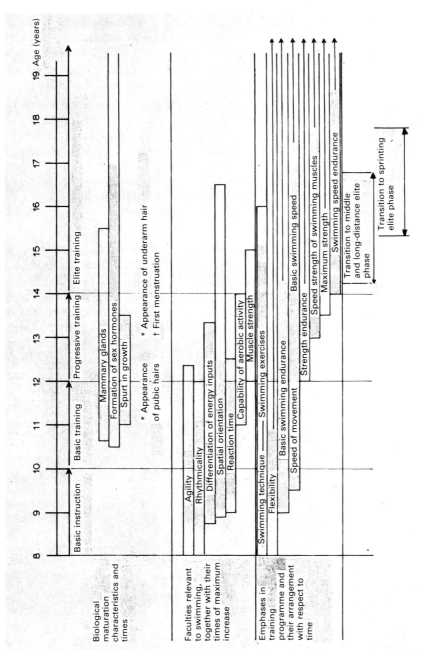

FIG. 3 Time relationship of maturation processes, development of capabilities significant to swimming, and emphases in a training schedule for girls

training could be increased to two to four sessions a week. It will be obvious from the example chosen that the later start naturally implies the compression of the coaching content and partial loss of the time needed to become accustomed to the gradually increasing training load. The result is that the child is from the outset subjected to a greater time commitment and to greater physical pressures, without the pleasant and enjoyable experiences associated with the water and the training group. It is precisely the latter which should predominate during the first two years of instruction, creating an emotional bond with swimming which helps greatly when the young person has suffered a temporary stagnation or even a deterioration in performance.

On no account should a late starter do the next training stage to its full extent and at the prescribed intensity until the essential coaching aims of the previous stage have been achieved.

Otherwise general coordination defects, faults in swimming technique and conditional weaknesses will slip through and later lead to unexpected dips in performance or obstacles to development.

It seems more favourable and more in keeping with the conditions of late starting to shift the entire training schedule for such swimmers through a time equivalent to the lateness of their start. The shortest times within the individual sections of the training schedule would of course be set. Late entry into swimming will be successful if the child has previously been active in sport generally or has changed over from another sport.

The danger with the later starter, as with the late developer, is not the actual absence of rapid sporting development. It is that, because of comparison of performance with that of early-developed swimmers and lack of patience on the part of parents and coach, there is hardly a reasonable chance of development. What is more, early failure will prematurely lose the social assistance essential for development.

The great expectations which are placed on early-developed (accelerated) young swimmers as a result of the early and steep rise in their performances not only put pressure on them prematurely to succeed, but also often cause interest to wane in the basic, comprehensive and development-oriented training programme of the late developer (retarded), and sometimes even of normally-developed boys and girls.

The consequences include, among others, a high percentage of youngsters prematurely giving up the sport. They have not been allowed the time necessary to cope with competitive swimming and its demands on a sound footing of sports coaching. What they have lacked during their first years of coaching has been the time and enjoyable

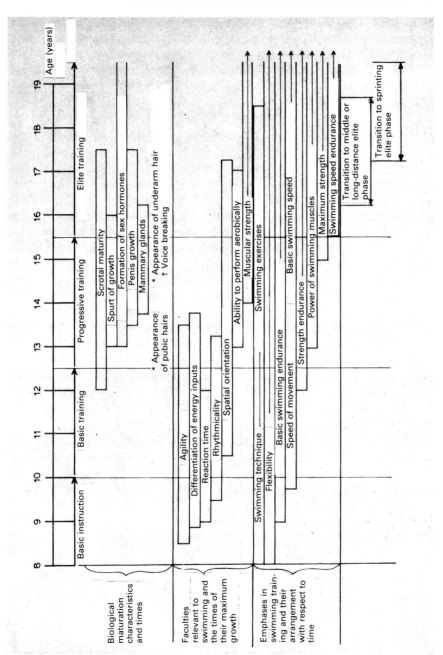

FIG. 4 Time relationship of maturation processes, development of faculties important to swimming, and arrangement of points of emphasis in a training schedule for boys

experiences which go into developing a sense of belonging and devotion to the sport and to its environment, which is so necessary for a life-long activity and sense of well-being in the sport.

A transition to the elite stage (cf. FIGS. 3 and 4) implies – assuming that the training programme has been followed systematically and in full – that the age-group swimmer should be capable of participation in national championship finals and show promise of aptitude for international competition.

Embarking on the elite phase is not synonymous with the swimmer's peak performance in his career. This peak usually comes later.

In the light of what has been said on the differing rates of development of young people and on varying starts on a long-term training programme, the transition to the elite phase may be delayed by up to two-and-a half years. It has therefore been given as a period. Outstandingly 'steep' early careers have not been taken into account, since they often cause further improvement in performance to be lost or suddenly fall away (Feige 1973).

On average, a distance swimmer will start the elite phase a good year earlier than a sprinter. This applies equally to boys and girls, of course with a sex-determined lead in the case of the girls.

The reason for the earlier elite stage of distance swimmers is the different stressing of the motor skills for endurance performances on the one hand and for speed-endurance performance (sprint distances) on the other. The motor skills primarily required also exhibit different times of maximum growth (FIGS. 3 and 4.)

3 Hints on mental development and mental-attitude coaching

DEVELOPMENT-PSYCHOLOGY AND SPORTS-EDUCATION TIPS FOR THE AGE-GROUPS

Age 8/9 years:
The child's freedom and urge to be on the move have to be directed. There is a great deal of liveliness and learning involving movement: both of these have to be taken into account using repeated instructions to perform movements, but also by frequent opportunities for free movement and for letting off steam. Besides trying out new movement patterns a lot can be learned by imitation. The child should not be asked to dwell too long on one task or to repeat the same movement pattern precisely. Never the less the main movement patterns of the basic strokes have to be ensured by repeated exercises, because the volatile receptivity of children tends to make them quickly forget what they have learned. For motivation reasons the child's striving to perform well calls for simulated races.

Emphasis is on the mental-attitude conditioning in the swimming instruction. Enjoyment of the water and of movement, as well as belonging to a group, and regular participation in exercise and training sessions should be to the fore. About a third of activity should be out of the water: simple gymnastics and athletics exercises, a great many catching and reaction games and simple ball games. Roughly half the time in the water should be devoted to learning the swimming strokes; the remainder to diving, underwater swimming and play (familiarity with water). A knowledge of hygienic behaviour, such as thoroughly drying one's hair, ears, etc, has to be imparted too and its observance checked. This is accompanied by instruction on the most important rules of competitive swimming.

Age 10/11 years (♂ 12):

A down-to-earth interest in the environment and in why things are done a certain way, and a critical attitude towards his or her own performance and the performances of others, are clearly apparent. Self-criticism is capable of appreciably damping the zeal for movement. The desire to be recognised and the urge for companionship can be satisfied by comradeship in sporting activities. There is an obvious thirst for knowledge and information in the field of sport too, e.g. sporting idols or successful teams. Deliberation with understanding leads to the development of know-how, but this is initially based on existing standards and follows conventional lines.

It is also a favourable motor-learning age for complicated swimming and turning techniques, particularly on the basis of good and accepted models. Regular training sessions for flexibility, basic swimming endurance and speed of movement are also accepted willingly, although in these too variety in the movements employed should be paramount.

At this age the individual ought to exhibit a fundamental will to perform well. The sporting performance itself can, however, be played out and experienced within the group. Failures are at first easier to stand and get over in common with others. Performance demands must expressly consist only of what has been learned and practised previously. The child has to learn the relationship between his own regular efforts and the resultant performance. He should experience the effect of sporting success and the necessity of cooperation and collaboration within the group. Intensive learning of the strokes should be conducted using simple mechanical explanations, calling for periods of theoretical instruction using a lot of visual materials. Rules of a sportsman's behaviour and life, a knowledge of warm-up procedures and what to do prior to a race should be introduced. The swimmer should be consulted on how the programme for the day should be broken down.

Age 12/13 years (♂ 14):

Personal striving towards independence and self-determination can only achieve the commitment of the growing person to a long-term training programme or to proposed races if he or she has been given and understood well-prepared logical explanations and been involved in both the decision and the planning. This presupposes a wide knowledge of sport. The desire to be an individual and to gain recognition at this stage of development is satisfied by the controlled introduction of individual races. A certain volatility and an alternation between overactivity and 'loafing around' often occur. In the sporting context these can be countered by regular training, provided there is a sufficient variation of challenge and quality of experience.

The swimming strokes have to be learned and consolidated by varied drills, but they must be kept flexible. In addition to increasing knowledge of the mechanics and techniques of swimming, a basic biological knowledge for sporting performance must be imparted. This should be followed by the simple methods of self-monitoring, such as measuring one's own weight, size and pulse-rate, keeping a training diary, observing sleeping and eating habits, as well as information on the organization of dry-land and water training.

The swimmer must voluntarily undertake all the associated aspects of the competition and training plans agreed with the coach. Trips taking long preparation (training camps, compensatory sports, races), more demanding sports (basketball, volleyball, water polo) and the involvement of equipment and technology in certain aquatic activities (ABC/skin-diving), satisfy this age-group's accentuated thirst for experiences and love of adventure.

Age 14/17 (♂ 18):

The self-awareness which starts at this stage of development is shown in abrupt alternation between enthusiasm for a project and lack of interest. This is aggravated by material dependence on the adult world and by its attitude to sexual behaviour at the age of incipient maturity. The high state of intellectual development finds no suitable individual responsibility outlet in everyday life, but it makes great demands (of a material nature too) on those around. This is expressed, among other ways, in an over-critical attitude towards adults, especially towards those directly surrounding them, and in an all-too-ready generalization of these critical observations. Systematically practised competitive sport offers a fine opportunity for satisfying the great demands arising from the desire for individual responsibility, from the state of intellectual development, from the desire for self-expression and from the quest for self-realisation (perfection).

Whereas the early years of youth and the critical peak around 15/16 years (♀) or 16/17 years (♂) are concerned with individualization, this is followed again by a communal striving, including the import-ance of sports social-education, e.g. mutual respect, comradeship, helpfulness, commitment and responsibility to the group.

This is the stage at which the decision has to be made for or against involvement in top-class swimming, because the young person is now conscious of the fact that his actions are the result of encouragement towards swimming training from outside and he has to acknowledge the fact. The decisions should accordingly be based on the essential driving forces of the stage of development (self-realisation, self-expression, quest for critical-intellectual orientation, social needs), combined with serious discussion, and on no account on mere habit, by being talked into it or as a result of external social pressures (parents, coach or club). Organic and muscular increases in strength and improved coordination as a result of the developing body proportions offer the best prerequisites for a good swimming perform-ance and for technical-stylistic perfection of the movement patterns. By virtue of physical and motor maturity, definitive specialization for swimming stroke and competition distance must be decided at this age.

In addition to sporting attitude, the young swimmer also has to acquire theoretical knowledge of special training methods and effects, performance tests, nutrition and recovery measures, simple methods of self-monitoring and tactics in competition. He or she should be encouraged to draw up part of the training programme in consultation with the coach. They should gradually determine the emphases both of sporting and professional education plans, coordinate them and plan them out over a long period. The observance, results and any necessary corrections to these plans must be dealt with by regular discussions between coach and swimmer.

4 Composition and emphases of a long-term training programme

The next few sections of the book deal with the demands made by competitive swimming on a young sportsman, and the training designed to satisfy those demands.

We have already expounded the theory behind such training and have considered the physical and mental development of the young person from nine to 20 years, if only in broad outline and describing only the most important features.

The overall plan, 'Composition of a long-term year training programme (covering a period of 8 to 10 years)' on pages 24–26 links the chapters which have gone before with those following. It is also intended to bring together:

1 the sporting and sports-education theories referred to;
2 the factors in the biological and mental development of children and young people;
3 the motor, attitude-related and intellectual demands increasingly made by competitive swimming;
4 the training methods which enable swimming to be practised successfully.

In the first place, the overall plan shows the time relationship, i.e. it relates stages in swimming instruction to the periods in which the average development of the young swimmer favours the learning, exercising or coaching of certain skills and movement patterns.

The composition and location of points of emphasis in the long-term training programme have been arrived at with the aim of linking all the above in as balanced a way as possible: a balance between the responsibility which every coach bears for the welfare and overall human development of his or her charges, and the hard and matter-of-fact pursuance of the demands and loads involved in successful competitive swimming.

TABLE 1 A long-term training schedule covering a period of 8 to 10 years

	START AT AGE OF	DURATION	TIME SPENT PER WEEK	SPORTS MOTOR COACHING AIMS
BASIC MOTOR LEARNING PERIOD	8±1 years to 10 years	2 years	In water: 3 to 4 × 40 to 50 min On land: 3 to 4 × 15 to 25 min	1 Variety of movement coordination in water: underwater swimming, diving, swimming. 2 Swimming-technique instruction: crawl, backstroke, breaststroke and butterfly. Grab start, backstroke start, flip turn and roll turn: 3 Varied general body-building: general endurance, flexibility, agility. 4 Swimming mobility. 5 Basic swimming endurance. 6 Ball games in water: games with partners and in groups.
BASIC TRAINING PERIOD	10±1 years to 12/12½ years	2–2½ years	In water: 5 to 6 × 45 to 60 min	1 Basic swimming endurance. 2 Swimming speed: changing speed of swimming and tempo over a few metres. 3 Swimming technique instruction: consolidating the four basic strokes; back 'flip' turn, medley tumble-turn and wind-up start; swimming exercises. 4 Improvement of conditioning skills, basic aerobic endurance, flexibility, speed and muscular endurance. 5 Aquatic agility, simple forms of diving, synchronised swimming and water ball games. 6 Relay races, team races. 7 Distance swimming at constant pace. *Annual training schedule taking account of race dates.*
PROGRESSIVE TRAINING	12/12½±1 to 14 years	2–3 years	In water: 6 to 8 × 70 to 90 min On land: 4 to 5 × 30 to 50 min	1 Basic swimming speed. 2 Specific (swimming) muscular endurance. 3 Basic swimming endurance (aerobic endurance). 4 Speed strength. 5 Start of stroke specialisation and classification as sprinter or middle/long-distance swimmer. 6 Individual and team races. 7 Tapering. 8 Varied pace over long distances.

AIMS IN ATTITUDE AND KNOWLEDGE AREAS	EMPHASES OF CONTENT AND METHOD
1 Enjoyment of water and of sporting movements. 2 Getting used to the group. 3 Getting used to regular participation in practice and training sessions. 4 Knowledge of swimming techniques. 5 Knowledge of the most important competition rules. 6 Adoption of hygienic behaviour before and after swimming.	In the water: – learning and practising all four strokes; – water polo, volleyball, water rugby in shallow water; – sculling: prone, supine, feet-first, head-first, in circles; – load alternation as a game; – interval swimming and steady swimming of long distances. On dry land: – gymnastic exercises on ropes, rings, bars, boxes and floor; – athletics exercises: running, jumping, throwing; – flexibility training: A and C exercises; – gymnastics with and without hand apparatus; – pairs exercises: shadow running, shadow boxing, lifting and carrying partner; – ball games: dodge-ball, rounders, ball bouncing.
1 Behaviour in relation to team. 2 Readiness to perform in group. 3 Discipline of sporting life. 4 Standards of sporting behaviour. 5 Timing of day's activities. 6 Knowledge of warm-up programmes and pre-race behaviour. 7 Responsibility towards group.	In water: – continuous method, extensive interval method, speedplay (fartlek); – accelerating and pace-variation swimming; – contrast, combination and feel-for-water exercises; – flipper swimming; water polo games with simplified rules; dives from 1-metre and 3-metre boards: somersaults and headers with run-up; synchronised swimming, e.g. wheel of six people. On dry land: – running in forest and country, cycling; – games, e.g. mini-basketball, mini-hockey, mini-volleyball; – throwing and playing with medicine ball; – general strength work: gym apparatus work; exercises with own body weight, elastic rope, dumbells and expanders; – circuit training; isometric exercises; – flexibility training: B exercises.
1 Willingness to perform as individual or team competitor. 2 Knowledge of fluid mechanics (basic). 3 Knowledge of mechanical basis of swimming techniques. 4 Knowledge of biological fundamentals of performance 5 Joint planning of training and competition schedule. 6 Self-monitoring and record keeping: training performance, weight, pulse, sleep, body reactions.	In the water: – sprints, spurts; – swimming with paddles, leg tube, resistance boards; – intensive interval training, over-distance swimming; – underwater swimming with A-B-C or compressed-air equipment; underwater rugby; proper-rules water polo. On dry land: – exercises with workhorse or Exergenie apparatus, long barbells, own bodyweight and additional load; – flexibility training with sustained stretching; – occasional games.

START AT AGE OF	DURATION	TIME SPENT EACH WEEK	SPORTS MOTOR COACHING AIMS
ELITE TRAINING	14–15½±1 years	1 to about 10 years	In water: 6 to 11 × 80 to 90 min On land: 5 to 6 × 45 to 70 min	1 Swimming speed endurance. 2 Maximum strength. 3 Muscular endurance specific to race. 4 Endurance specific to race. 5 Varied pace, depending on opponents. 6 Basic swimming endurance. 7 Hypoxic swimming. 8 Supplementary sports relevant to swimming. 9 Distance specialisation: sprinter, middle-distance or distance swimmer. 10 Intermediate and top competitions. *Transfer to national/international (♀) performance level*

While the sports-education theory and the swimming demands may remain constant for some time at least, the biological and intellectual development of each young swimmer will vary slightly. This is apparent not only from the differences in stature and weight between boys and girls of the same age, but is also manifested in differences in other maturation characteristics and modes of behaviour.

Finally, every young sportsman is in the process of developing their own immutable personality, and swimming should help to do so in as favourable a way as possible.

By referring to the overall plan, the coach can not only check just what the young swimmer is learning and which conditional skills should be being coached at a particular stage, but he should ask himself from time to time whether the physical and mental development of the swimmer is consistent with the particular training being done. The semi-diagrammatic representation of the biological maturation characteristics and the development of skills relevant to swimming (in FIGS. 3 and 4) can be used as a guide in answering this question.

The figures given in the column 'Time spent each week' for the length of training sessions represent average values. Depending on the relative position in the training year, or 'macro-cycle', the duration of the individual workouts can be shorter or longer than the average value (cf. Chapter 20: Sample training sessions, p. 246 ff.). Taken overall, the longer training sessions balance out the shorter ones.

AIMS IN ATTITUDE AND KNOWLEDGE FIELDS	EMPHASES OF CONTENT AND METHOD
1 Knowledge of special training methods and effects. 2 Knowledge of nutrition. 3 Behaviour prior to and during races, independent of coach. 4 Simple methods of self-monitoring. 5 Knowledge and application of time trials. 6 Drawing up training schedules. 7 Establishing points of emphasis and time-related planning for swimming and professional training over a long period. 8 Conditioning to and experience of risk in team.	In the water: – repetition training, continuous swimming; – swimming with retarding apparatus: resistance belt or trousers, tee-shirt, tights; – simulated races; – hypoxic training; On dry land: – circuit training and exercises with special – apparatus, e.g. mini-gymn, wheel-bench, – latissimus machine; – rowing, canoeing at camps; – mobility training: 3-S exercises; – mountain climbing, scout camp, cycling trips.

5 Skills essential to competitive swimming and their importance in planning the training programme

Training is a complex process: complex in the sense that it involves a large number of influencing factors. Ideally, the training process consists of the systematic variation of the stress structure, especially using increasing loads – and alternating contents and methods. Any training process must start from an analysis of the factors governing performance in the particular sport (requirement profile). The planning and execution of the training must be based on these influencing factors.

The questions to be considered are which

coordination (motor) skills,
conditional (motor) skills,
sports and swimming knowledge,
intellectual capabilities,
attitudes

in particular determine competitive swimming performance and to what extent they do so.

Only after these questions have been answered can attempts be made to improve the skills, knowledge and attitudes by appropriate training and coaching.

Let us, for the moment, leave aside the intellectual skills, knowledge and attitudes and turn to the motor skills. The motor skills relevant to swimming have been listed diagrammatically in FIG. 5. The importance of the individual skills in relation to competitive performance is indicated by the size of the particular box. Many of the skills are mutually dependent on others. (This is illustrated by arrows.)

The motor skills are divided into coordination and conditioning exercises. The state of development of the coordination skills primarily determines the extent to which the various strokes and their associated starts and turns can be mastered.

Water-related movement sensitivity is what is commonly known as 'feel for the water'. It refers to sensitivity to water pressure on the surfaces of the hands and feet, so that arms and legs can move with optimum dexterity in the water and encounter maximum water-resistance (cf. pp. 93 and 99).

Sensitivity to water pressure can be improved by special exercises (cf. p. 97 f.). If the swimming instruction is properly organized, water-related movement sensitivity will be included in the watermanship assignments for the beginner. These exercises should be continued and extended in all later stages of training.

Flexibility is mentioned in all general training textbooks both in relation to conditional and coordination skills. In the diagram flexibility is assigned to the coordination skills. It is defined as the extent of mobility of the joints. It depends on the nature of the joint, the flexibility of the muscles, tendons and ligaments pulling via the joint, and on muscular strength. In swimming flexibility of the shoulder joint is of crucial importance in the crawl, backstroke and butterfly, of the hip joint in breaststroke, and of the ankle joint in all four strokes (cf. p. 104). It is not a matter of simply developing the maximum possible flexibility, but also of improving flexibility to such an extent (and maintaining it), that the swimming movements can be executed in as 'friction-free' a way as possible. They then exert practically no adverse influence on the flat, low-resistance attitude of the body in the water (cf. p. 93).

The ability to relax applies to all cyclical sports as a contributory factor to performance. It relates to the muscular relaxation necessary in order to be able to execute repeated movements over a long period. Only by an uninterrupted transition between tension (e.g. of the driving muscles in the underwater phase of the crawl arm movement) and relaxation (e.g. in the out-of-water phase of the crawl arm movement) is it possible to ensure the energy supply via the blood (e.g. oxygen supply). The ability to relax thus constitutes one prerequisite for sustained performance.

The ability to relax affects flexibility too. For example, only if the chest muscles are suffiently relaxed can the butterfly swimmer lift his arms far enough out of the water in the recovery without increasing the angle of attack of his body and without putting uneconomic excessive demands on the energy output of his shoulder and back muscles in the recovery phase.

There are other links between the water-related movement sensitivity, the ability to relax and coordination skills: all three are dependent on the efficiency of the nervous system. Through the ability to relax, neuromuscular coordination and the flexibility of the nerve processes influence water-related movement sensitivity and coordination skills, and, in common with joint flexibility, determine the quality of swimming technique.

In other words, the better the coordination, the ability to relax and the water-related movement sensitivity, the more quickly and efficiently will the swimming techniques be learned.

The right-hand side of FIG. 5 shows the swimming-related conditioning factors and (represented by arrows) the relationship between them. The diagram demonstrates which factors or capabilities are the most important for competitive performance.

Starting from a basis of general endurance, maximum strength and speed, which are present in a healthy youngster, and which can be improved by all-round sporting activity, it is the specific swimming-oriented nature of the conditional skills mentioned that determines competitive performance as age and training experience is accumulated.

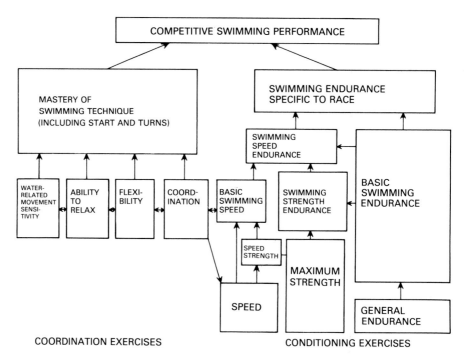

FIG. 5 The major motor factors and their importance in swimming

The overwhelming importance of basic swimming endurance (cf. p. 118) to competitive performance in swimming, regardless of distance, is illustrated by the size of the box.

Maximum strength (cf. p. 150) and swimming strength endurance (cf. p. 160) also contribute greatly to performance. Speed (cf. p. 138) and power (cf. p. 159), on the other hand, are not very important.

The dependence of basic swimming endurance on general endurance, that of swimming strength endurance on maximum strength, and the dependence of basic swimming speed both on the maximum strength, speed, coordination and also on power, is indicated by arrows.

Basic endurance, strength endurance and basic speed are prerequisites for swimming speed endurance, which in its turn, together with basic swimming endurance – depending on the length of the race – constitutes the universally decisive race-specific swimming endurance. A kind of requirement profile is thus obtained of the motor skills for swimming. The quality of swimming technique also determines competitive performance to a similar degree. In the final analysis, therefore, it is the mastery of swimming technique and the level of race-specific swimming endurance – varying according to the distance – that determine performance.

Although knowledge, attitudes and intellectual capabilities are not shown in the diagram, we need to be aware of them and be aware that their development is essential for an improving competitive performance. In particular, the quantities of determination and attitude to performance and towards the team should develop in parallel with the motor skills (cf. hints for the individual training years). Whereas technical knowledge calls for periods of regular instruction from the coach, attitudes and mental competitiveness are formed by the experience of races and of teamwork and by consistent training and daily self-conquest. By the same token, strength endurance training aids the development of mental staying power. Moreover, the only coaching measures available to the coach are occasional conversation and the grading of stress situations in competition and in training (cf. hints on intellectual development and mental attitude coaching).

It is obvious that the coordinative skills are equally important to every young swimmer, regardless of his preference with regard to stroke and race distance.

The constitution of the conditioning exercises, on the other hand, is of a different degree of importance for the distance swimmer from that for the sprinter. The distance man needs better basic swimming endurance than the sprinter: he does not need such a great maximum strength and does not need to be as sharp. Therefore, the training of the long-distance swimmer should be designed differently from that of the sprinter. This is illustrated, not in FIG. 5, but in Chapter 17 – 'Hints on training methods for the individual training years, distances and composition of training' (pp. 211 ff.).

It should also be borne in mind that the diagram shows the major swimming-related motor skills as a guide for controlling training, but it starts from the high-pressure area and does not constitute a time characteristic of training requirements. The skills included all have to be improved by training, but not all at the same time. The goals in the first year of training are different from those in the fourth year, and so on, as can be seen from the hints for the individual training years (cf. pp. 211–36).

Competitive swimming performance can be achieved with irregularly developed motor skills. This means that a slight weakness in one skill can to a certain extent be compensated by above-average ability in other skills.

Once a particular level of performance has been reached, quite often on skill alone, further improvement in competitive performance can only be achieved through a balance of all the individual factors which contribute to performance; i.e. the swimmer must now work on strength, or endurance, coming back to skill as increased strength permits technique change. The identification and integration of these factors gives control of training, and constitutes the hallmark of a good coach.

The starting point for training control is the requirement profile for swimming-related motor skills. During basic instruction and basic training, it is derived from the factual demands made by swimming on basically each and every competitive swimmer (e.g. learning all the strokes). During the progressive-training stage, the profile differs somewhat for the sprinter, middle-distance and distance swimmer (e.g. extent of basic swimming endurance). During elite training, consideration has to be given both to the peculiarities of the preferred stroke and also to the race distance. In control-system terms, the requirement profile constitutes a kind of training 'desired value' – what the swimmer knows should be done and perhaps wishes to do.

On the other hand, there is the reality of a personal starting level of sports performance capability, which varies from one young swimmer to the next. This personal performance condition can be determined by swimming-related training tests (cf. p. 262) and constitutes, as it were, an 'actual value' in relation to the requirement profile. Coaching mediates between the desired value and the actual value of the performance condition.

Training control consists in particular of:

1 *Drawing up training schedules*, from the long-term schedule (p. 13), through the year's schedule with its cycle (p. 200), down to the weekly training schedule (micro-cycle, p. 209) and the daily schedule with its individual training sessions (p. 201). For long periods the schedule can only give key dates. The shorter the period covered, the more precisely must the schedule be prepared. For example, the daily schedule will specify what training is to be done, how quickly, with what intervals, etc.

2 *Executing the training schedule*, i.e. implementation of plans. Correct execution of the schedule presupposes, apart from a certain amount of experience, good know-how in scientific fields related to training (training theory, sports medicine, pedagogics, psychology, etc.).

3 *Regular monitoring of performance development*, both by observation of training, by training tests and races, and also through daily self-monitoring by the young swimmer. All important data should be recorded in a training diary in preparation for the next step, i.e. evaluation.

4 *Evaluation and comparison of schedule and training done*. It is this fourth step that is often omitted, although it is essential for continuous and systematic training control.

If the coach observes, for example, that the schedule workout has been too hard, he should balance it by a correspondingly gentle session of basic endurance swimming (regeneration training, p. 273) on the following day at the latest, or even the same day, to prevent excessive energy loss. Conversely, a training intensity which has been chosen too light should be stepped up as soon as possible to avoid idleness and time-wasting.

For longer periods – of a week up to a monthly cycle – training tests and time trials are suitable methods of checking the effectiveness of the training schedule, as a basis for possible amendments to the schedule.

6 The four strokes, starts and turns

The aim of the basic instruction stage is the learning and practising of the four strokes, together with the associated starts and turns.

After the strokes have been roughly mastered, the learning process, in most cases, proceeds to swimming the complete action, aiming at all times to emulate an ideal action (stroke) presented as a model. This also includes sometimes isolating parts of the action and concentrating on practising them in various forms (swimming technique exercises).

Both the learning and practice of a stroke presuppose that the swimmer has a clear understanding of the required swimming movements. The crucial initial factor in this understanding is for the swimmer to see and appreciate the correct movements.

For this reason each swimming stroke has been represented diagrammatically in the following.

On the basis of the findings of Schleihauf/Counsilman (1980) and on training experience, we consider it necessary to draw two different views of the same movement patterns, depending on who is observing the action:

- the young swimmer observing his own action while swimming (swimmer's view),
- the coach observing the action of his swimmer as he swims past (coach's view).

The reference point for the swimmer's view is his own body, i.e. the young swimmer observes that his arms, following a curved path, are pulled backwards and then forwards again in the recovery. What appears to him to be important is to know whether, how and where his arm movement (and in the case of the breaststroke his leg movement too) is following a curve, and whether the movement is being executed at a varied speed. The latter is illustrated by the width of the hatched curve. The wider the hatched area, the faster the movement. This means that the swimmer ought to increase his energy input at the widest point of the curve.

The numbers in the small circles on the curves indicate important phases in the action. The smaller diagrams, numbered accordingly, give details of the movement at the phase concerned.

For the alternating pull strokes they provide information about
- arm movements, seen from the side (top left);
- body position and roll about a longitudinal axis (top right);
- leg movement: kick (bottom left);
- breathing (bottom right).

The simultaneous pull strokes give information on:
- arm movements, seen from the front (top left);
- leg or foot movement (top right);
- body position, seen from the side (bottom left);
- breathing (bottom right).

The reference point for the coach's view is the water, i.e. the observer remains stationary and the swimmer passes by. This is represented by the position of the swimmer's body, which changes in the direction of reading. The hand curves correspond to the actual path of the hands in the water: they overlap or intersect. Small arrows indicate the hand direction. In this connection it is best to imagine that the swimmer's hands (and the insides of the forearms) are trying to remain at a particular point in the water (roughly level with the observer) and that the body is being pulled away by the hands or forward past the hands. It is, incidentally, one of the duties of every coach to convey this concept to his swimmers again and again.

In this connection, the observer should be aware that the drawing only represents the sequence of movements in two dimensions, whereas the swimming action is in reality three-dimensional.

Thus, for the alternating pull strokes, the hand curve is presented as a side view. The observer, for example, sees the forward-and-backwards and the downwards-and-upwards components of the crawl arm action, but he is unable to see the outwards-and-inwards components. For the simultaneous pull strokes the view given of the hand curves is from above. This illustrates the forwards-and-backwards and the outwards-and-inwards components of the arm action, whereas the downwards-and-upwards movements cannot be shown from above. This applies both to the coach's view and the swimmer's view.

A swimmer's awareness of what his movements should be can be assisted to a limited extent purely by showing him two-dimensional stroke plots.

In order to develop his conception of movements still further, the swimmer must rely on experience and observation of his own body in the water.

He can increase that experience and the accuracy of those observations, amongst other things, by swimming technique exercises.

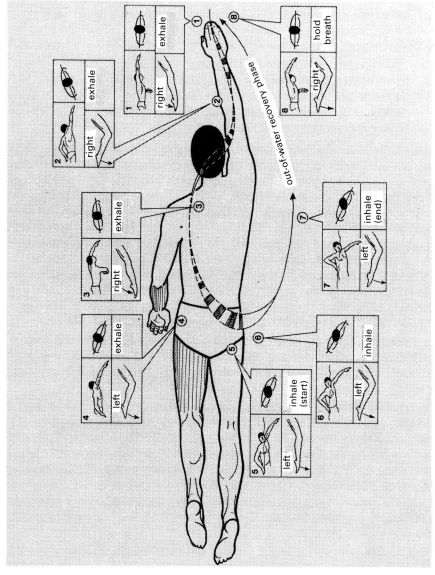

FIG. 6 Crawl action: swimmer's view

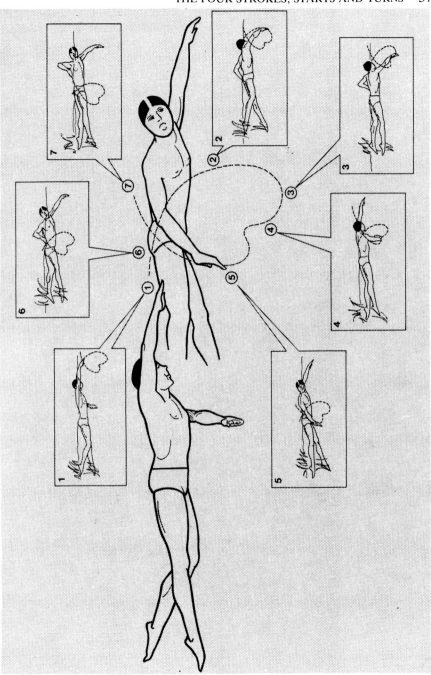

FIG. 7 Crawl action: coach's view

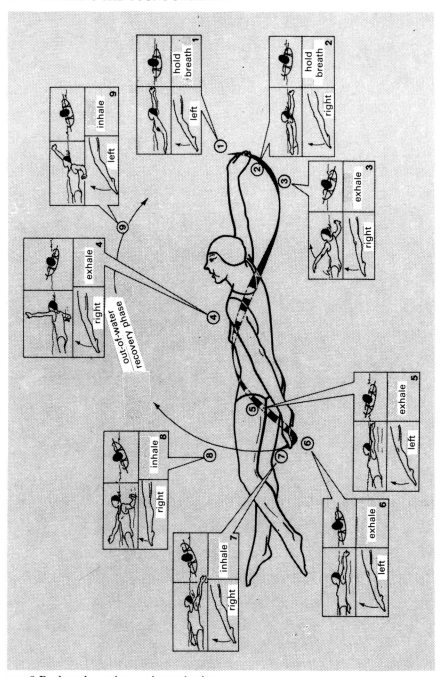

FIG. 8 Backstroke action: swimmer's view

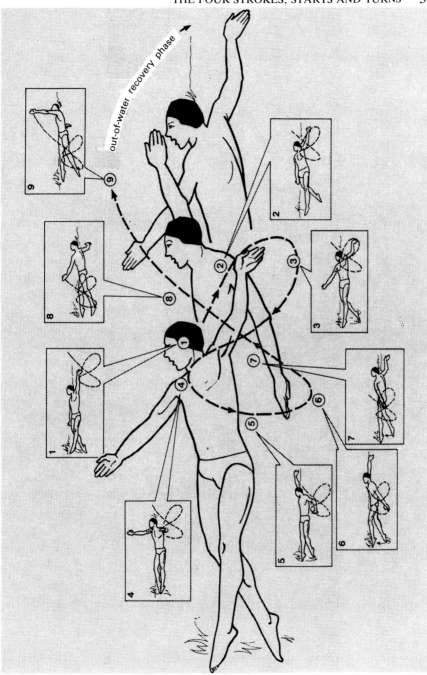

out-of-water recovery phase

FIG. 9 Backstroke action: coach's view

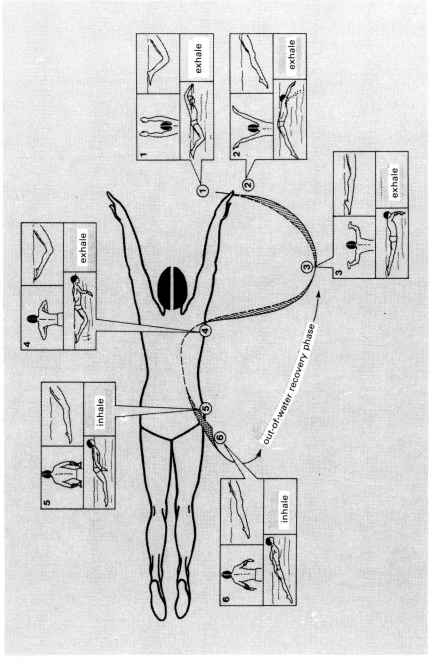

FIG. 10 Butterfly action: swimmer's view

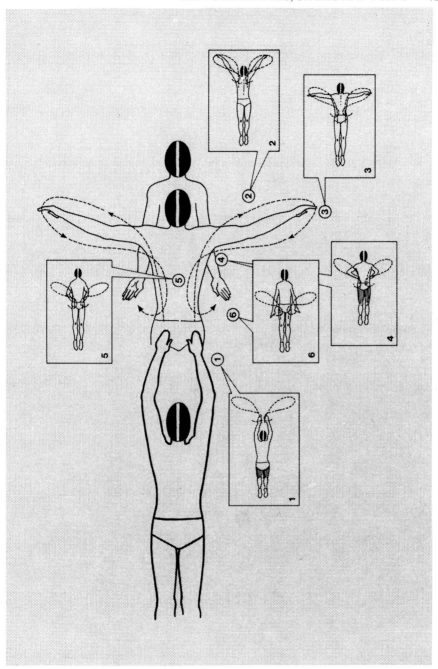

FIG. 11 Butterfly action: coach's view

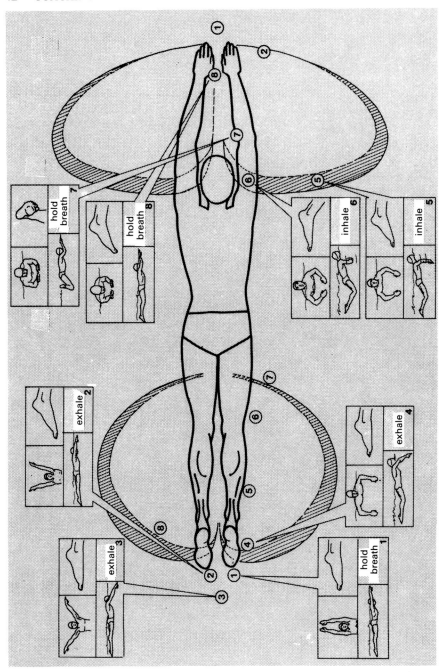

FIG. 12 Breaststroke action: swimmer's view

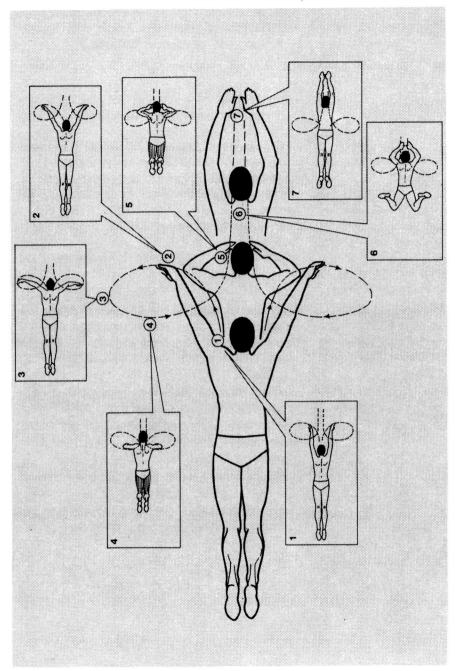

FIG. 13 Breaststroke action: coach's view

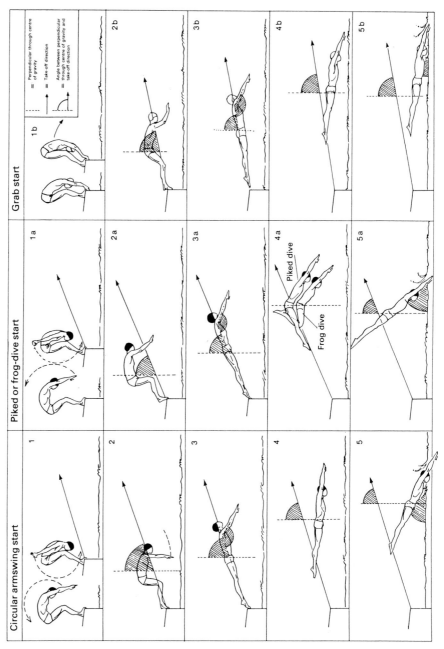

FIGS. 14a–c Sequence of movements in the dive start: conventional, pike and grab start (left to right)

FIGS. 14a to 14c show various starting techniques.

FRAME 1:   The initial position.

FRAME 2:   The position of the body and the relative position of the parts of the body shortly after the starting signal, i.e. after the swimmer has transferred his weight to in front of his feet.

Note: only in the grab start can the swimmer draw his centre of gravity actively forwards and downwards by bending his arms.

FRAME 3:   The position of the body and the relative position of the parts of the body at the instant at which the legs extend, i.e. when the push-off of the legs begins.

FRAME 4:   Position and attitude of the body shortly before the feet leave the starting block.

FRAME 5:   Position and attitude of the body roughly in the middle of the mid-air phase.

The arrow running forwards and upwards from the starting block is intended to represent the takeoff direction. The varied length of the mid-air phase for the three versions of diving start can be explained by reference to the different angle between the perpendicular through the centre of gravity and the direction of takeoff.

Another consequence of the takeoff angle is the different angle of entry (represented by a cross-hatched segment in FRAME 5).

In FRAME 3 the hatched angle indicates the point at which the arms are slowed down so that their centrifugal force can assist in extending the subsequent mid-air phase. *N.B.* The retarding of the arms occurs when the feet are still just touching the starting block.

The piked start can be performed directly from the starting position of the grab start, i.e. without a circular armswing.

FIG. 15 illustrates the starting technique for backstroke.

FRAME 1:   The initial position for the start (= starting position).

FRAME 2:   The position and attitude of the body after the arms have been actively extended as the first step.

FRAME 3:   Position and attitude of the body at the instant at which the legs push off from the wall.

FRAME 4:   Position and attitude of the body shortly before the feet have left the wall.

FRAME 5:   Position and attitude of the body during entry.

The arrow in the swimming direction and slightly upwards indicates the takeoff or diving direction.

The shaded areas indicate the angle between the prependicular

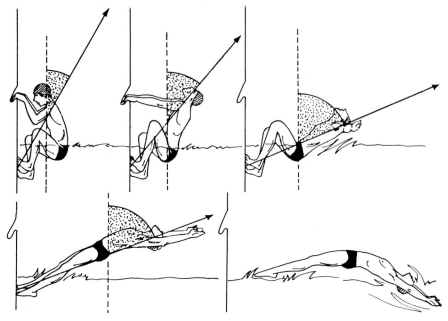

FIG. 15 Sequence of movements for backstroke start

through the centre of gravity and a line from the feet to the shoulder. In FRAMES 3 and 4 this line coincides with the pushoff direction.

FIGS. 16a to 16d illustrate five essential consecutive phases in the action of the breaststroke/butterfly turn, the freestyle flip turn and the backstroke tumble and roll turns (from left to right).

FRAME 1:   The behaviour of the body during or just before reaching the wall.

FRAME 2:   The body position and attitude preparatory to the actual change of direction (= turn).

FRAME 3:   Shows how the directional change comes about, i.e. which movements are executed by arms, legs and head.

FRAME 4:   The position of the body shortly before pushoff.

FRAME 5:   The position of the body during the glide, shortly before reverting to the action of the swimming stroke.

The arrows in the bottom right or top right in the individual frames are intended to represent the rotational axes, the direction of rotation and the extent of rotation to take place next.

The arrows against the swimmer show the direction of movement of parts of the body, e.g. of the arms and legs, which in the final analysis permit the change of direction of the entire body (= turn).

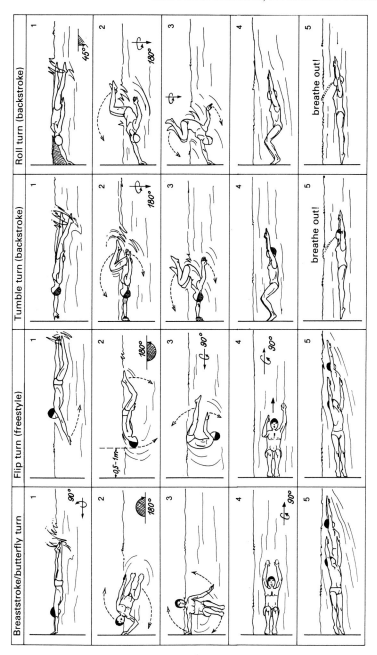

FIGS. 16a–d Turns: sequence for breaststroke/butterfly turn, freestyle flip turn, backstroke tumble and roll turns (left to right)

7 Swimming technique exercises

The purpose of swimming technique exercises is primarily to impress on the memory the movement patterns for the individual swimming strokes (stroke consolidation) and, secondly, to improve the ratio of energy expenditure to swimming performance (action economization).

In both cases the exercises are designed to increase the efficiency of the action, i.e. they are intended to convert the energy expended by the swimmer into a greater forward-propulsion power, rather than increase the amounts of energy themselves. For this reason, swimming technique exercises are often referred to as technique training, in contrast to condition training, whose aim is in the main that of increasing reserves of energy and of making such reserves readily available.

After the four swimming strokes have been learned, swimming technique exercises are the focal point of swimming instruction during the first years of training for the age-group swimmer.

On the one hand, the aim of frequent repetition of identical swimming movements is to ensure that the correct action is maintained even when, in the course of subsequent training, it is impossible to concentrate all the time on accurate technique. The exercises thus have the effect of preventing the shift of attention, say to hard training requirements or interference from races, opponents, excitement, etc., from causing the practised swimming technique to fall apart.

On the other hand, the multiplicity and variation of swimming technique exercises stimulate the learning ability of the young swimmer in relation to new patterns of movements (and, within limits, to movement patterns not directly related to swimming). This nascent learning ability in particular enables swimming technique to be adapted to different external and internal conditions.

Different external conditions which may occur are, for example, different depth of water or quality of water, turbulence, strange starting blocks or pushoff positions, different pool shape, a different coach or new training programme. Changes in internal conditions relate to the effects of growth, i.e. limb growth occurring in a short period, larger hand and feet areas, larger muscles, increased size of rib cage and displacement of the body's centre of gravity in relation to its length.

Training effects relating to strength, speed and endurance can, however, also affect the internal conditions for swimming technique. It is obvious that arm growth of 3 to 5 cm in one year, with a simultaneous increase in hand area, will appreciably alter lever ratios. Adapting to this change by accentuated bending of the elbow during the pull will be achieved more quickly and with greater success by a swimmer who has trained using a maximum range of swimming exercises than by one who has limited himself to only a few movement patterns and is set in these.

The internal conditions also include changes in the nervous system, new knowledge, views and attitudes.

Even in cases where there is really little variation in the external and internal conditions, it can be claimed that, in the context of the movement pattern being aimed at for a particular stroke, repetition and variation of technique exercises will have a favourable influence on the relationship between energy expenditure and swimming performance.

Searching, probing variation of a movement pattern, using a wide range of exercises, is more certain to bring the swimmer closer to his personal ideal movement pattern than will a monotonous repetition of the same swimming action.

This also explains how many top-class swimmers have only achieved mature performances in their discipline after trying other strokes and widening their repertoire.

By no means the least important feature of a varied exercise programme is that it prevents monotony and boredom in training sessions during the early years of training of the age-group swimmer. In this respect, most dry-land sports offer more variety than swimming, which results in many talented boys and girls prematurely giving up swimming. A good programme for age-group swimmers should introduce at least three new technique exercises or combination exercises each week.

The following exercises are classified as 'special':

- exercises for frontcrawl, backcrawl, butterfly and breaststroke, arranged within each stroke as exercises for leg action, arm action and coordination;
- exercises for diving start and backstroke start;
- exercises for turns.

In addition to these, there are the general but equally important:
- exercises for 'feel for the water';
- contrast exercises;
- combination exercises.

The exercises described below are not individually substantiated, although the individual exercises have a somewhat different effect on the swimming action. They represent a collection from which it is possible to select and to which new exercises should be continually added. The order within the sets of exercises is arbitrary. The use of sets of exercises with particular goals (e.g. contrast exercises) is governed by the training schedule and can be derived from the hints for the individual training years (p. 211).

SWIMMING TECHNIQUE EXERCISES FOR FRONTCRAWL

Exercises for leg action

Flutter kick in prone position
1 With kickboard: arms on kickboard and head raised.
2 With kickboard: the hands grasp the end of the kickboard, the head is in the water between the outstretched arms, and turns to one side to inhale (FIG. 17).

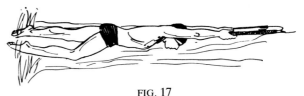

FIG. 17

3 With a kickboard as a resistance device: the hands hold the side of the kickboard vertical in the water, with the head between the arms in the water.
4 With a leg tube (tube from a motor-scooter tyre or a PT tube): the hands grip the tube from the inside (FIG. 18).

FIG. 18

5 With arms held out in front: the arms are extended at shoulder width with the face in the water.
6 With hands together: as in the previous exercise, but with the thumbs of the touching hands interlocked (FIG. 19).

FIG. 19

7 With arms by sides: the palms of the hands rest on the thighs, the face is in the water.
8 With hands on back: the fingers are interlocked on the back or across the buttocks, with the head in the water (FIG. 20).

FIG. 20

Variation: the head is raised, looking forwards.
9 With one arm extended: the other arm is held against the body and the face is in the water. The position of the arms is swapped after each length or set distance or number of kicks.

Flutter kick on the spot
1 Against the pool wall: one hand grips the gutter, while the other hand is placed against the wall lower down (fingers pointing downwards).
2 Raising upper body: with both hands on the gutter or edge of the pool, the legs kick for 10 seconds hard enough to raise the swimmer's back out of the water (FIG. 21).

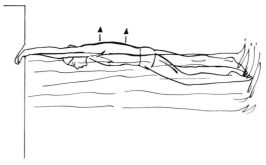

FIG. 21

3 From the vertical: the arms are extended, the body is suspended vertically (forwards and backwards). The body is raised to a horizontal position by powerful kicking (FIG. 22).

FIG. 22

4 Against the wall: the swimmer pushes off feet-first from the wall with his arms and propels himself back to the wall by kicking strongly, and so on.
5 In vertical position: the arms are held against the body, and the swimmer raises his head and arms out of the water by kicking.
Variation: one arm or both arms are held up above the surface of the water.

Varied applications of flutter kick
1 On side: the lower arm is held out in front and the upper arm against

the hip. After six kicks, the body is rolled onto the other side and the arms swap their positions. (FIG. 23).

FIG. 23

2 With flippers: the arms are stretched out together in front, the head is kept raised.
3 Underwater: swimming underwater for distances of 10 to 25m; arms in front or paddling alongside the body.
4 As a two-man contest: two facing swimmers grip each other's shoulders with their outstretched arms and attempt to force each other backwards.
5 As a team relay: two to four swimmers in each team, using only leg kicks, push a beam about 1.5 m long, or a barrel, up to a mark where other swimmers take over (FIG. 24).

FIG. 24

Exercises for arm action

Arm movements using apparatus
1 On dry land in front of a mirror: the swimmer stands with his body inclined forward in front of the mirror and watches himself as he executes alternate arm movements (FIG. 25).

FIG. 25

Variation: execution sideways-on to the mirror.
2 With a kickboard: one arm pulls as in the crawl, while the other arm is stretched out in front on a kickboard. The legs swing loosely and the head is in the water. The swimmer breathes at each pull. The arms change roles after half a length.
Variation: breathing after every second or third pull.
3 With pull-buoy: swimming with a continuous alternating pull with a pull-buoy between the thighs.
4 With leg tube: as in the previous exercise, but with a leg tube round both ankles.
5 With flippers: the thumbs engage in the armpits. The swimmer executes the alternating crawl stroke with arms shortened into 'chicken wings'. The legs give support by kicking (FIG. 26).

FIG. 26

6 With paddles: almost all the exercises for the arm action can be performed using paddles.

7 On an elastic rope: the rope (stretch-cord, strong elastic rope) is attached to the side of the pool at one end and is tied round the swimmer's waist at the other (FIG. 27). This is known as 'tethered swimming'.

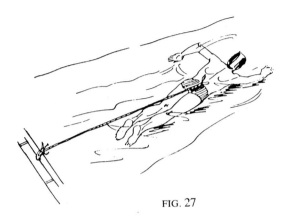

FIG. 27

Variation: the first end of the rope is tied round the waist of a second swimmer. The two swimmers try to tow each other in opposite directions.

Arm movements without apparatus
1 One-sided pull: one arm pulls as in the crawl, while the other is stretched out ahead. The legs swing loosely, and the head is in the water. The arms change roles every half-length.
   Variation: the inactive arm is held against the hip.
2 'Snatch': alternate pull with accentuated raising of elbow. The tips of the thumbs and fingers stroke the side of the body from the thigh up to the armpit (FIG. 28).

FIG. 28

3 Close to the wall of the pool: the swimmer rolls his body sharply onto its side and raises his elbows high.

4 'Duck stroke': the upper arms are held against the rib cage, while the forearms are bent forward, the hands forcing the water backwards from waist level to legs (FIG. 29).

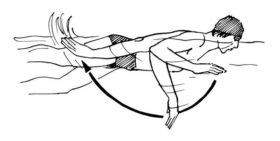

FIG. 29

Variation: as the previous exercise, but the arms execute the duck stroke from shoulder level to waist level.

5 Armswing over back: during the out-of-water recovery phase of a slow crawl, each arm reaches its highest elbow position and stretches across the buttocks to the opposite side of the body, so that the back of the hand strikes the water (FIG. 30).

FIG. 30

Exercises for coordination

1 Standing in shallow water: the leg on the breathing side is set back a pace and the head and torso are inclined forward on the water. The breathing arm performs the crawl action, with body roll and regular breathing, while the other arm is extended, gripping the edge of the pool (FIG. 31).

FIG. 31

Variation: exercising the other arm and exercising the breathing side, accompanied by a two-arm crawl action.
2 Breathing each arm cycle: alternate-pull swimming, breathing at movement of breathing arm.
   Variation: breathing on unaccustomed side, with change of sides every half-length.
3 Bilateral breathing: as in previous exercise, but with breathing at every third pull, alternately on right and left.
4 Bilateral breathing: as in previous exercise, but alternating with two-pull to left, three-pull, two-pull to right, etc.
5 One-pull breathing: swimming a very slow crawl with an uninterrupted alternation of left and right breathing.
6 'Dog paddle': the arms are alternately thrust forward under the surface of the water and pull to below the shoulders (FIG. 32).

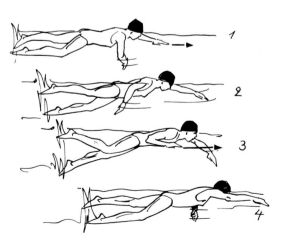

FIG. 32

7 'Catch-up stroke': crawl, in which the advanced arm is delayed in the extended forward position until the other arm catches up with it and touches it.

8 Synchronised swimming: two or more participants swim the crawl alongside a 'lead swimmer' and match the timing of his movements (FIG. 33).

FIG. 33

9 Variation of leg-beat rhythm: swimming a continuous crawl, every other length is swum with a six-beat kick or a two-beat kick.
Variation: the leg-beat rhythm is changed every half-length, after a set number of pulls (10:10, 8:8, 6:6), or at a signal from a whistle.

10 Body rolling: swimming in a narrow lane marked off by two lane-dividing ropes (or pool wall and a rope), with accentuated sideways roll of body and with high raising of elbows (FIG. 34).

FIG. 34

11 Coordination variation: the swimmer does a series of crawl exercises, such as 6 kicks with arms held out in front, 6 kicks with two arm movements on the right, 6 kicks with two arm movements on the left, 6 kicks with one alternate pull, etc.

12 'Blind swimming': after the pulls needed for a length have been counted, the participants swim with their eyes either closed or blindfolded, counting their pulls until they reach the wall.

SWIMMING TECHNIQUE EXERCISES FOR THE BACKCRAWL

Exercises for leg action

Flutter kick in supine position without apparatus
1 Arms beside body: flutter kick with back of head in water. The arms paddle alongside the hips.
   Variation: the arms are held with the palms resting on the thighs.
2 With arms folded: flutter kick, with arms folded on chest (FIG. 35).

FIG. 35

Variation: the hands are clasped under the buttocks or the arms are interlocked behind the back.
3 Arms extended above head: flutter kick with arms extended side-by-side on the water in the swimming direction, with the thumbs interlocked.
   Variation: the extended forearms are held just above the surface of the water (FIG. 36).

FIG. 36

4 One arm back: flutter kick with one arm held back just above the surface of the water, the other resting against the hip. The arms change roles every half-length (FIG. 37).

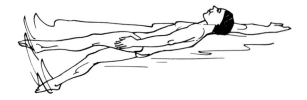

FIG. 37

5 With body roll: as in previous exercise, but the body is rolled through 45 degrees towards the side of the arm held back, this arm being stretched back just below the surface. As the arm position changes, the upper arm pulls powerfully through the water and the body rolls through 90 degrees to the opposite side.

With apparatus/in different body positions
1 With flippers: flutter kick with flippers, with both arms stretched back just above the surface. The palms rest one on the other with interlocked fingers, or the back of one hand rests in the palm of the other (FIG. 38).

Fork grip

FIG. 38

2 On side: the legs kick well past each other to front and rear, the lower arm being extended in the swimming direction and the upper arm resting on the thigh. After half a length, the sides are changed.
3 Continuous change of position: as in the previous exercise, but the body rotates continuously about its longitudinal axis during the large kick.
4 One arm held high: flutter kick with one arm held vertical out of the water, the other arm resting on the hip. Arm positions are interchanged after half a length.
Variation: the other arm lies in the swimming direction just under the surface.

5 Both arms held high: powerful flutter kick with both arms extended upwards.
6 Underwater kicking: the two arms are extended and locked together as an extension of the body. The flutter kick during the underwater swimming starts from underwater push-off or from a backstroke start (FIG. 39).

FIG. 39

Exercises for arm action

Arm movements with apparatus
1 On dry land in front of a mirror: the swimmer stands upright in front of the mirror. He observes himself as he executes the alternating arm movements.
Variation: execution sideways-on to the mirror.
2 One-sided arm pull at edge of pool: the swimmer lies in the water parallel to and close up against the side of the pool, with the arm nearest the pool side resting on the edge of the pool or in the gutter, while the other arm executes the complete action above and in the water. The eyes watch the arm being used (FIG. 40).

FIG. 40

3 Double arm pull with paddles and pull-buoy: with paddles on the hands, both arms are swung back simultaneously over the water and pull as far as the thighs, at the same time bending and pressing. The body is extended in a supine position and the pull-buoy is held between the thighs.
 Variation: a pulling tube replaces the pull-buoy.
4 One-sided pull with paddles: one arm executes the complete backcrawl arm movement with a paddle, while the other arm rests against the hip. When the working arm above the water enters the water, the body rolls towards the pulling arm. The arms interchange their positions after half a length, with the legs swinging loosely in a flutter kick.
 Variation: the inactive arm is stretched backwards in the water.
5 Alternate pull with paddles: the arms perform alternate gentle arm movements above and under the water. The legs swing loosely.

Arm movements without apparatus
1 Simultaneous arm pressure: the swimmer lies stretched out in a supine position, with his head on the water in line with his body. Both arms are drawn to shoulder level with the elbows to the fore. From there they press down to the thighs with finger tips pointing outwards, the legs swinging loosely.
2 Complete simultaneous pull: as in the previous exercise, but the arms are thrust in the direction of travel under the water to a position in front of the head and then pull from there, at the same time bending and pressing.
3 Simultaneous pull on back with gentle flutter kick: as in the previous exercise, but the arms are simultaneously swung over the water in the direction of travel and from there they pull to the thighs, at the same time bending and pressing (FIG. 41).
4 Alternating-side arm pressure: the arms are alternately moved underwater as far as the shoulders and press from there to the thighs. The upper arms are held against the rib cage and the legs swing loosely.
5 Alternating-side underwater pull: as in previous exercise, but before the pull each arm stretches underwater past the shoulder in the direction of travel. The body rolls onto the side of the extended arm.
6 Single-sided arm movement: one arm executes the complete action above and under the water, the other arm resting against the hip; the body rolls towards the side of the rear arm, and the legs swing loosely.
 Variation: as in the previous exercise, but the inactive arm is extended along the surface of the water in the direction of travel.
7 Alternate pull with touching hands: the arms pull alternately through

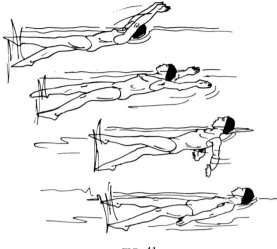

FIG. 41

the water and swing back over the water. The swung-back arm waits extended in the direction of travel until the other arm catches up with it, and so on. The legs move loosely.

Variation: the arms wait and are 'released' at hip level.

Exercises for coordination

1 'Reverse dog-paddle': complete backcrawl action, but with the arms under the surface all the time (FIG. 42).

FIG. 42

2 Use of shoulders: the legs kick in a supine position, with the arms held against the body. The shoulders are alternately raised and then drawn back in the direction of travel, with the body rolling towards the side of the dipping shoulder.
3 Regular breathing: as in the previous exercise, but inhaling each time the right shoulder is raised and exhaling as it enters the water.
4 Complete action with breathing: as in the previous exercise, but inhaling during lift-out and reverse recovery of the right arm, and exhaling while pulling and pressing (two-pull breathing).

5 Four-pull breathing: as in the previous exercise, but breathing at every second movement of the right arm.

6 One-pull breathing: a very gentle backcrawl is swum with un-interrupted breathing. Inhalation at lift-out and reverse recovery of each arm.

7 Coordination variation: the swimmer executes a series of swimming movements, such as 6 kicks with stretched-back arms, 6 kicks with arms at sides, 6 kicks with one arm back and the other at the side of the body, 6 kicks with same-but-opposite arm position, 6 kicks with alternate arm pull.

Variation: 6 kicks with arm movement on right but other arm stretched back, 6 kicks with same-but-opposite arm movement, 6 kicks with alternate arm pull.

Variation: as in previous exercise, but with inactive arm held against hip.

8 Backcrawl exercise length: third of a length with flutter kick and simultaneous arm pull, one third with alternating arm pull accompanied by body roll, and one third in full backcrawl.

9 Synchronised swimming: two or more participants swim backcrawl alongside a 'lead swimmer' and match the timing of his movements (FIG. 43).

FIG. 43a   FIG. 43b

FIG. 43b Example of an exercise for breathing rhythm: the backstroke swimmer rolls only one shoulder upwards and inhales, drops the shoulder and exhales. He then rolls the other shoulder in alternation but the breathing rhythm is still related to the first shoulder

10 'Blind swimming': after the number of strokes needed for a length has been counted, the participants swim along a roped-off lane with closed or blindfolded eyes, counting their strokes until they reach the wall.

Warning: use partners to avoid accidents!

SWIMMING TECHNIQUE EXERCISES FOR BUTTERFLY

Exercises for leg action

Leg action in prone position without apparatus
1 Snaking: the swimmer executes any number of dolphin leg movements
   with his head in the water controlling the movements, i.e. at each kick
   the head is bent towards the chest. The arms are held with the palms
   on the thighs, breathing by raising the head when required.
   Variation: the head is thrown back at every second kick and the
   swimmer inhales (FIG. 44).

FIG. 44

   Variation: as in the previous exercise, but with the head continuously
   out of the water.
2 With hands on back: the fingers are interlocked on the swimmer's back
   or across the buttocks, and his head is in the water.
   Variation: the head is raised and the eyes are directed forwards.
3 With arms held in front: the arms are extended at shoulder width, with
   the face in the water.
   Variation: the head is raised with the eyes looking forwards.
   Variation: head and arms 'pre-control' the leg kick and the swimmer
   breathes at every second kick (FIG. 45).

FIG. 45

With apparatus/in different body positions
1 With flippers: dolphin kicks are executed with flippers and with the arms at the side of the body. The head is in the water, controlling the movements.
Variation: at every second kick the head is raised out of the water and the swimmer inhales.
Variation: the arms are held out in front.
2 With kickboard held in front: the hands grasp the sides of the board and the head is in the water (FIG. 46).

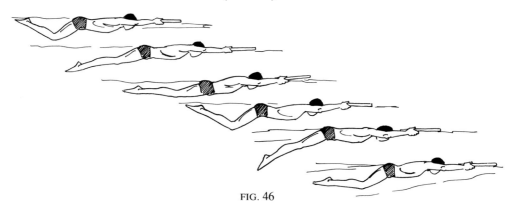

FIG. 46

Variation: the head is kept above the water all the time.
3 With kickboard and head steering: before every second stroke, the hands press the tip of the kickboard under the water, and the head is inclined towards the chest. During the first stroke the tip of the board and the head steer downwards (FIG. 47).

FIG. 47

4 Leg-kick rhythm: the swimmer executes dolphin kicks with the kickboard held out in front and with the head permanently raised. Every second kick is accentuated by putting more effort into it.

Variation: the head is lowered into the water before the first kick and is raised before the second.

5 With a kickboard used as a resistance board: the hands hold the sides of the kickboard, vertical in the water, and the head is in the water between the arms.
   Variation: the head remains above the surface of the water (FIG. 48).

FIG. 48

6 Underwater: swimming underwater for distances of 10 to 25 m. The arms are out in front or paddle alongside the body.
7 In supine position: both arms are extended in the water beyond the head (FIG. 49).

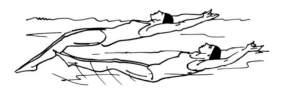

FIG. 49

Variation: the arms are held against the hips.
8 On side: the lower arm is held out in front, the upper one being held against the hip. The head rests on the lower arm (FIG. 50).
   Variation: after 6 kicks, the body rolls to the other side and the arms exchange positions.
   Variation: both arms are extended in the swimming direction.

FIG. 50

9 With rotation about the body's longitudinal axis: the swimmer executes continuous gentle dolphin kicks with the arms held against the hips. After every 2 to 4 leg movements, the body makes a quarter rotation about its longitudinal axis (FIG. 51).

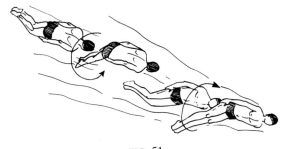

FIG. 51

Exercises for arm action

1 On dry land in front of a mirror: the swimmer stands in front of a mirror with his upper body inclined forward. He observes himself as he executes the dolphin arm movements.
Variation: execution sideways-on to mirror.
2 From a push-off: after a short glide, the swimmer performs rapid dolphin arm movements. The head is on the water and the legs remain extended.
Variation: after a diving start.

3 With a pull-buoy: the pull-buoy is between the thighs, with the head in the water. The arms are thrust forward under the water and pull towards the thighs, executing an exaggerated keyhole pattern (FIG. 52).

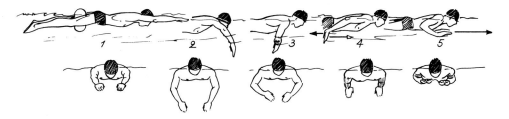

FIG. 52

Variation: at the end of the pulling phase the head is raised and the swimmer inhales.
Variation: the arms are swung forward above the water (FIG. 53).

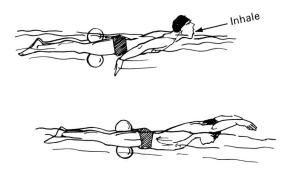

Inhale

FIG. 53

Variation: the head steers the body deeply down and up.
4 With leg tube: the tube is placed round the ankles. Rapid arm movements are performed over short distances (maximum 25 m), breathing at every third pull.
5 With a partner hanging on: the swimmer performs powerful arm movements for 10 to 15 m, keeping his head in the water. A partner holds on firmly to the swimmer's ankles and is pulled along (FIG. 54).

FIG. 54

Variation: the partner executes a powerful crawl kick.
6 With paddles: all the exercises listed for the arm action can be performed using paddles.

Exercises for coordination

1 As a simplified movement pattern: the swimmer glides stretched out, with his arms against his sides and his head in the water. The forward thrust of arms underwater and the first kick are simultaneous; also the end of the 'keyhole' arm pull and arm pressure towards the thighs and the second kick are performed simultaneously (FIG. 55).

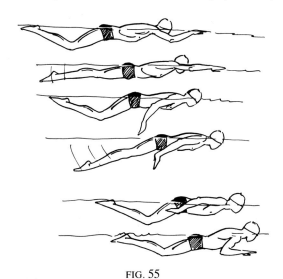

FIG. 55

2 Simplified sequence with breathing: as in the previous exercise, but inhaling at end of pressure phase of arms towards the thighs.

3 Single-arm butterfly: one arm is extended forward, while the other executes the complete action in conjunction with two kicks.
First kick: arm enters water and is extended. Second kick: arm ends its 'keyhole' pull and stretches towards the surface of the water. Inhalation every other time the arm presses and leaves the water (FIG. 56).

FIG. 56

Variation: breathing at each arm pull.
Variation: after every half a length the arms swap positions.
Variation: arm change after every two arm movements.
4 With arm against body: as in the previous exercise, but the inactive arm rests on the hip, and the head controls the accentuated undulation of the body.
5 Single-arm 'catch-up swimming': the swimmer performs a single-arm butterfly with two kicks. The other arm is extended in front and takes over the arm action after it has touched the first hand.
6 Coordination variation: the swimmer does a series of single-arm butterfly exercises with forward-stretched arm, such as: 4 kicks with both arms held out in front, 4 kicks with 2 arm movements on the right, 4 kicks with 2 arm movements on the left, 4 kicks with an arm movement to right and left.
Variation: the same series is executed with the arm resting on the hip.

7 Coordination variation for complete action: as in previous exercise with forward-stretched arm, but every two arm movements, to the right, left and alternating, are followed by two complete butterfly movements.
Variation: the alternation is between 6 kicks with arms stretched out in front and three complete movements.
8 Three-kick: a butterfly arm action is combined with three kicks. During the third kick the arms trail (FIG. 57).

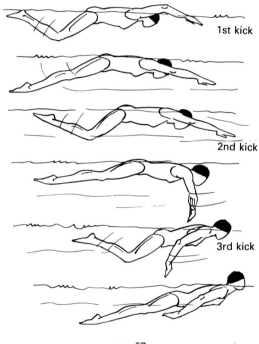

1st kick

2nd kick

3rd kick

FIG. 57

9 Rhythm alternation: series consisting of 6 kicks with arms held in front, 6 kicks with two arm movements (two three-beat strokes), 6 kicks with three arm movements (three normal movement cycles).
10 Two-pull breathing: a breath is taken at every second normal complete butterfly cycle.
Variation: alternation of two-pull and one-pull breathing.
11 Three-pull breathing: a breath is taken at every third complete cycle.
Variation: alternation of three-pull and one-pull breathing.

12 With large dolphin wave: the complete action is performed slowly with a large undulation upwards and downwards. The head steers exaggeratedly from the front (FIG. 58).

FIG. 58

Variation: a movement pattern in which a large dolphin undulation is followed by 6 to 8 kicks underwater and with the arms extended in front.

13 With small dolphin undulation: the complete action is executed quickly with the body all but stretched out and the legs trailing.

14 On an elastic rope: one end of the rope (stretch-cord, strong elastic rope) is fixed to the edge of the pool while the other is attached to the swimmer's waist. After swimming forward to stretch the rope, the swimmer attempts to swim on the spot without being pulled back by the rope.
Variation: the first end of the rope is attached to the waist of another swimmer. The two swimmers try to pull each other in opposite directions.

15 Synchronised swimming: two or more participants swim the butterfly alongside a 'lead swimmer' and match his movements.

16 'Blind swimming': after the number of pulls needed for a length has been counted, the participants swim with their eyes closed or blindfolded, counting the pulls until they reach the wall.

SWIMMING TECHNIQUE EXERCISES FOR BREASTSTROKE

Exercises for leg action

1 With a kickboard: with outstretched arms, the hands grasp the middle of the sides of the board, the swimmer's head being in the water. 10 to 15 m are swum on each occasion, without breathing.
Variation: the head is held out of the water.

2 As in the previous exercise, but the arms rest on the kickboard, gripping it at the front edge, with the head held high (FIG. 59).

FIG. 59

3 With a kickboard: the head is held out of the water. The leg action is executed with the knees held close together, possibly with a pull-buoy gripped between the thighs.
Variation: as in the previous exercise, with the knees initially close together during the kick, but gradually increasing the gap between them up to shoulder width.

4 Against a resistance board: both hands grip the board at the sides and hold it vertical in the water with the arms outstretched, the head being held above the surface of the water (FIG. 60).

FIG. 60

5 With arms held out in front: the arms are opened out to shoulder width with palms down and with the head held out of the water.
Variation: as in the previous exercise, swimming 10 to 15 m with the head in the water, then raising the head to inhale.

6 With hands by the sides: palms touching the thighs and the face in the water.
Variation: the head is kept out of the water the whole time (FIG. 61).

FIG. 61

Variation: as in the previous exercise, but with the arms thrust slowly forwards from the hips while swimming.

Leg movements on the spot
1 At the edge of the pool: one hand grips the gutter, the other hand being held against the wall lower down (fingers pointing downwards). The head is in the water (FIG. 62).

FIG. 62

Variation: as in the previous exercise, but with the head held high.
2 Raising the upper body: both hands grip the gutter or edge of the pool, and the legs kick sufficiently strongly for 10 seconds for the swimmer's back to be raised out of the water.
3 Against the wall: the swimmer pushes off feet-first from the wall with his arms and propels himself back to the wall by powerful breaststroke kicks, and so on (FIG. 63).

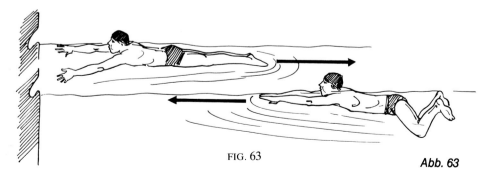

FIG. 63

Abb. 63

4 Vertical: the arms are held against the hips and the head is kept permanently out of the water. The head and upper body are forced out of the water as far as possible by breaststroke kicks.
   Variation: in addition, one arm is extended out of the water. The arms are swapped.
   Variation: both arms are extended completely out of the water (FIG. 64).

FIG. 64

5 Treading water: both arms are held against the hips and the head is out of the water. The right leg and left leg alternately perform breaststroke kicks.
   Variation: as in the previous exercise, but with one arm extended upwards.
   Variation: both arms are stretched upwards out of the water.

   Leg movements in a variety of applied forms
1 In a supine position: arms against the hips, head on the water with the chin slightly inclined towards the chest. The swimmer checks his knees visually, as they appear symmetrically just above the surface of the water (FIG. 65).

FIG. 65

Variation: both arms are extended at shoulder width behind the head.
2 In supine position with kickboard: the board is clutched to the stomach and chest with both arms (FIG. 66).

FIG. 66

Variation: the kickboard is held under the head and neck with both hands at the sides of the board.
3 Underwater: swimming underwater with breaststroke kicks for 10 to 25 m. The arms are held against the hips or paddle in that position.
Variation: as in the previous exercise, but with the arms stretched out in front.
4 As a contest: two facing swimmers grip each other by the shoulders with their outstretched arms and attempt to drive each other back using breaststroke kicks (FIG. 67).

FIG. 67

Variation: as in the previous exercise, but with both swimmers' heads held continuously out of the water.

Exercises for arm action
1 With pull-buoy: swimming with smooth arm movements, holding a

pull-buoy between the thighs. The head is in the water, being raised briefly every 10 to 15 m to inhale (FIG. 68).

FIG. 68

Variation: as in the previous exercise, but breathing initially at every third arm pull, and subsequently at every second pull.

2 Feet first with pull-buoy: in a supine position, the swimmer propels himself feet-first, using breaststroke arm movements. The body is stretched out and the arms, holding the upper arm against the body, execute lateral paddling movements against the hips.
   Variation: the same exercise performed without a pull-buoy.

3 At the side of the pool: one foot in the gutter, the other lower down the wall with leg outstretched. The swimmer executes 8 to 10 arm movements with his face in the water, before raising his head to inhale.

4 Towing a partner: the partner holds on firmly to the ankles of the towing swimmer and kicks gently. The towing swimmer has his head in the water and executes 10 to 12 powerful pulls before inhaling. After 25 m the partners swap roles (FIG. 69).

FIG. 69

Variation: as in the previous exercise, but the towing partner breathes at every second breath.

All the exercises can be performed using paddles.

Exercises for coordination

1 Leg action with variation of breathing: the arms are extended forwards shoulder-wide, the head being lowered into the water after each inhalation. Inhaling at each kick, then at every second, third, fourth, and so on, up to the sixth pull. Then begin again.
Variation: arms against the hips.
Variation: arms interlocked behind the swimmer's back or grasping each other over the buttocks.

2 Arm action with breathing variation: the legs are extended in the water or hold a pull-buoy between the thighs – no dolphin kicks! Breathing at each arm pull, then at the second, third, fourth, up to the sixth pull. Then start the breathing variation afresh.

3 Gliding swimming: the swimmer tries to execute as few full breast-stroke movement cycles as possible in covering one length.

4 Arm/leg combination: two kicks to one pull, with the face in the water. The first kick is coordinated with the arms in the complete action, while the second kick occurs during the glide with the arms outstretched. Breathing during the complete action.

5 Leg/arm combination: two pulls to one kick, breathing at every second pull in the complete sequence. The second pull takes place with outstretched legs and with the face in the water.

6 Breathing variation in the complete action: breathing at every second movement cycle, then at every third, then at every fourth. The face is in the water during complete actions with no breathing.

7 Submarining: an underwater breaststroke is performed about half a metre under the surface. This is followed by inhalation with the head thrown back, when the hands are against the thighs. The swimmer submerges when his arms are extended in conjunction with the kick (FIG. 70).

FIG. 70

8 With an elastic rope: the rope (stretch-cord, strong elastic rope) is attached at one end to the edge of the pool, the other end being tied to the swimmer's waist. Using the full breaststroke action, the swimmer stretches the rope and then attempts to swim on the spot without being pulled back to the wall by the rope.

Variation: two swimmers are coupled together with an elastic rope attached to their waists and attempt to pull each other in their 'own' direction (FIG. 71).

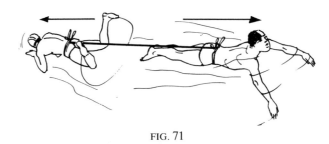

FIG. 71

9 Synchronised swimming: two or more participants swim alongside a 'lead swimmer'. They match the rhythm and speed of his breaststroke action (FIG. 72).

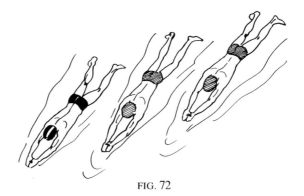

FIG. 72

Precision exercises for coordination

The following exercises make extreme demands on coordinative abilities. They are exercises for the advanced swimmer, and care should be taken that:

a) the basic coordination of arms and legs in breaststroke swimming is preserved;

b) the body is not rotated about its longitudinal axis (spinal-column axis);

c) the arm individually and the leg individually maintain their correct movement patterns.

1 With one leg: in a prone position and holding a kickboard in front, the swimmer performs a one-legged breaststroke kick. His head is raised and his inactive leg is loosely extended. After every half a length the active leg is changed.
Variation: the leg is changed after one movement.

2 With one arm: in a prone position and with a pull-buoy between the thighs, the swimmer pulls with one arm only, the other arm being extended forwards in the water. The arms are swapped after half a length, breathing at every third pull (FIG. 73).

FIG. 73

Variation: the arms are interchanged after two pulls.
Variation: the arms are changed after each pull.
Variation: as in the previous exercise, but the passive arm is held against the hip.

3 With single leg in action as a whole: the other leg is extended loosely, the legs being interchanged after half a length (FIG. 74).

FIG. 74

Variation: the leg change takes place after two movements, and subsequently after each movement.

4 With single arm in movement as a whole: the passive arm is extended forwards in the water, the arms swapping roles after half a length (FIG. 75a).

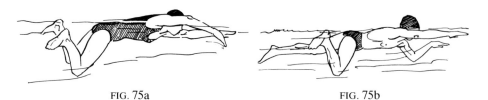

FIG. 75a   FIG. 75b

FIG. 75b Example of a demanding coordination exercise: the breaststroker moves his left arm and right leg in the normal action while his right arm and left leg are extended and idle; the next movement pattern is executed in a diagonally opposite manner

Variation: the arms are swapped after every second movement and subsequently after each movement.
Variation: the passive arm is held against the hip.
5 One-sided swimming: the breaststroker swims with his right arm and right leg, the left-side limbs remaining loosely extended. The active side changes over after half a length.
Variation: the change of sides takes place initially after every second movement, and subsequently after each movement.
6 With diagonal coordination: breaststroke is performed with right arm and left leg, the left arm and right leg remaining loosely extended. The side change takes place after half a length.
Variation: arms and legs are initially swapped after every second movement, and then after each movement.
7 Coordination variation: the swimmer performs a series of breaststroke exercises, such as three complete movements with right arm alone, three complete movements with left arm alone, three complete movements with both arms, three complete movements with right leg only, three complete movements, three diagonal sequences with right arm and left leg, three diagonal sequences with left arm and right leg, three complete movement patterns.

SWIMMING TECHNIQUE EXERCISES FOR DIVE START AND BACKSTROKE START

1 Dolphin dives: the dive is made from the bottom of a pool waist-deep to chest-deep, followed by a downward and upward glide (FIG. 76).
2 Backward dolphin dives: the arms are against the swimmer's sides, his head is thrown back and his hips upwards.

FIG. 76

3 Jumping-in in tuck position: the swimmer jumps as far as possible from the edge of the pool or from a starting block, making energetic use of the arms (FIG. 77).

FIG. 77

4 Running dive: after running quickly along the 1-m board, a header with arms outstretched is followed by a long glide (FIG. 78).

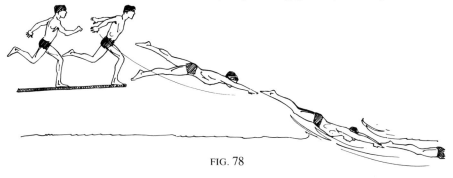

FIG. 78

5 Plunging: from a squatting position on the edge of the pool or on a starting block, the swimmer dives powerfully forward with his outstretched arms in front (FIG. 79).

FIG. 79

Variation: as in the previous exercise, but the starting position is standing with knees well bent, and with a 'tuck' on the up.
6 Starting dives with different takeoff angles: the swimmer dives over an imaginary cord stretched across the pool, the height of the cord and its distance from the edge of the pool being changed after each dive.
Variation: the swimmer alternates high-arc starting dives and straight-line mid-air phases, without using an imaginary cord.
7 'Boxing dives': the starting dive is performed with clenched fists and with the arms extended during takeoff, the fists being held against the chest in the initial position (FIG. 80).

FIG. 80

8 Alternate starting dives: the swimmer first of all performs a dive start with a circular armswing, alternated with a grab start.

9 Short-long starting dives: continuous alternation between dive starts with a long glide and starts with an early take-up of the swimming action; the stroke is also changed after two dive starts.

10 Dives through a hoop: the hoop floats or is held on the surface of the water; immediately after entry, the swimmer steers his body parallel to the surface (FIG. 81).

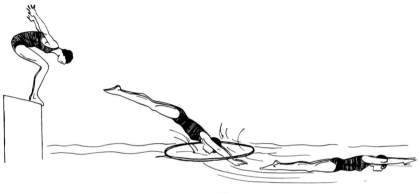

FIG. 81

11 High-arc dives: the dive is made upwards, the legs being tucked up immediately after takeoff and then extended backwards and upwards. The swimmer enters the water at a comparatively steep angle (FIG. 82).

FIG. 82

Variation: as in the previous exercise, but the body is steered parallel to the surface of the water immediately after entry.

12 Starting dives with half-twist: takeoff is forwards, the body rotating in the air about its longitudinal axis into the supine position (FIG. 83).

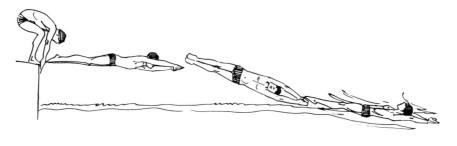

FIG. 83

Variation: the diver takes off backwards and twists into the prone position in flight.

13 Backward starting dive: the swimmer dives backwards from a squatting position at the edge of the pool, his arms gripping the starting block or the edge of the pool (FIG. 84).

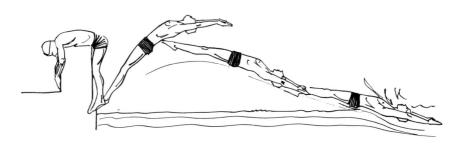

FIG. 84

14 Back start with arms at sides: entry and gliding curve are controlled only with the head, the swimmer gliding as far as he can.
   Variation: the start is performed with extended arms and with a long glide.

15 Backward starting dive: from a squatting position on the starting block, the swimmer falls backwards and takes off in a high arc (FIG. 85).
   Variation: as in the previous exercise, but the swimmer's hands are held by a partner during the backward fall in a squatting position. The

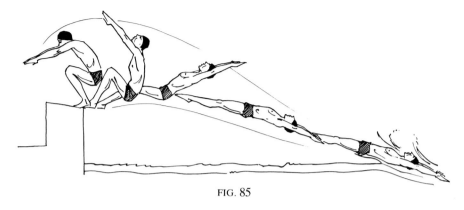

FIG. 85

partner stands behind the starting block or on the edge of the pool
(FIG. 86).

FIG. 86

16 Alternating back starts: alternately diving in a high arc and with a flat
   trajectory.
17 Short/long back starts: the swimming action is initiated early after a
   short glide; at the next diving start a long glide is combined with a late
   pick-up of the swimming action.
18 Dolphin glide: the back start is followed by a long glide underwater
   and by dolphin kicks.

SWIMMING TECHNIQUE EXERCISES FOR TURNS

1 In waist-deep water: the swimmer tilts to one side in a squatting
  position, then presses hard with his hand on the bottom of the pool,
  tipping his squatting body over to the other side (FIG. 87).

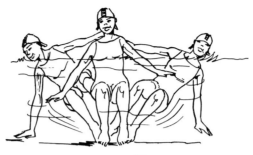

FIG. 87

Variation: as in the previous exercise, but tilting from one side to the other repeatedly without a break.

Variation: as in the previous exercise, but after the push-off from the bottom, the free (i.e. not pushing-off) arm, with palm uppermost, pulls from the hip to the shoulder to accelerate the tilting process (FIG. 88).

FIG. 88

2 In shallow water at the side of the pool: the swimmer tilts from the squatting position towards the wall and fully bends (passively) his turning arm. By pressing against the wall with the turning arm, the body is tilted sideways and the swimmer can push off.

Variation: as in the previous exercise, but tilting and turning are executed on the other side.

Variation: the 'grab' or 'throwaway' turn (the term customarily used in breaststroke and butterfly) is executed after a glide almost up to the wall. The swimmer adopts the side position beforehand and looks fixedly at his turning arm.

3 From the crawl: the side position (towards the turning arm) is adopted at the instant the hand touches the wall. After push-off the turning arm performs an arc over the head into the water.

4 From a prone position: the swimmer glides in the prone position and touches the wall with both hands simultaneously with arms extended, the side position having been previously adopted by rapid withdrawal of the free arm with the elbow advanced (FIG. 89).

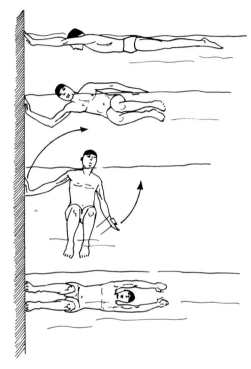

FIG. 89

Variation: two-arm grab turn from breaststroke.
Variation: two-arm grab turn from butterfly.
5 Turning in open water: the grab turns are executed from the glide in open water without a wall, with the turning arm pushing off against the water.
Variation: the grab turns are executed in open water from crawl, breaststroke and butterfly.
Variation: all the turns should also be performed on the unaccustomed side.
6 With twist: the swimmer makes his grab turn at the wall and pushes off. During his glide on his side he executes a quarter-rotation about his longitudinal axis, gliding into the prone position.

Variation: as in the previous exercise, but carrying on swimming in a prone position: crawl, breaststroke or butterfly.

Variation: a quarter-twist from the side-position glide and the transition to the swimming action are executed on the unaccustomed side of the body.

7 Into the supine position: from the pushoff in the side position, a quarter-twist into the supine position is executed during the glide, and the back crawl is adopted (FIG. 90).

FIG. 90

8 With half a forward roll: during the glide there is a double arm pull to the thighs. The head is then quickly inclined towards the chest and the tucked-up body executes a half-roll. The swimmer swims back to the wall on his back (FIG. 91).

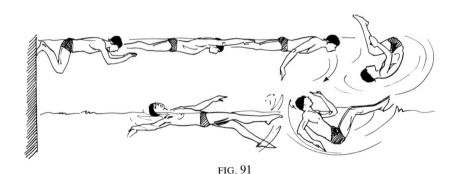

FIG. 91

9 With a half-twist: from the glide in the prone position with arms extended in front, the swimmer rotates about the extended longitudinal axis onto his back and continues with the backcrawl.

10 With half a backward roll: after pushoff and glide in a supine position with the arms extended backwards, one arm performs a backstroke

pull. The head is then thrown back sharply and the body performs a half-roll. The swimmer then swims back to the wall on his back (FIG. 92).

FIG. 92

11 With a quarter-twist and half-roll: pushoff and glide in supine position; during the glide the extended body rotates about its longitudinal axis into the prone position. This is followed by a half forward roll and backstroke to the wall.
12 From an inactive prone position at the surface of the water: the arms are held against the hips with palms downwards, and the face looks forwards. The head bends forward energetically towards the chest, and the arms press strongly downwards. The buttocks move upwards and the swimmer performs half a forward roll with extended legs into the supine position (FIG. 93).

FIG. 93

Variation: as in previous exercise, but at the same time as the head movement, a dolphin kick from the bent knees initiates the roll.
13 Turning on a 'turntable' in supine position: after pushoff and a short glide in supine position with extended arms, execute backstroke pull

with one arm and tuck up legs toward the chest out of the water. Then rotate the tucked-up body with slightly raised head (lying as if on a turntable) through 180 degrees about an axis through the navel. The upper arm presses against the direction of rotation (FIG. 94).

FIG. 94

Variation: as in the previous exercise, but the non turning arm supports the rotation by pressing with the palm firstly outwards and then towards the head.

Variation: the turntable turn is performed in the opposite direction.

14 Half-twist and half forward roll: the swimmer glides from the pushoff on his back with arms extended and rotates about his longitudinal axis into the prone position. Using his head, legs and arms, he changes to a supine position via a half-roll and swims the backcrawl back to the push-off point (FIG. 95).

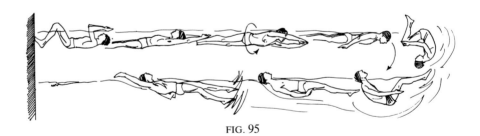

FIG. 95

15 As a two-arm roll turn: from breaststroke, pull both arms in a double pull towards the thighs. Turn onto back by a half-roll and swim back doing the backcrawl.

Variation: perform exercise, starting from butterfly.

Variation: perform exercise, starting from crawl, after one arm has been halted in front and the other taken to it.

16 As a one-armed roll turn: after the arm pull of the crawl, one arm is held against the hip, the other following suit after its pull. A forward

half-roll is initiated by bending the head and a dolphin kick. The arms press powerfully downwards and then bend up towards the head (FIG. 96).

FIG. 96

17 Half-twist and half forward roll: the swimmer swims the crawl and turns onto his back (half-twist) as his right arm leaves the water and swings in the swimming direction. As soon as the right arm enters the water backwards, the head is thrown back into a half backward roll. This is followed by swimming breaststroke or crawl back to the side of the pool (FIG. 97).

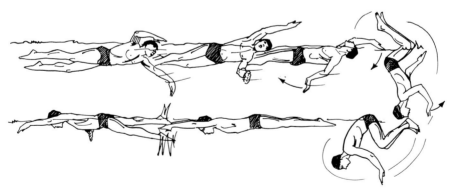

FIG. 97

EXERCISES TO IMPROVE 'FEEL FOR THE WATER'

Exercises to increase a swimmer's feel for the water do not relate so much to particular swimming strokes. They are intended, rather, from time to time, to increase the sensitivity of the young swimmer to a propulsive performance making maximum utilisation of the properties of water.

Sensitivity related to pressure, position and muscle force is covered in the main by contrast exercises. Exercises for feel for the water are aimed at two additional areas:

a) sensitivity which can minimise the water resistance retarding the swimmer (gliding exercises);
b) sensitivity to the fact that curving arm movements and favourable angles of pitch of the hands can increase propulsion (sculling exercises).

Whereas the relevance of gliding exercises to competitive swimming is readily apparent, an acceptance of sculling exercises calls for an explanation of the effect of hydrodynamic lift. This is the phenomenon, whereby, by analogy to the blades of a ship's propeller, movements of the hand and forearm at right angles to the direction of travel can propel the body through the water. This assumes, of course, that the hand and forearm exhibit a sufficient velocity and exhibit an angle of pitch (between palm and its direction of movement) of approximately 37 degrees (Schleihauf 1977).

The term 'sculling exercises' originates from the sculling action of the Italian gondoliers. To propel their gondolas, they waggle an oar backwards and forwards transverse to the direction of travel, adjusting the position of the blade of the oar so as to produce an angle of pitch in relation to oar movement. In swimming, these lateral movements and the pitch of the hand occur in the curving patterns for the crawl, butterfly and backstroke, but especially in the breaststroke.

Gliding exercises

1 Diving start, followed by gliding as far as possible: body well extended, head as an extension of the body between the outstretched arms, shoulders thrust forward, legs closed and extended to the toes. This is known as the 'plunge' dive.
2 As 1, but several times from a running start over the edge of the pool or from a 1-m board (FIG. 98).
3 Glide as far as possible after pushing off from the wall of the pool: in prone position and on side, to right and left.
4 Glide as far as possible after pushing off from the bottom of the pool (dolphin dive).
5 From a position standing leaning well forward, dive head-first into the

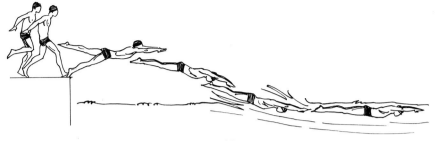

FIG. 98

deep part of the pool (diving area) and down to the bottom: from the side of the pool, 1-m board, 3-m board or platform (FIG. 99).

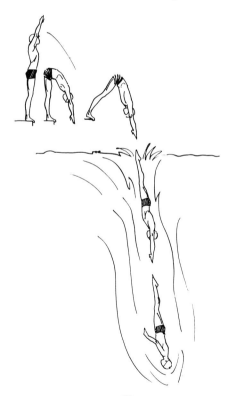

FIG. 99

6 Push off with an underwater pull and glide out:
   a) with arms stretched out in front,
   b) with arms at sides.

7 Push off and glide on back.
8 Back start and glide on back.
9 Dolphin dive backwards from bottom of pool and glide with arms at sides.
10 A partner pushes the swimmer, and with a final push at a specified point causes him to glide as far as possible (FIG. 100).

FIG. 100

11 One swimmer in prone or supine position pushes off from the edge of the pool at a distance of 0.5 m parallel to the long side, and glides until after about 5 m a partner grasps him by an arm and a leg and propels him further on. Other helpers at 3-m intervals 'float' him to the end of the pool in the same way (FIG. 101). The exercise is also possible in deep water if the 'floaters' stand on the step and hold on to the edge of the pool with one hand.

FIG. 101

12 Starting from a sprint crawl or sprint backcrawl lay the arms forwards in succession at a specified point and glide as far as possible. With the exception of Nos. 5 and 11, all the exercises can also be performed in the form of contests.

Sculling exercises

1 Swim head-first in a supine position, using only side-sculling hand movements, possibly with a pull-buoy between the knees (FIG. 102).

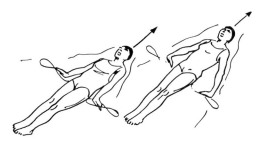

FIG. 102

2 As 1, but swimming feet-first.
3 As 2, but sculling the arms inwards and outwards behind the head, propelling the body feet-first (FIG. 103).

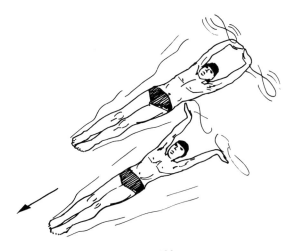

FIG. 103

4 Using sculling movements, first of all at shoulder height, then at the side beside the body, raise the body vertically in the water (FIG. 104); particularly suitable for breaststroke and butterfly swimmers.
5 Swim head-first in prone position by sculling with hands beside the hips, with pull-buoy between the knees.

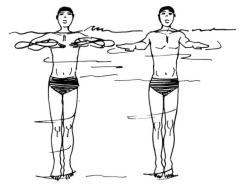

FIG. 104

6 As 5, but sculling with forearms and hands at shoulder level (FIG. 105); particularly suitable for breaststroke and butterfly swimmers.

FIG. 105

7 Swim feet-first in prone position; to do so, scull with arms behind head.
8 As 7, but sculling with forearms and hands at shoulder level.
9 In prone position, with head and upper body lying on a large float in such a way that the arms are supported ahead as far as the elbows: simultaneous sculling movements of the forearms outwards and inwards (FIG. 106).

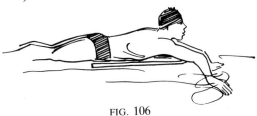

FIG. 106

10 As 9, but forearms 'sculling in parallel', like car windscreen wipers.
11 Breaststroke arm action with pull-buoy between thighs: execute only inward sculling movements with both arms, and extend the arms outwards again with the hands in front (FIG. 107).

FIG. 107

Variation: a pull-buoy is also held under each armpit.
12 As 11, but feet-first on back.
    All the exercises can be performed with paddles.

CONTRAST EXERCISES

By 'contrast exercises' we mean exercises which enable a swimmer to experience the contrast between incorrect (unfavourable) and correct (favourable) movements within the swimming strokes. They could consequently also be called wrong/right exercises. This type of exercise is designed to sharpen up the young swimmer's perception of a considerable part of his action.

Thus, for example, after the intentional incorrect execution of the arm pull with clenched fist, the swimmer will be appreciably more aware of the pressure surface inside his hand than he would be without the preceding contrast. In this way it is possible, in the early years of training, to train in particular the sense of pressure or touch (haptic sense), positional sense (vestibular sense) and muscle (force) sense (kinesthetic sense). Such exercises also contribute to the ability at an early stage to compile the movement sensations of the swimmer's own limbs into a space-related image of his own body (body diagram).

This image of the body, together with the pressure, positional and muscle-force senses, determine the quality of swimming technique. They act as reference points for subsequent improvements and corrections to movements.

It is important that the incorrect execution should always be followed by the contrasting correctly execution of the exercise. It is an advantage if the young swimmer learns to describe his perception in words during the correct exercise.

The appearance of the exercise is such that the complete action, e.g. of the breaststroke, is performed in the normal body position and with the full action, but the hands or fingers should be:

a) clenched into a fist (FIG. 108);

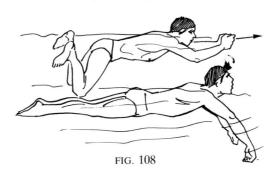

FIG. 108

b) curved;
e) spread (FIG. 109);
d) pressed firmly together.

FIG. 109

On each occasion a short distance of 10 to 15 m is swum in the above manner. This is immediately followed, without a break, by a longer stretch of 20 to 25 m with the hands held in the normal manner.

The contrast exercises can be performed in exactly the same way in butterfly, crawl and backstroke. Another possibility is:

e) with everted or inverted palms (i.e. using the edge of the hand), cut the water from front to back, in order subsequently to 'catch' the water better with backward-facing palms.

In the following exercises the young swimmer swims with the correct hand and finger configuration, but in this instance the arms should be pulled back:

a) extended;
b) slightly bent;
c) very bent.

Breaststroke can be practised in contrast to the correct technique by:

a) drawing the arms back far beyond the shoulder line;
b) only opening the arms briefly to pull in front of the body.

Contrast exercises can, of course, also be performed for the leg actions. With an otherwise correct arm action, the legs, during crawl, backstroke or butterfly, should either:

a) beat up and down fully extended, or
b) bend at the knee up to the buttocks and stretch.

In breaststroke:

a) the knees could be drawn well under the stomach;
b) the legs could be not bent at the hips at all, but only at the knees;
c) the legs could be widely splayed;
d) the legs could move with the thighs tightly closed-up.

These contrast exercises too should always be followed by the correct execution of the action.

All the strokes can, moreover, be attempted either with:

a) dorsiflexed feet (drawn-up toes) (FIG. 110), or
b) plantar-flexed feet (pointed, ballet-like).

FIG. 110

The otherwise correct execution of all four strokes also allows contrast by swimming:

a) with the head permanently raised above the water;
b) with an exaggeratedly deep head position.

The exercise naturally ends with the correct head position.

COMBINATION EXERCISES

These combine components of different swimming strokes. In addition to assisting coordination, they fit in well in training for basic swimming endurance, particularly to provide variety in an extensive interval training series. They should, of course, only be used once a week and only at the beginning of a session. Combinations with butterfly arm action are unsuitable for endurance training.

Arm action combined with leg action in prone position

ARMS	LEGS
− breaststroke	+ crawl
− breaststroke	+ butterfly
− crawl	+ breaststroke (FIG. 111)
− crawl	+ butterfly
− butterfly	+ crawl
− butterfly	+ breaststroke

FIG. 111

Arm action combined with leg action in supine position

ARMS	LEGS
− backcrawl	+ breaststroke
− backcrawl	+ butterfly
− symmetrical pull (to hip)	+ breaststroke

– old English backstroke   + backcrawl (FIG. 112)
  (two-armed out-of-water
  recovery)

FIG. 112

– old English backstroke   + breaststroke
– old English backstroke   + butterfly
– sidestroke   + breaststroke on side (FIG. 113)
  (right and left)
– sidestroke   + crawl on side

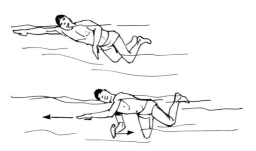

FIG. 113

8 Flexibility training

Flexibility, or 'mobility', training, is designed basically to increase the range of movement in joints for the benefit of swimming technique. In addition, such training promotes both muscular relaxation (reduction of myostatic stretch reflex) and effective muscle contraction (pre-stretching). Its effect is based on the fact that it extends or stretches the muscles pulling via the joint, together with their connective-tissue sheaths and tendons, and also increases the deflection of the joint in opposition to the limitation from ligaments and joint capsule (suppleness).

Flexibility exercises should be performed for at least 10 to 15 minutes before every swimming training session, as well as before warming up for a race. They can be repeated in modified form without a partner before the start. Flexibility exercises are absolutely essential before strength training and circuit training, particularly because of the stretching effect; 5 to 10 minutes of preparatory flexibility exercises is the minimum.

All flexibility exercises in which the young swimmer has to sit, kneel or lie on the floor require a soft base, e.g. a thick towel.

In order to avoid strains or torn tissue, the body should be warmed up beforehand by running, hopping, skipping, arm circling, squat or star jumps, body twisting, press-ups, etc. This should be followed first of all by flexibility exercises without a partner (type-A exercises), then by exercises with a partner (type-B exercises), and finally individual dynamic exercises (type-C), e.g. swinging arm-crosses in front of and behind the body.

Exercises with a partner should always be performed with great care and attention: the assisting partner should control movements gently and sensitively; he must slacken off immediately the exercising partner shows pain in any way.

It is therefore advisable, whenever possible, to have the same partners working alternately with each other.

As training experience is accumulated, the type-B exercises can be considerably refined. On the basis of comparative research, two methods of stretching with a partner helping have been shown to be particularly effective (Hartley-O'Brien 1980):

Static stretching

'This method consists purely of passive stretching, e.g. the leg of the partner (lying on his back) is passively raised and gradually pulled to its limit. The limit, which is just below the pain threshold, is held passively for about 60 seconds' (Hogg 1978, p. 116). Exercises of this nature are suitable for the build-up stage of training; at that age and training experience the age-group swimmer should be responsible enough to handle the partner properly.

Passive 3-S stretching exercises

In this case a partner also raises the passive leg of the swimmer and, counting out loud, gently pulls it in 6 seconds to the limit of leg deflection. In this position, for over 6 seconds, the swimmer performs an isometric muscle contraction against the partner's resistance, i.e. he attempts with all his strength to press his leg downwards, without being able to move it from the spot. This time it is best for him to count the seconds out loud. He then relaxes the previously contracted muscles without changing the position of the leg. The partner can now force the swimmer's leg a few centimetres further down and back. This he again does while counting the 6 seconds out loud, and so on, up to 60 seconds.

It is recommended that 3-S exercises (Scientific Stretching for Sport) be performed only at the elite training stage, firstly because isometric strength training has to be coped with, and secondly no further development-related mobility changes are to be expected. In other words, maintaining or increasing flexibility is only then possible by means of flexibility training. This means a daily minimum of 10 to 15 minutes.

Since boys are generally less supple than girls, they need to do more flexibility training. The same applies, of course, to girls who are exceptionally inflexible and to swimmers who are prone to frequent injuries, particularly to torn muscles. A training schedule should also take into account the fact that a breaststroke swimmer should devote about half of his training time to the flexibility of his hip and ankle joints.

It should be pointed out that the following exercises are only a selection, which may be extended as required, either on the basis of the reader's own ideas or from literature. The basic considerations applicable to stretching and suppleness must, of course, be borne in mind.

FLEXIBILITY EXERCISES (STRETCHING AND SUPPLENESS)

Type-A exercises

1 One hand grasps the elbow of the other arm and pulls it behind the head to the opposite side (FIG. 114).

FIG. 114   FIG. 115

2 The same exercise is performed with a direct alternation of right to left and left to right, for which purpose the arms are folded above and slightly behind the head (FIG. 115).
3 Starting with arms raised with everted overlapping palms, the arms are pressed to the side with the smallest possible lateral movement of the torso (FIG. 116).
4 One arm is held out in front, palm uppermost and the hand bent downwards; the other hand grips the fingers of the first from beneath and bends them firmly back (FIG. 117).
5 The same exercise is performed on the downward-bent hand, so that the back of the hand and forearm are stretched (FIG. 118).
6 After adopting a hurdling position, the torso, head and arms are slowly bent forward and, after straightening up again, are slowly bent to the sides (FIG. 119).

FIG. 116

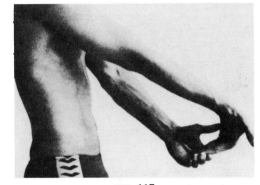

FIG. 117

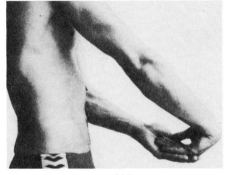

FIG. 118

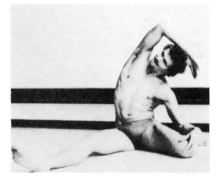

FIG. 119

7 Sitting with legs slightly apart, with knees fully bent and toes pointing outwards, slowly lower the buttocks to the floor between the lower legs, so that the toes are pointing forwards and outwards and the arch of the instep is resting on the floor (FIG. 120).

8 The same exercise can be made more difficult if, after the buttocks touch the floor, the upper body is slowly lowered backwards (FIG. 121).

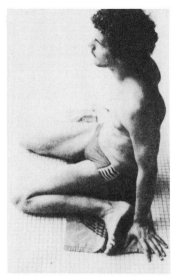

FIG. 120

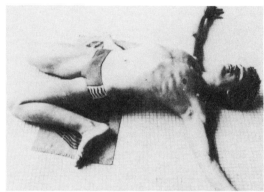

FIG. 121

9 With the same initial exercise, instead of lowering the torso grip the toes from outside with the hands and pull them forward and inwards (FIG. 122).

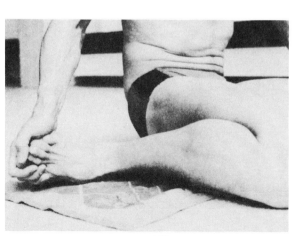

FIG. 122

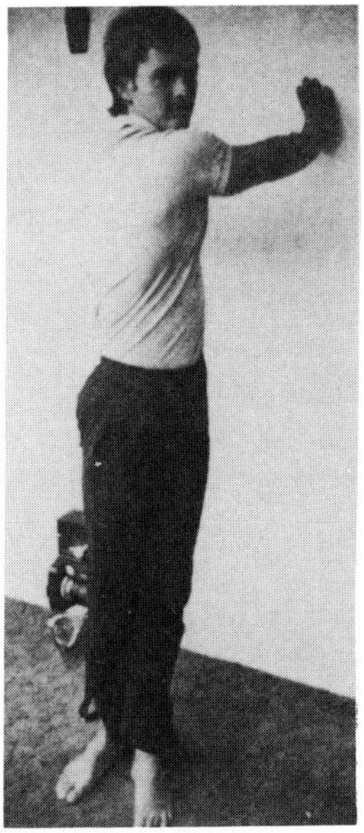

FIG. 123

10 In a sitting position, tuck up the legs and place the soles of the feet together; support the forearms on the insides of the knees and slowly force the knees to the floor.

11 Sitting with outstretched legs, cross one leg over the other and place the foot on the floor: supported on the floor by both hands alongisde the buttocks (both on the side of the crossed-over leg), slowly turn the body over into a press-up position.

12 Standing with outstretched arms, place the palms on the wall: without letting go, rotate the body to one side by small steps on the spot, and then in the opposite direction (FIG. 123).

13 Stand about 1 m from a wall (or a partner), supporting yourself with your hands. With extended body, lean further and further against the wall, keeping the heels firmly on the ground. Then increase the distance between feet and wall (FIG. 124).

14 Sit with outstretched legs and place the hands behind the body about shoulder-width apart. Slowly slide the hands as far back as possible, so that when the arms have gone as far as they can, the torso continues to lay back (FIG. 125).

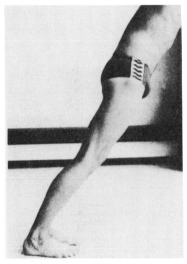

FIG. 124

FIG. 125

15 Sitting on the heels, slowly lower the upper body backwards; the arms can initially support the body at the sides (FIG. 126).

16 In a supine position, raise the legs and lower body to the vertical. Then bring the legs down to touch the floor alongside the head to right and left (FIG. 127).

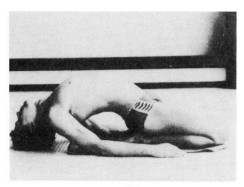

FIG. 126

FIG. 127

Type-B exercises

1 Sitting with legs outstretched, interlock the fingers behind the neck, so that the elbows are pointing outwards. A partner places his everted knee between the shoulder blades of the seated swimmer and pulls his elbows back with his hands (FIG. 128).

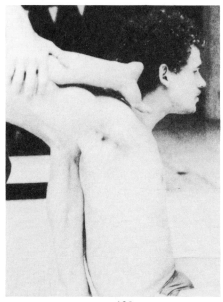

FIG. 128

FIG. 129

2 In a standing position, a partner slowly presses the backward-stretched arms (with interlocked fingers) upwards as far as possible. To prevent cheating, the person actually doing the exercise can be made to stand against a wall (FIG. 129).

3 The same effect of this exercise can be achieved to a magnified extent if the extended arms of the partner lying on his stomach are raised slowly upwards and forwards from the buttocks (FIG. 130).

4 In prone position, the partner stands astride the buttocks and, facing the exercising swimmer's feet, grasps his legs and lifts them (FIG. 131).

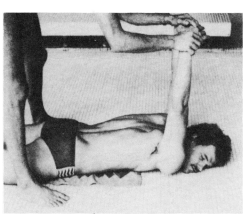

FIG. 130

FIG. 131

5 Sitting with legs outstretched, the swimmer passes his interlocked hands round the neck of a partner behind him standing with one leg in front of the other and with his body inclined slightly forward, supporting himself with his outstretched arms on the shoulders of the seated swimmer. The partner forces the shoulders of the seated swimmer forward with a bounce, at the same time pulling his arms back and up with his neck.

6 Force the arms back at just below shoulder height and cross them (FIG. 132).

7 Bring the extended arms together just behind the buttocks until there is a gap of 20 to 30 cm between the hands, then raise the arms slowly and outwards slightly.

8 Sitting with outstretched legs or kneeling on the floor, raise one elbow

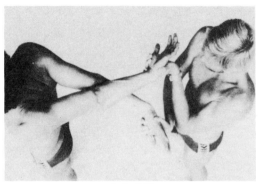

FIG. 132

FIG. 133

with the forearm hanging down, and pull this elbow towards the other side just behind the head (FIG. 133).

9 In prone position: partner forces the plantar-flexed feet on the bent legs down against the buttocks. The exercise can also be started initially with one foot (FIG. 134).

10 In prone position: bend the lower legs back and up, and draw the toes outwards. The partner grasps the instep and toes from behind and presses forward and down (FIG. 135).

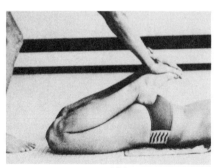

FIG. 134

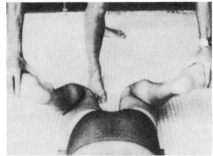

FIG. 135

11 Prone position: partner stands or crouches astride the buttocks and draws the elbows forcefully up and back. The exercising swimmer's hands are behind his neck (FIG. 136).

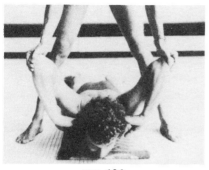

FIG. 136

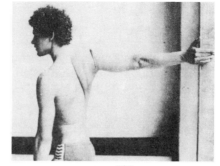

FIG. 137

Type-C exercises

1 Bending at the waist with legs slightly apart, arms stretched out at the sides: rotate the upper body and arms, touching the right foot with the left hand, and vice versa.
2 Standing with legs slightly apart, arms outstretched to sides: rotate upper body and arms, springing back in each direction.
3 Standing with arms folded above the head, with each hand gripping the elbow of the other arm: interchanging, suddenly, each elbow is pulled to the other side behind the head.
4 Standing sideways-on to a wall, alongside a tree, post, or the like, with the palm of the outstretched arm resting on the wall, etc.: thrust the shoulders forward and rotate the same side of the body forwards (FIG. 137).
5 With the upper body inclined forward and arms outstretched over a starting block, bench, fence, or the like, drop the torso and alternately with a bounce dip the right or left shoulder well down (FIG. 138).

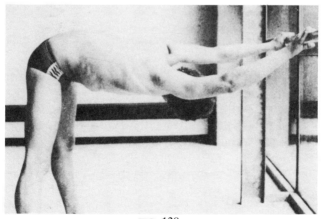

FIG. 138

6 Standing on one leg, bend the other leg and raise the foot to the buttocks. Grip with the hand from inside under the instep and powerfully flex the foot upwards and forwards against the thigh. Breaststroke swimmers grip from above (FIG. 139) on the sole of the bent foot and on the arch at the big toe and pull the toes out against the thigh (FIG. 139b).

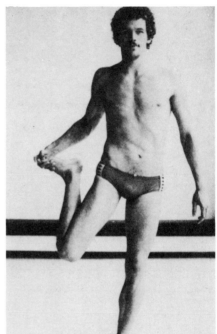

FIG. 139   FIG. 139b

7 Standing with legs slightly apart, grip a rope or towel at shoulder width: bend to sides with extended arms (FIG. 140).
8 Stand gripping a rope or towel at about twice the width of the shoulders, with one arm extended upwards and the other downwards behind the back: with the lower arm pull the upper arm as far as possible backwards and inwards (FIG. 141).
9 Hold the rope or towel high with the hands as close to each other as possible: with arms extended, move the rope continuously backwards to the buttocks and in the reverse direction, keeping it as horizontal as possible FIG. 142).
10 One arm held high: stretch arm and shoulder upwards to the limit and hold the position for 6 seconds.
11 Both arms held high: stretch arms and shoulders upwards to the limit and hold for 6 seconds.

FIG. 140   FIG. 141

12 Standing with the hands interlocked behind the buttocks: swing the
extended arms springily upwards and forwards, at the same time
bending the body well forward (FIG. 143).

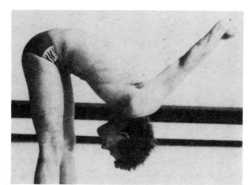

FIG. 142   FIG. 143

TABLE 2 Flexibility training within the framework of a long-term training schedule

METHODS/TYPES OF EXERCISES				
			(B) Stretching exercises with partner	
	(A) Gentle stretching using own body weight		(A) Gentle stretching using own body weight	
	(C) Ballistic stretching exercises		(C) Ballistic stretching exercises	
TRAINING YEAR	1	2	3	4
DAILY TRAINING TIME FOR FLEXIBILITY (IN MINUTES)	5	8	8–10	8–10
TRAINING STAGE	BASIC INSTRUCTION		BASIC TRAINING	

13 In a standing position, hold out the arms just below shoulder height: swing the outstretched arms alternately forward and back, swinging them across each other.

14 In a standing position, single-arm and two-arm circling forwards and backwards.

15 In a standing position, circle arms in opposite directions.

		3–S exercises	
Static stretching		Static stretching	
(B) Stretching exercises with partner		(B) Stretching exercises with partner	
(A) Gentle stretching using own body weight		(A) Gentle stretching using own body weight	
(C) Ballistic flexibility exercises		(C) Ballistic flexibility exercises	
5	6	7	8
		Spr 10	10
	Spr 10	MD 13	15
8–10	MD/D 13	D 15	20

PROGRESSIVE TRAINING   **ELITE TRAINING**

9 Endurance in relation to swimming

Endurance may be defined as resistance to fatigue under physical stress.

It is mainly limited by two factors:

a) A central factor, associated with the efficiency of the cardio-circulatory and respiratory system;

b) A local factor, related to the efficiency of the individual muscle cells.

Body movements are brought about by the contraction of individual muscle cells. Muscular contraction is a process involving energy. It can therefore only continue while energy is available.

This energy is supplied to the body through the intake of food in the form of carbohydrates, fats and protein. The energy contained in the food cannot, however, be used directly for contraction, but has to be converted beforehand.

The only energy-supplying substance which directly permits muscle contraction is so-called adenosine triphosphate (ATP), which is only present in the muscle cell in small quantities. It is only sufficient for a few muscle contractions and would be used up if the small store were not topped up again by other metabolic systems.

Depending on the extent and intensity of the physical activity, the ATP required for muscular contraction can be provided by the following three metabolic processes:

a) By splitting creatine phosphate (CP) and transmitting the energy thus produced to adenosine diphosphate (ADP). This process is referred to as anaerobic-alactacid energy provision, or the 'ATP-CP' ('phosphogen') system.

b) by glycolysis, an anaerobic-lactic acid energy provision process, based on the splitting of glycogen into lactic acid (taking place in the cell plasma);

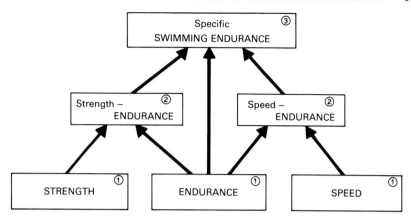

FIG. 144 The part played by conditioning motor capabilities of strength, speed and endurance in specific swimming endurance: 1 = basic capabilities, 2 = composite capabilites, 3 = applied capability. The quantitative composition varies according to the distance and intensity of the swimming

c) by breaking down carbohydrates and fats by means of oxygen (oxidation), which takes place in the mitochondria of the muscle cells and is called aerobic energy provision.

All three systems can basically provide the energy required during physical activity. In most cases, however, only one or two are operative at the same time or overlap in the course of physical stress. Which system supplies the energy is determined by two factors: with what intensity; and to what extent the loading is applied.

In a greatly simplified form, the three energy-supplying systems can be represented as three interconnected liquid reservoirs of different sizes (see FIG. 145).

As the diagram shows, energy can only be supplied to the muscle cells via the middle reservoir (1) by opening the valve (V). Reservoirs 2 and 3 are used to top up the middle reservoir as quickly as possible to prevent its being emptied as a result of physical activity.

At the beginning of any physical exercise it is consequently the first system (creatine phosphate and ATP) that supplies the energy required.

The energy-rich phosphates stored in the muscles have one big advantage: they can provide the energy for muscular contraction immediately and without a supply of oxygen (anaerobically). Their drawback is, of course, that this energy is only present in small quantities, which is indicated in FIG. 145 by the smallness of the

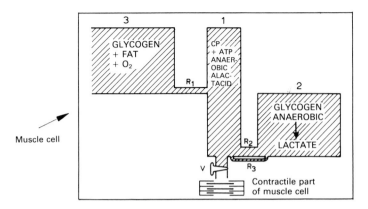

FIG. 145 Model of energy-supplying systems for muscular contraction in a muscle cell (hydraulic model after Margaria 1976)

reservoir. It is only sufficient for 7 to 12 seconds of the most intense activity.

If an extremely high-intensity physical loading is continued for more than 7 to 12 seconds, the first reservoir has to be continuously topped up. It is topped up from the second system. This system's 'energy reservoir' is larger than the first, but its energy flows in smaller quantities per unit time (the outlet R_2 has a smaller diameter). Physical exercise which brings the second system into play, i.e. lasting longer than about 12 seconds, cannot therefore be performed at the same high intensity.

The energy of the second system is obtained by splitting the glycogen stored in the muscle to form lactic acid. This process is referred to as glycolysis. Like the first process, it takes place without oxygen, i.e. it is independent of breathing. The second system overlaps the first, i.e. it begins to top up the first reservoir immediately its 'energy level' falls. This occurs in fractions of a second. The drawback is that the end product of the metabolic processes in the second system, namely lactic acid, accumulates so quickly as the physical loading continues that acidosis of the working muscles occurs, and, after a certain time (approx. 3 minutes), of the body too. Lactic acid is thus produced in the working muscles during very intensive exercise lasting longer than 7 to 12 seconds. It is then transmitted to the blood.

Lactic acid accumulation is measured in hundredths of a gramme of the molecular weight of lactic acid, related to one litre of blood (mmol/l). At rest, a person has on average a lactic acid accumulation of 0.5 to 1.5 mmol/l).

The efficiency of the second system (glycolysis) is exhausted after maximum exercise for about 45 seconds. This means that, after a maximum swimming load, the second reservoir is empty. The lactic acid produced in the working muscles is distributed over a large proportion of the body fluid. Acidosis of the body is produced. Since the distribution of the lactic acid over the body occurs within a few minutes, body fluid (e.g. capillary blood from the ear-lobe) can be painlessly sampled after the physical loading, and the lactic acid concentration can be determined. The highest lactic acid values are measured in sports and disciplines in which the load lasts for about 45 seconds: 22-25 mmol/l.

We know from experience that attempts to start the 400-m crawl at 100-m pace lead to an appreciable reduction of swimming speed at the latest after the turn at 100 m, and the participants collapse. The reason for this is the acidosis of the propelling muscles, involving muscular pain and causing loss of coordination. At a lactic acid concentration of 22-25 mmol/l the glycolysis is inhibited, since the second reservoir is empty. The activity can therefore only be continued if the first reservoir receives an energy boost from the third. As can be seen from FIG. 145, the connecting pipe R_1 is narrower than R_2. For this reason even less energy per unit time can flow through R_1 than through R_2. In consequence, the intensity of the loading has to be reduced still further.

The third system starts to provide energy roughly 5 to 8 seconds after the beginning of the activity. However, since this system can only supply energy under aerobic conditions, it is dependent on the swimmer's breathing.

The breathing needs a comparatively long time to get going: it takes approximately 60 seconds for the third system to reach 'full revs'.

During this period the second system contributes the energy lacking for a particular performance. Let us stay with the example of a 400-m race. For the reasons listed earlier (acidosis, coordination disturbances, etc.), nobody starts the first 100 m at top speed. If, say, a time of around 5 minutes is being aimed at, it is obvious that the first two systems cannot on their own supply the requisite energy. Since, however, the third system only comes into play slowly, it cannot help supply the energy required during the first 45 to 60 seconds of the activity. The shortfall in energy has to be covered by the first and second systems. This amount of energy, which consequently has to be covered anaerobically, is referred to as the 'energy deficit'.

The energy deficit can only be made good from the third system reservoir, involving breathing (aerobically), after the physical activity has ceased. This does not happen until no further energy is needed to cope with the continuous load. Because of the anticipation of the subsequent energy balance involving breathing, we talk of a so-called 'oxygen debt'.

Like the other two systems, the third also has one big advantage and one disadvantage.

The advantage is that if sufficient oxygen is provided by breathing, the energy produced by the consumption of glycogen and fatty acids is available for an almost unlimited time. The waste products water and carbon dioxide can be got rid of with no problem, instead of having them affect the body.

The disadvantage is that the amount of energy flowing from the third reservoir per unit time is comparatively small. For this reason, it is only possible to swim with a lower loading intensity than when the first and second systems are called upon. In addition, as has already been mentioned, breathing does not reach its maximum efficiency until after about 60 seconds.

Physical activity of long duration is consequently only possible with the involvement of the third energy-supplying system. This implies that swimming, exceeding 45 seconds in normal cases, always takes place with the assistance of breathing.

The first and second energy systems play a mainly bridging role in swimming: they permit intensive physical activity by ensuring the supply of energy until the third system can take over.

The efficiency of the third (aerobic) system depends on central and local factors.

Central factors
1 The quantity of air, in litres, which can be inhaled and exhaled by the lungs (breathing volume per minute);
2 The amount of oxygen transferred to the blood from the inhaled air in the lungs;
3 The amount of blood flowing through the lungs per unit time; this depends on the delivery rate of the heart (beat volume × beat frequency = heart volume per minute).

Local factors
The oxygen absorption capacity and oxygen utilisation capacity of the working muscle cells (so-called 'internal breathing').

10 Control of training using load norms

The application of accepted training fundamentals and methods, together with consideration of the special conditions in swimming, call for a control of training in the form of data concerning what speed, how long, with what intervals, etc., the swimmer is to swim in order to improve particular conditional skills or abilities.

Regardless of which particular swimming skill is concerned or whether the type of conditioning involved contributes only indirectly to improvement of swimming performance, training requires that standard values be laid down for the nature, duration, intensity, frequency and intervals of the swimming. These standard values are referred to in the following as 'load norms' and will appear in the same order in all the tabular training recommendations.

Since the nature and the magnitude of the load norms, as well as their relationship to one another, depend on which area of conditioning is to be improved, the objective is always stated before the data. The order of the information can be represented by the acronym ANDFIR:

A = Aim of training; conditional skill
N = Number of repeats
D = Distance of a repeat
F = Form of movement execution; movement pattern; swimming technique or stroke
I = Intensity; swimming speed
R = Rest interval duration; nature of rest interval.

The quantitative details of the load norms are in certain cases given as absolute values, e.g. the distance to be swum at the basic speed in training is indicated as 8 to 20 m. In other cases they have to be relative figures, e.g. a percentage of the race speed currently possible. The reason for this is the desire to make the load norms as easy to use as

possible, but without neglecting dependence on the personal performance factors of the swimmer (see TABLE 3).

AIM	IMPROVING BASIC SWIMMING ENDURANCE (AEROBIC CAPACITY)	IMPROVING SPEED ENDURANCE (ANAEROBIC CAPACITY)
NUMBER	20	4 sets of 5
DISTANCE	100 m	100 m
FORM	Crawl at steady speed	Crawl at steady speed
INTENSITY	Equivalent to lactate concentration of 4 mmol/l = e.g. 1.22 m/sec $\simeq$ 1:22 min	Equivalent to lactate concentration of 6 to 8 mmol/l = e.g. 1.44 m/sec $\simeq$ 1:09 min
REST INTERVAL	Approx. 23 sec, i.e. starting every 1:45 min	Approx. 1:15 min, i.e. on 2:30 min; 1 minute longer interval after every fifth repeat

TABLE 3 Example of application of ANDFIR load norms to the same training
swimmer or same training group, but with two different training objectives. These
different aims can be achieved either by changing all the load norms or, as in the above
example, by varying only two quantities. On the left it is the basic endurance that is
being improved, while on the right it is the speed endurance. As the example shows,
both the number of repeats (20) and the distance (100m), as well as the stroke, remain
unchanged. The different objective is thus here achieved only by greater intensity in
the speed endurance set (1.44 m/sec compared with 1.22 m/sec) and the consequently
necessary longer rest intervals between the repeats (1:15 min compared with 0:23 min)

11 Training for basic swimming endurance

The most important fitness attribute for competitive swimming is basic endurance (cf. FIG. 5, p. 30).

Regardless of the race distance, it constitutes the basis for each and every swimming performance and is essential to the execution of a systematic swimming training programme.

In a long-term training programme (cf. TABLE 1, p. 24), in addition to mobility, basic swimming endurance must be systematically trained as the primary factor in conditioning.

From as early as the second year of training, basic swimming endurance constitutes a large part of the training as a whole, and from the third year it occupies roughly half of available training time.

Right up to the end of the swimmer's career, improving and consolidating basic swimming endurance should take up between 30 and 60 per cent of the total training time, depending on whether the race distances are sprints, middle or long distance (cf. TABLE 19, p. 230).

There is a close relationship between basic swimming endurance and general endurance or stamina (cf. FIG. 5), which can form a non-sport-specific basis for swimming too, since in all sports in which at least one seventh to one eighth of the entire muscle mass of the body is used for protracted periods – and this includes swimming – the degree of development of general endurance greatly influences sporting performance.

In other words: increasing general endurance will benefit sport-specific basic endurance. General endurance can be improved by practising other sports, such as canoeing, running, cycling, rowing, etc.

Basic swimming endurance relates the endurance exclusively to swimming and not to any movement pattern or sport of a continuous nature.

This means that besides the central influencing factors, i.e. those of the cardiovascular and respiratory systems, which the swimmer could certainly improve just as well by running, the local influencing factors, e.g. oxygen supply to muscle cells involved in propulsive movements, accordingly acquire greater significance. It is not sufficient, using general endurance training, to make the body capable of absorbing a great amount of oxygen if that oxygen is not delivered to the propulsive muscles essential to swimming and utilised in those muscles. This can only be achieved by swimming.

Basic swimming endurance is thus dependent on the aerobic capacity, i.e. on the ability to absorb as much oxygen per unit time as possible and to convey it to the propulsive muscles.

This can only be improved by swimming. Only in this way are the cardiovascular system and muscles placed under stress and at the same time improvement of oxygen distribution and utilisation in the propulsive swimming muscles purposefully achieved.

If we now attempt systematically to improve basic swimming endurance, the training stimulus or the load acting on the body must:

a) last long enough for the breathing to reach 'full revs', and
b) the training intensity must be chosen at such a level that the load can be maintained for sufficient length of time to be effective.

How long the loading should last depends on the current fitness and on the number of years in training, the 'training age'. If 200 m 'continuous swimming' is sufficient in the first year of training to improve basic swimming endurance (duration approx. 5 min), it would perhaps need to be 1500 m in the eighth year to constitute an effective stimulus. That is to say that the distance for continuous swimming always has to be increased in accordance with the improvement in the state of endurance training. If basic swimming endurance is being improved on the interval principle, this implies a continual increase in the number of repeats of the distances.

In this way, either the sets are made longer or several sets are swum in succession (cf. TABLE 4, overleaf).

In this case it becomes very important for the coach to design such training sets with as much variety as possible, without losing sight of the objective of improving basic swimming endurance. Within certain limits (cf. TABLE 4), the rest intervals can be kept the same length in a set, but they can also be made shorter or longer. 20 × 50 m crawl can thus be swum as follows:

a) 5 repeats on 60 sec.
b) 5 repeats on 55 sec.

c) 5 repeats on 50 sec.

d) 5 repeats on 45 sec.

The set can also be swum in reverse order or 20 repeats with the same rest interval at the same speed, e.g. 'on' 55 sec. (starting off every 55 sec.).

Regardless of how the rest intervals are arranged, the swimmer must endeavour to keep his swimming speed constant.

A set can be swum in each of the four competitive strokes or as a medley, or alternating between two or more strokes. The change between strokes can be made after each repeat or after small sets of identical repeats. It is a good method, despite a limited water space and despite many swimmers having different favourite strokes, of doing justice to each participant and to adjust the training load according to current performance. In addition, a fixed number of repeats can be swum with a set in faster and faster times, starting more slowly again after the last repeat.

Such a set is variously described as 'progressive swimming', or a 'descending set'. For the 20 x 50 m already mentioned, for example, it can be swum with a load intensity such that a frontcrawl swimmer with a best time of around 30 sec. swims the first 50 m in 38 sec. and subsequent lengths one second quicker, so that the fifth repeat is swum in 34 sec. The sixth repeat begins again at 38 sec., the seventh in 37 sec., and so on, until all the 50-m repeats have been swum (cf. TABLE 4).

Experience has shown that a 1-sec. increase in speed is only beneficial over five repeats, in order not to place excessive stress on other areas of conditioning, e.g. speed endurance.

For as many repeats as possible to make a contribution to improving basic swimming endurance, the difference between the slowest and fastest repeat should not be excessive. The reason for this is that although the young swimmer must not, on the one hand, exceed the endurance-promoting speed, and on the other should be personally aware of the time jumps in the repeats, it is expedient if the speed is increased only a few times. After that the speed increase starts afresh within the set.

A descending set offers certain advantages over sets swum at a constant speed:

a) The fact that the swimmer has to swim each repeat at a speed appropriate to himself, a speed which is increased steadily over five repeats, forces him to check carefully on each occasion that the prescribed time has been achieved. In this way he gradually

METHODS	CONTINUOUS SWIMMING	FARTLEK (SPEED PLAY)
A	Improving local and central influencing factors: 90% stressing of aerobic energy system	Improving local and central influencing factors; alternate stressing of aerobic and anaerobic glycolitic systems
N	1 x	1 x
D	Depending on year and trained condition: 400–5000 m	Depending on year and trained condition: 400–2000 m
F	At even speed: – all strokes, also sep. arm – overdistance crawl	At variable speed in all strokes except butterfly
I	As % of currently possible race time over 400 m 87% 800 m 89–92% 1500 m 92–94% ›1500 m 95% or more (roughly equivalent to 4 mmol/l lactate level) TPF according to formula: TPF = (MPF-RPF) 4/5 + RPF	Gentle and fast swimming in ratio 4:1 to 2:1 (roughly equivalent to 2:6 mmol/l lactate level)
R	None	None

TABLE 4 Methods and load norms of basic swimming endurance training

develops great sensitivity to the energy expenditure required to swim as prescribed, and as expressed in the corresponding swimming speed. In technical circles this is referred to as a 'feeling for pace' or 'sense of pace'. The continual variation of speed per repeat in the set and the subsequent feedback of the time needed develops this pace-sense more quickly than sets swum at a uniform speed.

b) With speed variation it is highly probable that a considerable proportion of the repeats will be swum in precisely that intensity

EXTENSIVE INTERVAL TRAINING	INTENSIVE INTERVAL TRAINING
Improving central and local influencing factors: 80–90% stressing of aerobic energy system	Improving central and local influencing factors; stress 70–80% aerobic 20–30% anaerobic at transition to speed endurance training
Depending on distance: 10–100 x	Depending on distance: 5–30 x (poss. in sets)
25–400 m	25–200 m
All strokes (butterfly only for as long as perfect technique maintained), also sep. arm and leg action, as a set at even or variable speed.	All strokes (butterfly only for as long as perfect technique is maintained) at steady or increasing speed

As % of currently possible race time over
     25 m 77%
     50 m 80%
     100 m 83%
     200 m 85%
     400 m 87%
     800 m 89–92% as lower limit (roughly equivalent to 4–6 mmol/l lactate level) TPF as in formula under continuous swimming
	As % of currently possible race time over
	
	     25 m 85%
	     50 m 88%
	     75 m 89%
	     100 m 90%
	     150 m 90%
	     200 m 90%
	     (roughly equivalent to 6–8 mmol/l lactate level)

5–45 sec only for 800 m up to 60 sec	1–2 times load duration, max. 90 sec

range which helps improve basic swimming endurance (see FIG. 146 overleaf).

In a set swum at an even pace each repeat contributes to improving basic endurance, provided the intensity is equivalent to a blood lactate level of around 4 mmol/l. In this case the swimming speed is individually exactly right, so that the stimulus produces an optimal improvement in basic endurance. If, on the other hand, the intensity is too low (A in FIG. 146) all the repeats have no effect, or at best a

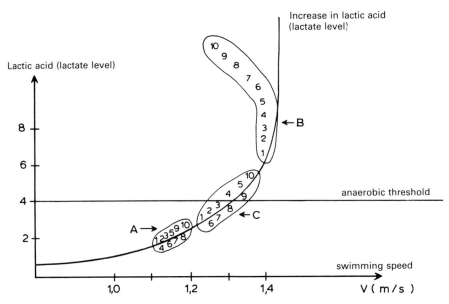

FIG. 146 Relationship between lactate accumulation and swimming speed during sets swum in a uniform manner (e.g. 10 × 200 m) at too low an intensity (A), too great an intensity (B) and during a decreasing set (10 × 200 m, speed increase over first to fifth and sixth to tenth repeats) (C)

recovery effect. This frequently applies to less keen swimmers, who generally swim too slowly.

The more ambitious swimmer often swims constant-speed sets too intensively (B in FIG. 146). The intensity is in that case above the anaerobic threshold during the first repeat. Attempting to maintain the times for the subsequent repeats leads to an accumulation of lactate. The blood lactate level increases sharply, causing muscular pain and loss of coordination. In consequence a disproportionate deterioration in performance occurs after six or seven repeats. The swimming times become slower (8, 9, 10 in B), because energy can only flow from the third reservoir referred to earlier. The swimmer himself perceives the load as being constant or even increasing, because the lactate built up during the first repeats cannot be dissipated: there is consequently a deterioration in the contraction capability of the muscles and in coordinative ability.

The effect of a set swum in this way is small, as far as improvement of basic endurance is concerned. What also happens is that in cases of frequent swimming of sets with the deterioration of performance referred to earlier, it is only a matter of a few weeks before the young swimmer finds himself in an overtrained condition.

When using descending sets, on the other hand (C in FIG. 146), the first and sixth repeats turn out to be rather too slow, with the fifth and tenth actually too fast. This is balanced out, however, by the sixth, slower repeat, during the course of which the lactate accumulation can be partially dissipated. The other repeats are in the correct speed range. This alternation between training loads that are slightly too intensive and loads that are less intensive has proved to be extremely beneficial in improving basic endurance. In addition the swimmer becomes more capable of adapting to the different speed requirements of competitive races, occurring in the form of intermediate spurts, finishing bursts, fast starts, or a faster second half. He also learns to recover more quickly, i.e. to remove accumulated lactate. A descending set has the following advantages:

a) Increasing intensity corresponds to the way in which nearly all competitive distances are swum nowadays.
b) Experience has shown that with the faster repeats very good times are achieved, with some young swimmers almost their best times. When this occurs it helps to improve the swimmer's self-confidence.

A further possibility in swimming sets for endurance improvement (interval training) consists in swimming the first and second halves of each repeat at the same speed, or the second half more quickly than the first. The latter form is extremely beneficial, both from the energy point of view and also in relation to races.

If every second repeat is swum quickly (approx. 6 to 8 mmol/l lactate level) and every intervening repeat in the recovery range (approx. 2 mmol/l), a similar effect can be achieved as with a descending set.

To a great extent, the load norms of all the sets mentioned can be intermixed, thereby producing an almost infinite variety of possibilities, in order to prevent monotony and boredom. It is quite possible to offer a fresh set every day in training, so that no set is repeated in a macrocycle.

Experience has nevertheless shown that it is advisable to repeat sets at particular intervals in order to illustrate changes in the trained condition. Even sets, such as 10 × 200 m, are particularly suitable for carrying out such checks on performance. For this purpose the times of all the repeats should be recorded for each swimmer, the average times calculated and the pulse taken immediately after the last repeat. Another pulse reading should be taken 60 seconds later and these values also noted.

By comparing such sets, their swimming times, training pulse and recovery values, it is possible to establish accurately whether basic endurance has increased, decreased or has remained static in the period between two identical sets. If no illness or injury has forced the swimmer to interrupt his training, if the training has been correctly carried out and if there has been no loss of motivation, the average times for such test sets should improve week by week. If this is not so, the remaining training should be analysed closely to detect any errors and to modify the training schedule accordingly.

The greatest problem with basic endurance training is to execute it at the correct intensity. As has already been mentioned for descending sets, the aerobic capacity is best increased when the intensity is at a blood lactate level of the order of 4 mmol/l, or whatever the anaerobic threshold may be.

It is consequently not sufficient to have sets swum in training, say 10 × 200 m crawl on 3:00 min and to embellish them with commands such as 'full effort', 'evenly', 'average intensity' or 'at pulse rate of 170', or the like. Intensity indications in such a crude form are no real help to the young swimmer. It will be by pure chance if he finds his individual 'training effective' speed in this way.

It is even more difficult when the water space is limited and a number of swimmers have to swim in a lane in single file one behind the other, virtually like a conveyor belt. Since, in such a case, all the swimmers try to keep up with their leader, it is highly improbable that the pace set by the leading swimmer will prove to be 'endurance effective' for all those following.

It is wrong to believe that all one needs to do is to try and hang on for as long as possible and everything will come right of its own accord. Such a policy may perhaps help to toughen up the swimmer, but it does nothing towards achieving the actual objective of training.

In order to improve basic endurance, it is not a matter of training as hard as possible but as correctly as possible. This means that the coach has to go to the trouble of determining the correct swimming speed for each swimmer at a particular time and to make him swim his repeats at that speed.

For training by the continuous method and for short-rest interval sets swum at a constant speed, the most difficult command should be to maintain the constant speed.

If the swimmer is intent on subjectively stretching himself to the full, but on swimming the full distance at an even pace, he must be induced to keep his speed down at the start in order not to 'blow up' after a few repeats. If the load as a whole lasts long enough (cf. TABLE 4, p. 128), the intensity naturally fluctuates within the correct range. The only danger is that the swimmer may in fact swim evenly but at too low an intensity to reach the endurance-effective threshold between the aerobic and anaerobic processes. To prevent this happening, the pulse rate can be taken as an objective load indicator, especially in extensive interval training.

The intensity is correct when the individual pulse rate immediately after a repeat corresponds to the numerical value calculated from the following formula: training pulse rate = 4/5 × (maximum pulse rate – rest pulse rate) + rest pulse rate.

$$TPR = \tfrac{4}{5}(MPR - RPR) + RPR$$

The maximum pulse rate is best measured immediately after a hard set of fast repeats, and the rest pulse rate in the morning before getting up. Both measurements can be done over 10 seconds, extrapolated to 1 minute. If a swimmer exhibits a maximum pulse rate of 200 and a rest pulse rate of 60, then his training pulse rate is calculated as follows:

$$\tfrac{4}{5}(200 - 60) + 60 = 172$$

If we now use the third control possibility, i.e. the percentages in TABLE 4 of the best time for the particular repeat distances valid at that point in training, the individual's correct training speed can be determined comparatively accurately.

It should be borne in mind that the correct training speed changes continuously when it is calculated using percentages of the current best times. This is because, assuming that our training is having the right effect, the basic swimming endurance is improving, and the training speed has to be adjusted accordingly, i.e. increased.

A further possible reference point for the training speed in basic endurance training is the racing speed over 800/1500 m.

The average time per 100 m in a 800/1500-m distance can, for extensive interval training, be taken as a good guide for the pace for all repeats of between 50 and 200 m.

If the coach uses all the suggested possibilities for speed control in basic endurance training, he can, without too much effort, arrive at a relatively accurate determination of the effective swimming speed for each swimmer. He must, of course, take frequent measurements of times and pulse, and he must, in addition to calculations for the individual swimmer, occasionally investigate the speed that can be swum over long distances and must be ready to make frequent speed adjustments.

Currently the most accurate method for determining the intensity of basic endurance training is the so-called 'two-distance test' after Mader (1976). The swimmer has to swim 400 m twice or 100 m twice with a rest interval of about 20 minutes between. Immediately before and after each swim a sample of capillary blood is taken from the swimmer's ear-lobe, from which the lactate concentration is subsequently determined in the laboratory. The blood sample should of course be taken by medical personnel.

The first test-distance should be swum at below maximum speed (training speed for extensive interval training), if possible at an intensity equivalent to a blood lactate level of 4 mmol/l. The second distance should be swum as fast as possible.

In FIG. 147 an example is given of two swimmers, A and B, who have undergone different endurance training; this can be used to illustrate the two-distance test.

Let us take as our starting point that A and B are two sprinters who swim 2 × 400 m in the test. Both swim the first 400 m at an intensity

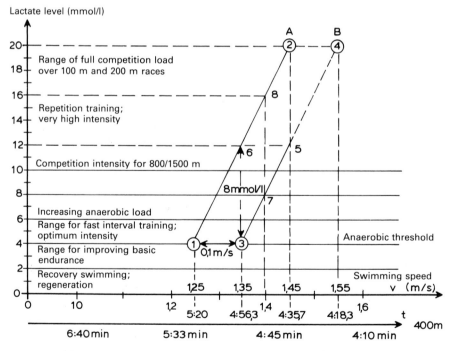

FIG. 147 Relationship between lactate accumulation (mmol/l) and swimming speed (m/sec). Left: intensity ranges, measured in relation to the stressing of anaerobic capacity by differing training methods and forms of training. Right: example of two crawl swimmers (A and B) at different stages of endurance training

corresponding to a lactate accumulation of 4 mmol/1. A does the 400 m in 5:20 min., i.e. at a speed of 1.25 m/sec (point 1 in the diagram).

B achieves 4:56.4 min., equivalent to a swimming speed of 1.35 m/sec (point 3 in diagram). On the second 400-m swim both A and B achieve the same speed of 1.40 m/sec.; they swim 4:45.7 min (points 7 and 8 in diagram).

Up to a lactate accumulation of approx. 4 mmol/l, there is a balance between the generation and dissipation of lactate during the load: the lactate concentration does not therefore continue to increase if the load intensity is kept constant.

However, at the very moment the limit of 4 mmol/l is exceeded, i.e. the swimmer swims faster, the lactate accumulates very quickly and, even with small increases in speed, quickly rises to the level of acidosis just tolerable for that individual.

This lactate behaviour is represented in the diagram by the steep straight lines connecting points 1 and 2 and points 3 and 4. Although A and B in our example swam their second 400 m at the same speed, A was only able to manage the 4:45.7 min by using his entire anaerobic capacity (16 mmol/l blood lactate). B, on the other hand, only had to call on his anaerobic capacity up to a lactate level of 8 mmol/l to achieve this speed: he did not fully extend himself.

If we were only to use this last 400 m to estimate the requisite training intensity, we could arrive at the false conclusion that the two swimmers ought to swim at the same speed in training. Swimmer A, a strong-willed dogged competitor, only needs to tag on to swimmer B until he drops. And we wouldn't have to wait long for this to happen in this case. For swimmer B a swimming speed of 1.35 m/sec would be just the right training speed to increase his basic swimming endurance. In a set of, say, 6 × 400 m crawl on 5:30 min, he should attempt each time to swim the repeat in around 4:56 min.

Should A attempt to match his pace, he would already have a lactate level of 12 mmol/l after the first 400 m (point 6 in FIG. 147), i.e. around 8 mmol/l more than B. At the start of the second 400 m swimmer A would have to cope with a lactate accumulation of approximately 10 mmol/l. His attempts to cover the second 400 m at the same intensity would lead to a level of approx. 16 mmol/l. Under training conditions, i.e. without the competitive stimulus, swimmer B would in all probability not be able to summon up the willpower to do the second swim at this intensity at all. This implies that even the second 400 m would not be swum by A in under 5:00 min. The remaining 4 × 400 m would, if at all, only be swum considerably more slowly, probably at a speed of around 1.2 m/sec, i.e slower than 5:30 min.

Even if A and B were both to do 400 m in 4:45 min in a race (points 2 and 5 in FIG. 147), this could not be interpreted as implying that both swimmers should also swim at the same speed in training. For the same race time A accumulates 20 mmol/l of blood lactate, while B has a build-up of only 12 mmol/l. For training, a speed of 1.25 m/sec should be recommended for swimmer A (point 1 in FIG. 147) and B should swim 0.1 m/sec faster if both swimmers are to increase their basic endurance in the best possible way.

How far a person can extend himself, i.e. how great a lactate accumulation he can overcome, again depends to a great extent on training.

The body has to be forced, through appropriate loads, to tackle large accumulations of lactate. Experience has shown that this is physically and mentally far more unpleasant and painful than, say, basic endurance training. The most effective way of executing these desirable adaptation processes is speed endurance training. There are of course biological limits to the effect of speed endurance training. Since lactate is virtually synonymous with lactic acid, which as an acid can only be partly buffered by the blood, lactate accumulations displace the pH-value of the blood in the acid direction: the pH-value falls.

The greatest lactate concentrations occur in track athletics after the 400 m (up to 25 mmol/l). Such acidosis causes the pH-value to fall from 7.4 (normal value) to 6.85. The pH-value in the muscles falls to 6.3, leading to inhibition of the glycose enzyme and, because of the attendant lack of energy-rich phosphates, rendering further muscle contractions impossible. The lactate and pH-values quoted constitute the extreme limits compatible with life. They cannot be shifted, either by training or by medicaments or other methods.

These limits can in fact be reached by special training, but any further increase in performance can only be achieved by improving basic endurance by other methods and forms of training and by attention to the other conditional skills or abilities.

As a generalisation one could therefore state that after appropriate speed endurance training at the full-load level, no excessively large individual differences exist.

Since blood lactate increases very steeply above 4 mmol/l (cf. FIG. 147), an additional lactate accumulation of 2 mmol/l only produces a comparatively small increase in swimming speed (cf. FIG. 147).

The essential fact to emerge from the above is that even for a sprinter, who only swims 100 m in competition, basic swimming endurance has a quite decisive significance.

Since lactate builds up at almost the same rate for every swimmer above 4 mmol/l and also has roughly the same upper limit, a further improvement in race time can only be brought about by an additional increase in basic endurance. With reference to FIG. 147 this means that the curves are shifted further to the right. If swimmers A and B are again compared it will be seen that, at the same level of 20 mmol/l, swimmer A cannot swim faster than 1.45 m/sec and B roughly 1.55 m/sec. At this same lactate concentration, A can consequently never beat B. For A, the only chance of catching B is to raise the threshold speed (to be read off for him as point 1).

By correct basic endurance training, it is possible to raise the speed (shift of curve to right) which the young swimmer is able to maintain before he has to call increasingly on his anaerobic capacity and the lactate level starts to rise sharply.

It is important to know that the better a swimmer is trained for basic endurance the less lactate he produces. The distance swimmer, when fully extended, reaches considerably lower lactate levels than the sprinter, mainly on the basis of the extensive endurance training he has to undergo.

The often surprisingly good 100-m times of distance swimmers are achieved through the fairly high lactate-free speeds they can maintain as a result of their outstanding aerobic capacity.

Many years of experience of intensity control using lactate measurements have shown, however, that in the long run it is not possible to cope with basic endurance training at an intensity corresponding to the anaerobic threshold. Training for one week at a constant and even appropriate intensity apparently leads to 'Addisonoid' overtraining (cf. p. 280).

To prevent this, only about 60 per cent of the basic endurance training should be carried out in the region of the anaerobic threshold and around 40 per cent at an intensity corresponding to a blood lactate level of 2-3 mmol/l.

In particular the long distances of 400 m and above should be swum at a lower intensity. The intensity of the basic endurance training over a week can be divided up as follows:

Monday	Tuesday	Wednesday	Thursday	Friday	Saturday
4 mmol/l	4 mmol/l	2 mmol/l	4 mmol/l	2-3 mmol/l	3-4 mmol/l

Basic endurance training requires that long distances are swum continuously, or a large number of shorter distances swum with short rest intervals. It should again be pointed out that in a large training group this is only possible by organising a continuous 'conveyor belt'.

12 Training for basic swimming speed

Basic swimming speed can be measured as the maximum speed at which a short distance of 15-20 m (possibly even 25 m) can be swum. It is the type of movement through which pure human speed is seen and must clearly differ from speed endurance, which must be regarded as a combination of speed and endurance.

In sport, speed is basically the motor skill which, more than any other, is dependent on the natural aptitude (talent) of the sportsman or woman.

The reason for this is the great influence which the human nervous system exerts on the execution of rapid movement patterns and on the possibilities of improving them. The efficiency of the nervous system cannot be improved by training to the same degree as, say, the muscles or the cardiovascular system. However, the influence of the nervous system on swimming speed is apparent in several ways:

a) in the reaction time when starting;
b) in selecting the most appropriate and effective swimming technique, which is also to be maintained at high speed;
c) in the rapidly alternating tension and relaxation of all the muscles involved in swimming movements;
d) in the contraction speed of the muscles and thereby the tempo.

'While the movement frequency (or 'tempo'), as a function of the central nervous system, is predominantly a nerve problem within the framework of well learned movement, making progress through the water depends primarily on the power efficiency of the muscles' (Blaser 1978, 445).

Both the power utilisation of the muscles at starts and turns, and also the maintenance of effective use of the propulsive muscles during sprinting, are only achieved with good coordination of the movement patterns, i.e. with good nerve control, monitoring and adaptation of the energy inputs. For these reasons, speed is classified among the conditional and coordinative motor skills (cf. FIG. 5, p. 30).

This view is reinforced by the pronouncements in general training theory that it is precisely with increasing involvement of movement technique in measurable sporting performances that prospects improve for an improvement in speed (Letzelter 1978, 187 f.). It is made clear that, in swimming, the emphasis in speed training should always be on correct technique. Training is only in movement patterns that have been largely mastered. Training to increase speed of movement and frequency can be done very effectively with little effort. This would be the case, for example, with a swimmer being drawn forward on a rope but sprinting (cf. FIG. 148, p. 147).

The neuro-coordinative aspect of speed training can also be covered by two recommendations for the swimmer's programme:

1 Speed training (over distances of 12–15 m) should start as early as basic swimming instruction and basic training, i.e. when the development processes in the nervous system are proceeding apace and the promotion of speed is highly effective.

2 Speed training in the form of a few sprints should be included in every workout from the very first year, not at the end of the session before an important meet (Counsilman 1980).

Only in this way does the nervous system acquire the necessary coordinative ability to convert conditioning and training improvements in muscle power, cardiovascular efficiency and muscle metabolism, into faster swimming.

Speed training for swimming relates primarily to increasing basic swimming speed – which is the greatest possible speed that can be swum for approximately 7–12 sec. Maximum physical performances over such a short period are made possible by oxygen-less (anaerobic) and lactate-independent (alactacid) energy-provision processes (cf. p. 120).

Accordingly, distances suitable for the basic swimming speed are 15 m up to a maximum of 25 m. They have to be sufficiently short for neither fatigue of cardiac, circulatory and respiratory processes in the propulsive muscles to reduce the swimming speed. A 50-m distance is too long. Training forms for basic swimming speed should only be imposed for up to 12 sec., and at most 15 sec.

In contrast to basic speed, we refer to the ability – despite the occurrence of the fatigue factors listed – to maintain a high swimming speed over 50 m or 100 m as 'speed endurance'. It already presupposes a high basic speed. In contrast to basic speed, the hard training of swimming speed endurance belongs to later in the elite training stage and calls for a physically mature sportsman (cf. TABLE 1, p. 24).

Of the factors which are relevant to basic swimming speed, we are particularly concerned with those that can be influenced by training. They are interrelated and mutually influence each other. They are in particular:

a) reaction time at start;
b) swimming technique;
c) strength or power of propulsive muscles;
d) rapid alternation of tension and relaxation of muscles;
e) stroke frequency.

The reaction time at a start depends both on mastery of the dive start or backstroke start and on reactive capability. It can be improved on dry land by means of general reaction exercises, such as

a) shadow running;
b) shadow boxing;
c) 'catch' (on thigh);
d) numbers race;
e) starts at a signal, from sitting, prone and supine positions;
f) ball games, e.g. dodge-ball.

Exercises in the water to improve reactions include:
a) game of catch;
b) ball games;
c) spurts of 3–5 m from gentle swimming at command from coach;
d) spurts from stationary prone position;
e) 'black/white'*.

The swimmer can also improve his reaction time by preparing himself intensively mentally before performing the start (anticipation) or by systematically imagining his movement pattern many times over (mental training).

Swimming technique plays a decisive role in basic speed and propulsive efficiency (compared with the energy expended) must not fall away during the sprint. The ability, at a high swimming speed, to achieve an optimally favourable ratio of energy expenditure to propulsive movement patterns (stroke efficiency) cannot be developed in a few sprint exercises before races.

---

* In the reaction game 'black/white', there can be any number of swimmers in two rows 2 m apart. On the command 'black' or 'white', the appropriate swimmers attempt to 'catch' their opposite numbers before they reach the edge of the pool. The two rows should not be more than 12 m from the sides of the pool.

For this reason, a few forms of speed training should be practised throughout the training season, even when races are not imminent or when strength and speed endurance are still in early stages of development in the training programme.

The importance of strength or power of the propulsive muscles increases with swimming speed, because the water resistance they have to overcome increases roughly with the square of the speed.

When all the possibilities for improving coordination and swimming technique have been exhausted for a swimmer, a further increase in his basic swimming speed can only be achieved by increasing the propulsive muscle power.

The comprehensive chapter on strength training (see pp. 149 ff.) takes this into account. In such a case, the more a swimmer has specialised on the sprint distance and the greater his basic speed already is, the more extensively and frequently will exercises for speed training and maximum-strength training have to be used in order to increase the functions of the fast-twitch muscle fibres and the anaerobic alactacid muscle metabolism (cf. TABLE 5, overleaf). Despite the high load-intensity (weight or resistance), the movement patterns of strength training should be performed as quickly as or even slightly more quickly than the movement patterns in swimming. Up to now, and with the training equipment available, this is unfortunately only possible with an elastic rope.

Despite the high swimming speed, the rapidly alternating tension and relaxation of the propulsive muscles forms the prerequisite for a rapid, less energy-consuming action, which does not cause fatigue to set in until a comparatively late stage.

This is therefore in an extended sense a swimming technique quality. Over the period of basic speed, i.e. when the speed endurance has an effect, it makes a proportionate contribution to the determination of swimming performance.

An important condition for a smooth alternation between tension and relaxation is above-average mobility, especially the elasticity of the muscles. This can be improved by flexibility training (see pp. 104 ff.). Switching to muscle relaxation can, however, also be promoted by rhythmic gymnastics, especially swinging exercises with and without hand apparatus (clubs, bar, rope, ball), in which a powerful upward swing gives way to subsequent gravitational and centrifugal forces. Rhythmic-accoustic or musical accompaniment can be used to support the alternation.

In sprint training in the water, after the maximum starting acceleration, the swimming speed and pull frequency should occasion-

TRAINING PHASE	AIM OF INCREASE	MAXIMUM STRENGTH		MUSCULAR ENDURANCE			EXPLOSIVE POWER	
		GENERAL	SPECIAL	GENERAL	SPECIAL	RACE-SPECIFIC	GENERAL	SPECIAL
Basic instruction		Only general strengthening by other sports						
Basic training		(25) Only general strengthening		40	10	–	(25) Only expl.-power, movements in games, running and jumping	10
Developmental training	Sprinter	(30) Predominantly general strengthening		20	10	10	20	10
	Non-sprinter			30	20	10	10	–
Elite training	Sprinter	10	30	10	10	20	10	10
	Middle-distance	10	20	10	20	25	5	10
	Long-distance	10	10	10	30	30	–	10

TABLE 5 Distribution of strength training over the various objectives, training phases, partially as a function of race distance. The figures represent percentages of time spent within strength training

ally be deliberately maintained, but reducing the applied effort slightly.

The swimmer thus behaves like a car driver, who has accelerated his car up to its maximum speed and then carefully slackens his pressure on the accelerator, with the car still maintaining its speed.

The stroke frequency, i.e. the number of pulls (both arms) per minute (cycles/min), constitutes an essential influencing factor in basic swimming speed. It is generally measured with a frequency watch over four cycles. It can also be determined with a normal stopwatch by measuring the time the swimmer takes for four complete cycles, and from that time calculating the movement frequency. For example, if the stopwatch reading for four cycles is 5.5. sec., the frequency is

$$\frac{4 \times 60 \text{ sec}}{5.5 \text{ sec}} = 43.6.$$

The stroke frequency actually provides information about the movement speed, since the higher the frequency (with a constant stroke quality), the less time the swimmer takes for the individual pull (cycle). In the above example the time for the individual cycle is 5.5/4 sec = approx. 1.4 sec. Olympic champions Mike Wenden (1968) and Mark Spitz (1972) took 0.92 and 1.24 sec. respectively for a crawl cycle (Makarenko 1978). Of course, with two swimmers having the same cycle time, there can be different time distributions of the out-of-water, pulling and pushing phases.

As a basic requirement, either the stroke frequency or the cycle time should be periodically measured for each swimmer when sprinting.

The stroke frequency of the age-group swimmer, however, represents only one important influencing factor for basic speed for the coach to measure. A second and no less important factor is the pull length, i.e. the distance covered per swimming cycle.

Reference to the pull length explains how Mark Spitz came to swim faster than Mike Wenden despite his lower stroke frequency: he covered a greater distance per arm pull.

The size of the pull length depends on the effectiveness of the propulsive phases of a swimmer. This is a question of mastering technique, as has already been mentioned. Strength also plays a vital role. Reischle (1978), for example, determined pull lengths in excess of 1.6 m for dolphin-butterfly swimming on national level age-group swimmers. Basic speed cannot therefore be increased simply by stepping up the stroke frequency, particularly since the pull length generally decreases when a swimmer raises his stroke frequency.

Increasing the frequency only becomes worth pursuing when a

swimmer's pull length is greater than twice his arm length. What is more, both the strength available and the swimming technique proficiency must enable this pull length to be maintained.

In this case, of course, slightly raising the stroke frequency will be accompanied by an increase in basic speed (Reischle 1978).

Before doing so, the swimmer should deliberately be made to swim at different frequencies, so that, on the basis of the best sprint times, the currently most favourable relationship between stroke frequency and pull length can be determined for that swimmer. The stroke frequency is measured, in addition to the sprint time, and the pull length calculated (distance covered in a two-arm movement cycle), e.g. 9 cycles for 20 m from push-off from the wall correspond to a pull length of (20 m − 3 m push-off) = 17 ÷ 9 = 1.88 m. It is thus not a matter of finding the maximum frequency, but the frequency that is optimal in relation to the pull length.

In these frequent sprints over 15–25 m it should again be ensured that, despite the maximum basic speed being aimed at, the swimmer does not swim flat-out each time, but that, after maximum acceleration, pressure on the 'accelerator' is almost imperceptibly reduced.

Swimming technique details should also occasionally be considered in these forms of basic speed training:

a) The intensity of the kick is increased in order to counter the forces which, on the basis of the greater movement speed, destroy the streamlined body position.
b) Despite the intensive arm and leg movements, body extension should be repeatedly emphasised.
c) Finally, restriction of breathing frequency contributes to the low-resistance position of the body in the water (Holmer/Gullstrand 1980). The swimmer does not breathe for at least two or three movement cycles after a start, after pushoff and before touching. In the short sprint distance of 50 m breathing can be limited to one or two inhalations.

Training for basic swimming speed stresses mainly the nervous system, in addition to the anaerobic alactacid metabolism.

The great concentration required and the control of the rapid tension and relaxation of large groups of muscles can quickly cause fatigue of the nervous system. This training should therefore not last very long. It should not include too many different exercises in one training session or too many repeats of the same kind. Twelve repeats should be the maximum. As a fundamental rule, the repeats should also be interrupted if fatigue obviously no longer permits the maximum speed.

At 0:45 to 1:15 min, the rest intervals are sufficient for the creatine phosphate to be topped up again and thereby to permit anaerobic-alactacid energy-provision again. Nevertheless the swimmer must also be emotionally prepared to start the next sprint with full concentration and maximum effort. In such cases the rest interval can be extended to three minutes.

It should finally be pointed out that only a well-tuned and warmed-up swimmer can train for basic speed. In a fatigued state, too, the swimmer will not be prepared for speed training. For this reason, speed training, which is carried out all the year round, should be arranged either after a long warm-up or at the latest in the middle of a workout. A few hard sprints to finish off a tiring session in fact interrupt the uniformly steady coordination, say, of endurance training. They also constitute an extra load and do not serve the actual objective of basic speed improvement.

The main form of training for basic swimming speed is the repetition of sprints organised in a similar way to repetition training. The load norms are as follows:

A	Increasing basic swimming speed.
N	4–12 (if necessary, in 2–3 sets).
D	8–20 m (max. 25 m with dive start or pushoff).
F	Sprints in a well-mastered stroke; Spurts: acceleration from gentle swimming or from swimming on spot.
I	Maximum (to begin with, then maintain stroke frequency and speed) (max. speed)
R	1–3 min (until subjective recovery of swimmer or until breathing is steady and pulse below 100)

TABLE 6 Load norms for training for basic swimming speed

Further forms of training:

Spurts in middle of pool
While swimming gently over a distance of 100 m, the swimmer regularly accelerates to top speed in the middle for 5–8 m. In a 50-m pool there are two acceleration points, roughly at 15 m and 35 m.

Spurt, quick turn, spurt
The acceleration in the repeat begins approx. 5 m before the turn and ends 5 m after it.

Irregular spurts
At a shout or whistle from the coach, or at his hand signal in the case of backstroke swimmers.

Different sprints in set of four
12 × 20 (25) m on 2 minutes;
a) half length max. – half length gently;
b) half length gently – half length max.;
c) gentle start and accelerate to max. speed in a spurt;
d) whole length max.;
e) repeat a), and so on.

Sprint with frequency variation (timed)
a) sprint at normal stroke frequency;
b) sprint at slightly increased stroke frequency;
c) sprint at greatly increased stroke frequency (as many pulls as possible);
d) sprint at normal stroke frequency;
e) sprint at slightly reduced stroke frequency;
f) sprint at greatly reduced stroke frequency (as few pulls as possible).

Sensitising sprints (timed)
a) sprint with maximum effort start to finish;
b) sprint with maximum effort at start, then maintain speed and frequency at reduced effort;
c) sprints as in b) but the last few metres at full effort until touch.

Sprints with restricted breathing
Each sprint is swum with more severely curtailed breathing, starting with normal breathing (no inhalation after start and before touching) and ending with one (or no) inhalation.

Assisted sprints
The sprinting swimmer is towed forward on an elastic rope, tied round his waist or chest with the free end on his back. Using this loose end, which is about 6 m long, the coach or a training partner pulls the swimmer forward without disturbing the action (see FIG. 148). The pull in the direction of travel is maintained for 15–18 m. The

FIG. 148 Training for basic swimming speed using a rope

swimmer's cycle frequency, which is slightly increased in this way, should be maintained for up to 25 m. The time swum is 0.5–1.0 sec below the best unassisted sprint time.

Forms of training in a group

Relay over short course (10–15 m)
Two or more teams swim in relay against each other, so that each swimmer has to sprint 8–12 times. Because of the necessary rest intervals, the minimum number per team is six.

Relay with points awarded
Sprint relay as above, but with points awarded from time to time, i.e. the swimmer in each team who is the first to set off after a clear signal (whistle) has his time individually measured. The fastest swimmer collects a time bonus of 3 (5, 10) sec. for his team.

Handicap relay
Sprint relay as above; the weaker team is given half a length or a length start. With teams that are equally strong, every third swimmer must set off without a dive start (from a pushoff).

First one eliminated
Group short-course sprints on command; the first in each sprint is

eliminated. In order to give swimmers with a low basic speed a chance, four sprints can be organised as a medley, i.e. one sprint in each of the different strokes. The order of the strokes can, however, be chosen arbitrarily by each swimmer himself.

Sprinting with the 'current'
The swimmer swims with the 'current', which in small pools can be generated by a group running or swimming in a circle (oval). The sprinter swims individually, possibly timed.

'Bumping' race
On a 25-m course, eight to ten swimmers swim a gentle 300 m at equal intervals behind each other ('conveyor belt'). The last swimmer spurts until he catches up with the swimmer in front and 'catches' him by touching him on the leg, then continues to swim gently. The caught swimmer in his turn spurts to catch the swimmer in front of him, and so on.

It should be borne in mind that such forms of training in a group will only be effective if the swimmers cooperate in a disciplined way. For example, in the bumping race, the swimmers must swim at a gentle pace and maintain the original intervals. If necessary, the coach can regulate the gaps at the turns by holding back swimmers who are too close to the one in front.

13 Strength training and swimming

The shortest Olympic distance, the 100-m freestyle, lasts some 50 to 56 seconds. On average 100 arm movements are executed: 50 with each arm.

An international level 1500-m freestyle swimmer executes about 1500 arm movements in a swimming time of 15–16 min. There is an inverse ratio between the resistance to be overcome in a movement pattern and its possible repetition frequency: i.e. the more repetitions, in our case arm movements, that have to be executed, the less strength can be applied to each repetition. On the other hand, it is maximum strength that determines performance when the strength input per arm movement constitutes more than 50 per cent of the maximum strength available for a single repetition of this sequence of movements.

What conditioning is peculiar to swimming? What strength requirements must be reckoned on? Do the repetition frequencies mentioned above make maximum-strength training necessary, or is it primarily muscular endurance that determines swimming performance?

Up until a few years ago, the starting point in the discussion was that a freestyle swimmer capable of swimming at a speed of 1.5 m/sec (equivalent to 1:6 min for 100 m), had to apply a force of approx. 6 kgf per arm pull (Karpovich 1933, Alley 1952, Counsilman 1955, Mosterd/ Jungbloed 1964, etc.).

More recent experiments (Holmer 1974, Di Prampero et al. 1974, Schleihauf 1977, Clarys 1978, and Bulgakova/Vankov 1980) indicate that the passive drag measured in the earlier experiments, which was used as the basis in calculating force expenditure, constitutes, in the case of frontcrawl swimming, only about half the active resistance generated when swimming.

A freestyle swimmer, swimming at 1.5 m/sec, must therefore apply not 5–7 kgf per arm pull, but around 12 kgf. When swimming at 2.0 m/ sec, he must even be capable of applying a mean pulling force of around 24 kgf per arm pull. These figures naturally include any (small) propulsion from the legs which can hardly be isolated in measurements. Swimming training on its own is not sufficient to produce this average pulling force. In order to achieve a sufficiently great reaction the swimmer has to resort to strength training on dry land.

Since the water resistance or drag increases roughly with the square of the swimming speed, it is understandable that sprinters in particular have to possess the greatest maximum strength for their high speeds. According to Miyashita (1972), the fastest speed possible increases linearly with the maximum strength propulsive muslces. This explains the significance of maximum strength for a sprinting swimmer.

Even for a distance swimmer, who naturally has a lower racing speed than the sprinter, the maximum strength becomes of increasing importance as the swimmer's career develops, since, as he climbs the ladder, swimming speeds increase, as does the water resistance.

The greater the percentage strength expenditure by the swimmer per arm movement in relation to his currently available maximum strength, the more significant for his performance will be the increase in maximum strength.

It can consequently be claimed that a present-day top-class swimmer, regardless of his race distance, just cannot get by without strength training on dry land. The importance of maximum strength and muscular endurance to competitive performance naturally depends on the distance (or on the swimming speed = magnitude of drag = force expended per arm movement): the shorter the distance, the more important the maximum strength.

Besides the maximum strength and the yet-to-be-explained muscular endurance, there is another form of force, the explosive power which can play a limited part in determining competitive performance. This applies to the racing start, to the pushoff after a turn, to the kick in breaststroke, and to the sharp acceleration of propulsive movements such as occur during the short sprint or (more rarely nowadays) during a spurt. According to Zanon (1973), the speed of a movement is a function of maximum strength. Speed and explosive power depend to a great extent on the given force ratios.

Maximum-strength training also has a beneficial effect on speed endurance: it not only thickens up and strengthens the muscles, but also increases their glycogen and creatine phosphate reserves (Saltin 1973).

For a sprinter, this means that his maximum-strength training increases the force required for the pull. By virtue of the increasing reserves of creatine phosphate, the anaerobic alactacid energy possibly lasts longer. In this case the lactic acid metabolic processes are not called upon until later.

The ability to maintain an average swimming speed over a long period in a race or in training without fatigue of the muscles involved causing the speed to drop, is referred to as 'muscular endurance'. It can be improved by various forms of training on dry land and in the water. After a certain level of performance and age have been reached, strength training on land to increase maximum strength, explosive power and muscular endurance is therefore essential for the competitive swimmer. It produces an indirect improvement in basic swimming speed, muscular endurance and speed endurance. On the whole it is the methods of maximum strength and muscular endurance training that predominate (cf. FIG. 149).

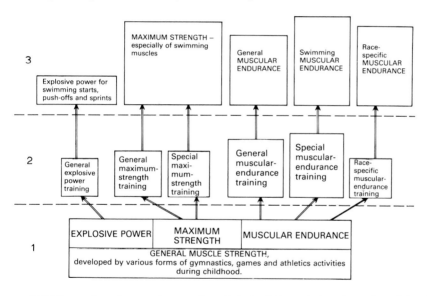

FIG. 149 The various forms of strength and their differentiation through training for improving competitive performance

TABLE 5 (p. 142) provides suggestions for dividing up swimming strength training according to the criteria:

a) the different reasons for developing the swimmer's muscle strength;
b) correlation with the four stages of the long-term training programme.

A different distribution will be obtained at the developmental training stage for the sprinter and non-sprinter, while the elite training stage also provides different training proportions for sprinters, middle-distance and distance swimmers. The percentages given relate to the total time devoted to strength training, thus simply representing the time ratio of maximum-strength training to strength training and explosive-power training.

The word 'general' in the table means that neither the muscle groups stressed, nor the three-dimensional (kinetic) movement pattern, nor the force-time (dynamic) sequence of training exercises are identical to the swimming action, e.g. raising the upper body from the supine position for the abdominal muscles, or bench press-ups for the arm extensors.

The swimmer's 'specific' strength training mainly stresses the propulsive muscles. Unlike the general training, it includes three-dimensional movement components which occur in the four competitive swimming strokes, e.g. pulling exercises on Workhorse Exergenie apparatus or pull over exercises with a barbell from the back of the neck to over the head.

The swimmer is carrying out strength training in a manner specific to competition, or 'race-specifically', if both (a) kinetically and (b) dynamically the movement patterns in training exercises are the same as those in racing and (c) account is taken of the duration of competitive strength involvement. This can be achieved only when training to develop muscular endurance.

A 200-m backstroker, for example, who needs about 160 arm pulls for his race distance, trains for these movement patterns on pulling apparatus at swimming speed against a resistance just in excess of the corresponding water resistance. He begins with eight sets of 20 repeats, which he gradually builds up to a series of 160 backstroke pulls, passing through the stages of 4 x 40, 3 x 60 and 2 x 80.

He must execute the following:

a) movement pattern corresponding to the swimming stroke;
b) stroke frequency as in race (insofar as available apparatus permits);
c) execution without a rest interval;
d) intensity 5–15 per cent above the water resistance at race speed.

When the swimmer has managed the 160 repeats, observing the above, the next aim is to repeat this series once up to a maximum of five times, with a rest interval between the series of two to four minutes.

In strength training, too, a start is basically made with general forms, with a subsequent transition to exercises specific to swimming (FIG. 150). Apart from a few special explosive-power exercises for dive

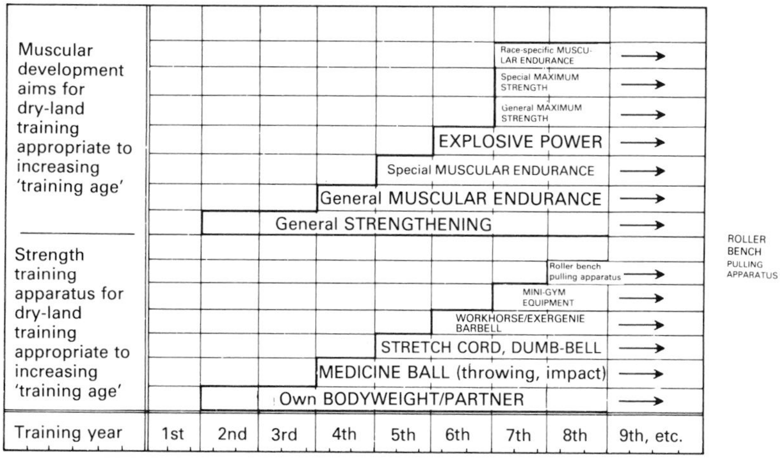

	1st	2nd	3rd	4th	5th	6th	7th	8th	9th, etc.
Muscular development aims for dry-land training appropriate to increasing 'training age'						Race-specific MUSCULAR ENDURANCE →			
						Special MAXIMUM STRENGTH →			
						General MAXIMUM STRENGTH →			
					EXPLOSIVE POWER →				
				Special MUSCULAR ENDURANCE →					
			General MUSCULAR ENDURANCE →						
		General STRENGTHENING →							
Strength training apparatus for dry-land training appropriate to increasing 'training age'						Roller bench pulling apparatus →			
						MINI-GYM EQUIPMENT →			
					WORKHORSE/EXERGENIE BARBELL →				
				STRETCH CORD, DUMB-BELL →					
			MEDICINE BALL (throwing, impact) →						
		Own BODYWEIGHT/PARTNER →							
Training year	1st	2nd	3rd	4th	5th	6th	7th	8th	9th, etc.

ROLLER BENCH PULLING APPARATUS

FIG. 150 Increasing specificity of strength training throughout the duration of a long-term training schedule for an age-group swimmer

starts, pushoffs at turns and the breaststroke kick, the swimmer should train for explosive power chiefly in a general manner.

Regardless of the particular objective, every strength training session should be preceded both by a warm-up and stretching exercises (cf. p. 106 ff.). The swimmer can warm up by running, skipping and jumping in any form. After a slow start, the intensity should be stepped up over a period of a few minutes to an extent which causes the swimmer to perspire slightly and his pulse rate to reach over 120. He should employ as many different movements as possible to warm up the entire body. To maintain his body heat during subsequent strength training, he should without fail wear a tracksuit, particularly during the maximum-strength training. As a protection against muscle injuries and to prevent cooling off, he should at least wear a tee-shirt, but a tracksuit is better.

MAXIMUM-STRENGTH TRAINING

'Maximum strength' is the force which the neuromuscular system is capable of exerting against an immovable resistance at the greatest possible voluntary contraction.

The first thing to be improved by maximum-strength training is the ability to employ a large number of muscle fibres (intramuscular coordination). Only through training are the muscle fibres thickened, leading to an enlargement of the muscle cross-section and thereby to an increase in muscle circumference.

As has already been mentioned, the importance of maximum strength to swimming performance depends to a great extent on the length of the race, i.e. on the number of repeated movements and on the resistance to be overcome. The sprinter will therefore spend more time and the distance swimmer less time on increasing it. On the whole though, only a relatively small amount of time can be devoted to this aspect because of other training priorities. What time is available, however, must be fully utilised on effective strength training methods.

Maximum strength naturally falls off quickly during the long-duration muscular endurance training at low intensity and during water training, because of the large number of movements against low resistances. It is therefore recommended that sections of the maximum-strength training be repeated at intervals (training cycles), striving for the greatest possible strength increases. This can be achieved by using the different modes of muscle contraction and the training methods founded on them, applying the appropriate load norms (A-N-D-F-I-R).

In addition to warming-up, stretching and clothing the body, the coach must watch that the young swimmer is wearing securely laced sports shoes during maximum-strength training and that he always keeps his back straight in order not to incorrectly load the spinal column.

The purpose of the shoes is to prevent the unaccustomed load of the weight or apparatus placing excessive demands on the plantar arch. The swimmer's feet are not used to heavy loads, since they beat against the water in a fairly relaxed manner. These preventive measures apply not just to the strength exercises themselves but also to the preparations, e.g. carrying weights. When swimming the upthrust of the water relieves the spinal column of stress, so that, because of the habitual low muscular tension in the trunk, the swimmer is prone to injury to the spine. This is particularly applicable when he lifts heavy weights with his back bent.

The danger is greatest at the period of maximum height growth. This alone is sufficient grounds for delaying maximum-strength training until the seventh year of training (14/15 years of age for girls; approx. 16 for boys). In order to eliminate the risk of injury completely, the young swimmer should initially carry out strength-training exercises with heavy dumb-bells in a supine or sitting position.

In this way the spine is supported on a firm base (bench, floor, mat), or, in the case of strength exercises in a sitting position, is resting firmly against a back support or the wall. If, as strength and familiarity with weight training increase, barbells are later to be lifted to the fully stretched position above the head (in order, for example, to include the muscles of the trunk in the strengthening process), this must on no account be done with the torso inclined forward and the back curved.

Instead, the upper body including the head should be erect above the hips with the lumbar section of the spine arched forward. The weights should be lifted from the floor with extended arms by powerfully extending the legs, before the arms raise them to the chest or above the head.

The swimmer's desire to manage as heavy a weight as possible is most safely satisfied by the bench-press exercise. Of course, as in all maximum-strength exercises using free weights (barbells, dumb-bells, 'yoke' barbells), a partner or 'spotter' must be present to hold in readiness the weights for the training swimmer in the starting position. The partner protects him from mishaps during the exercise and takes the weights from him at the end of the exercise.

Finally, attention should also be paid to regular breathing during strength training. As a general rule, there should be one inhalation for each repetition of an exercise. Missing out every second inhalation or holding one's breath over several exercises should be discouraged, in order to prevent pressurised breathing. It has proved favourable in maximum-strength training to inhale before each execution and to exhale towards the end of the main effort phase, i.e. when the weights have arrived at the top or the resistance of the apparatus has just been overcome.

Remember the importance of the 'five Ss':

1 Sufficient clothing
2 Shoes
3 Stretching and warm-up
4 Spine
5 Safe breathing

In order to increase the swimmer's maximum strength, he can 'overcome' and 'give way' to the resistance of a machine, a weight or an elastic traction apparatus (dynamic training) or he can hold his position against that resistance (static training).

In static strength training the involvement of the muscles concerned occurs at even intervals. Despite the increasing tension, the length of the muscles does not change: we consequently talk of isometric strength training. The training swimmer withstands a high resistance for 6 to 10 seconds. An increase in strength can be achieved in this way in a comparatively short time with 3 to 5 sets of withstand exercises.

The drawback with an increase in strength achieved in this way is the absence of the cooperation between nervous system and muscles (neuromuscular coordination), which is required in all sporting actions. The disadvantage can be countered to some extent by simulating the swimming action in three to five typical positions, and holding each one.

It is also isometric training if two swimmers try with all their might to force back each other's hands (see FIGS. 178–82). Their hands stay in one spot for a while because their forces are mutually balanced out.

If, on the other hand, the strength of one of the swimmers fails so that he has to give in, this is again a form of dynamic training. During submission, despite the great force applied, the muscle insertion (attachment) becomes further away from its origin, this consequently being termed eccentric dynamic training. In this sense, for example, an athlete is training eccentrically if an excessive weight is handed to him, which he cannot hold and which, despite his utmost efforts, he has to lower slowly to the ground. The snag with this method of training is that the muscle tension constituting the stimulus for the thickness increase is, at every point of the entire movement pattern, greater than when overcoming work. The muscles involved consequently have to develop maximum force at every angle of the joint. In addition, 'negative work' requires less energy and therefore offers the possibility of training more.

Most dynamic maximum-strength training chosen for swimming involves overcoming resistance, because it simulates the mode of contraction of the muscles during swimming actions.

An example of this is lifting a weight: it consists of the active bending or stretching of the arms or legs against a manageable weight. The muscle length is shortened and the muscle insertion (attachment) is closer to the origin, which is referred to as concentric strength training. Since it was originally assumed that in the course of their movement the muscles involved maintained the same tension level, the term isotonic training is also encountered. In actual fact, the tension does vary in the course of the movement because of the moments of inertia and the varying lever ratios.

When lifting a weight from the floor, the muscle tension increases until it is equivalent to the weight (isometrically). The muscle then contracts and changes its tension. The nature and magnitude of the change in tension are governed by the angle of the joint during the action, i.e. by the resultant force/load ratio. For this reason, it is more accurate, in dynamic concentric strength training, to speak of isotonic muscle contraction. The state of tension increases, i.e. changes.

The muscles clearly contract isotonically when the athlete extends a stretch cord or expander, because their resistance and thereby the muscle tension increase continuously the wider the elastic devices are extended.

It should not be overlooked that maximum strength training with isotonic or isometric contractions does not develop the swimmer's strength in the way in which he executes swimming movements in the water. For this reason, a strength training method has proved particularly appropriate for swimming, in which the muscles develop just as much force as is possible at each point in the movement pattern.

This is achieved by strength exercises against a mechanically or electrically braked resistance. The apparatus used prevents both the resistance increasing towards the end of the action and also the initial acceleration from bridging weak points in the movement. Such equipment forces the swimmer to pull at an even rate. Assuming that he is actually under load, his pulling (or pushing) muscles receive such a strong stimulus at every point in the action as a whole that the training effect is achieved to increase maximum strength, explosive power or strength endurance. Because the speed is constant, this training is called isokinetic.

For training with weights or other resistance apparatus, the instantaneous 100 per cent performance is initially established. To do so, each athlete is made to lift his greatest possible load or to overcome the greatest possible resistance in the action concerned.

From this individual 100 per cent, 85 per cent is calculated, which is used as the load intensity in maximum-strength training. The swimmer should repeat the exercises at this intensity at least three times.

If he is to perform more than eight repeats within the prescribed two or three sets it is essential that the swimmer's (100 per cent) maximum force, which has improved in the meantime, be determined afresh.

The load norms for maximum-strength training can be effectively varied by giving the intensity the shape of a pyramid: instead of repeats at a constant intensity of 85 per cent, the training continues with a set each at a load of 70, 80, 90, 95 and 100 per cent, and then back through 95, 90, 80 and 70 per cent. The repeat numbers inside the load pyramid prescribe sets of 8, 6, 4, 2 and 1 exercises and again up through 2, 4, 6 and 8 exercises.

One very important aspect in performing swimming-related maximum-strength and muscular-endurance training is that the force/time characteristics of the contractions referred to and of the training apparatus used are different. This means, for example, that expanders require very little force when one starts to stretch them, but that the force increases. On the other hand, lifting a heavy barbell calls for the greatest force at the start of the movement, in order to overcome inertia. The force/time curve of the arm action of the butterfly, for example, exhibits a power-input peak roughly in the middle. This in turn differs from the curve for the breaststroke arm action (see FIG. 151).

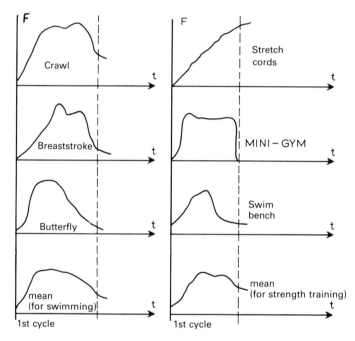

FIG. 151 Force/time characteristics for swimming and strength training (after Absalyamov, Bashanov, Danilochkin and Melkonov 1979)

The force/time characteristic and the three-dimensional movement pattern of a strength exercise must never be so deeply impressed on the swimmer that his swimming coordination is thereby disturbed or impaired. Constant strength training exercises, repeated too frequently over a long period using the same apparatus, should therefore be avoided.

Systematic training to improve maximum strength and muscular endurance is consequently carried out on a variety of apparatus. The force/time characteristics and the contraction modes of the items of equipment used should differ, if possible. None of the apparatus is used on its own with sufficient frequency for the movement pattern associated with it to come into conflict with the movement pattern of the swimming stroke in the water.

EXPLOSIVE POWER TRAINING

The explosive power training of the age-group swimmer on dry land embraces comparatively general forms of movement, such as jumping and short-distance running. Game-type sports are particularly useful in addition to the athletics disciplines of long jump, high jump, 30-m to 80-m sprints, shot putt and javelin.

Volleyball, for example, contains the elements of jumping, sprinting and of explosive stretching of the whole body. It additionally places great demands on reactive capacity and coordination. Playing basketball (sometimes with modified rules) makes similar demands and, particularly through jumps at the basket, promotes the explosive power of the leg and trunk extensor muscles.

Stationary high jumps with or without supplementary loads are especially suitable for increasing explosive power. The athlete stands sideways on to a wall and reaches up as high as possible with the hand nearest to the wall, without lifting his heels from the floor. Jumping upwards from this standing position, he tries to touch the wall as high up as possible. The aim is to generate as great a difference as possible between the point touched when standing and the highest point of the jump (FIG. 209, p. 242).

Standing high jumps can be performed with or without arm swings and after synchronised kneebends. One can even take a short runup. The supplementary load may be in the form of sandbags on the shoulders, a weighted jacket or an old windcheater with sand-filled pockets.

Identical conditions should of course always be used in order to permit regular monitoring of performance. Very low values or a complete absence of progress indicate the need to undertake maximum-strength training for leg and trunk extensors. The increase in jumping power is of greatest importance to sprinters, breaststroke and medley swimmers.

Counsilman (1980) claims to have established a reliable relationship between the height of the standing vertical jump and the swimmer's sprinting ability. The explosive power of the legs appears to be particularly important for breaststroke swimming: besides the explosive extension, it involves the rapid closing (adduction) of the legs. For this purpose, explosive power exercises against the resistance of elastic ropes can be used, the ropes being fixed laterally and running outwards at right angles to the swimmer (FIG. 197, p. 187). A pulling apparatus can be used instead of the rope if a deflecting pulley exerts the pull from outside on the swimmer's leg or foot. A suitable preparatory maximum-strength exercise is isometric training against the resistance of a partner, who holds the swimmer's splayed legs apart with his hands.

Explosive power training of the arm, shoulder and trunk muscles is only relevant in the rare case of a swimmer not being sufficiently capable of sprinting (cf. basic speed). Although adequate maximum strength is available, there may be a coordinative shortcoming. This can be countered with swimming technique exercises and by basic speed training.

It is generally sufficient for the young swimmer to do two-armed overhead medicine-ball throws to develop the requisite explosive power of his arms. This can be incorporated in the form of a game, e.g. throwing the ball over a high rope. During the basic and progressive phases of training, it is recommended that light weights, baseballs, slingballs or javelins be occasionally thrown with both hands and alternately with the left and right hands.

MUSCULAR ENDURANCE TRAINING

Of all the strength properties, muscular endurance is the closest to the competitive swimming application. This is particularly applicable to race-specific muscular endurance. The training is done mainly on dry land, but with regard to load duration and intensity and to movement pattern and frequency, it should be related to the main competitive discipline.

Swimmers are often unable to stand the load duration, or, to be more exact, the number of movements equivalent to the race distance. Experience has shown that race-specific muscular endurance can be developed more successfully and more easily if a broad foundation of general and swimming-related muscular endurance is laid down in the years of progressive training and at the start of each macro-cycle.

General muscular endurance training embraces as many different exercises and forms of apparatus as possible. It relates to every group of muscles in the body. It should be carried out at a load equivalent to 50–70 per cent of maximum strength and contain between two and four sets of up to 30 repeats (cf. load norms).

One common type of muscular endurance training is circuit training, with various exercises arranged at stations in a circuit. The athlete carries out his series of exercises at one station and moves on to the next. There are generally 10 to 12 stations, which consecutively stress the muscles of the arms, legs, front of trunk, rear of trunk (cf. FIG. 212). This sequence of stressed muscle groups is repeated two or three times in the course of a circuit. Each station offers facilities for at least two individuals to exercise, so that 20 to 24 swimmers can train at the same time.

This basic form of circuit training can of course be modified, if the space and time available or the number of swimmers make this desirable. For example, a ring of simple apparatus, such as gymnastics mats, boxes, benches, medicine balls and skipping ropes, at each station can offer simultaneous exercising facilities for three or more athletes. This is particularly applicable if a large number of simple exercises using personal bodyweight is to be included: press-ups, stretching jumps, jack-knives, jumping jacks, knee bends, etc. The number of stations can also be reduced (in small rooms or with limited apparatus), which would then involve several circuits.

From the USA we also know of combinations of circuit training at the pool edge and swimming programmes in the water. While one group is engaged on circuit training, they are leaving the pool free for another training group. Despite the need for or expediency of modifications, the fundamentals of circuit training and their organisational forms should not be underestimated.

The following two types of organisation are employed to regulate repetition numbers and rest intervals. The first arrangement uses signs to indicate precisely the number of repeats for each station according to degree of difficulty and dictates a minimum time for the athlete to complete a circuit. Increased loading is effected by repeating the complete circuit again or even twice. If an athlete does this at training pulse values below 180 per minute, the number of exercise repeats per station is increased by about 25 per cent (second load stage). As the swimmer gradually adapts to this increased load, load stages 3 and 4 can be arranged by increasing the numbers of repeats. After illness or a long lay-off from training, the swimmer should start again from the first stage.

The advantage of this arrangement is that swimmers with different muscular endurance performances can train on a circuit at the same time. This assumes, of course, that the number of stations is greater than the number of swimmers, to prevent them getting in each other's way. Only if there are enough free stations is it possible for those doing their circuits more quickly to overtake.

The second kind of organisation simply stipulates the exercise periods and rest intervals, which are uniformly applicable to all the stations. Initially as many repeats as possible are executed in 30 seconds at each station. This is followed by a rest interval, during which the athlete passes on to the next station. Each participant continuously counts his exercise repeats in one circuit. If, for example, he has done 15 repeats at the first station, he begins counting from 16 at the second. After a complete circuit there is a rest interval of 1:30 to 2 min. During this pause, the athlete takes his pulse and makes a note of the total number of exercise repeats for the circuit. It should be the individual's aim to steadily increase the number of repeats.

The ratio of exercise times to rest intervals can also be staggered in stages from 30:30 sec to 40:20 and 45:15 sec. This results in greater total repeat numbers executed on the circuit in the same time.

If the circuit is modified so that every second station stresses the arm and shoulder muscles, the emphasis is shifted from the general to the special swimming muscular endurance. The sequence of the exercises is then in the order of muscular loading of arms, legs, arms, front trunk, arms, rear trunk, arms, and so on. The specialisation is complete if the circuit only includes movement patterns which train the propulsive muscles for swimming. It is even possible to specialise with regard to race distance.

– distance swimmers repeat the exercises at each station for 50 sec and pause for only 10 sec (transfer to next station);
– sprinters observe a ratio of 30:30 sec for exercises and rest interval;
– medium-distance swimmers do as many repeats as possible in 40 sec and then rest for 20 sec.

Despite the different exercise times all swimmers must aim to do as many repeats as possible.

With particular regard to training the propulsive muscles continuously and more intensively than by swimming, a few sports with similarity to swimming must also be considered. These are basically endurance sports, in which the movement patterns exhibit a rhythmic alternation of muscular working and relaxation phases similar to those in swimming, i.e. rowing, canoeing and cross-country skiing.

By virtue of the similar movement requirements, human-propulsion water sports are particularly relevant: 'Just as in swimming, canoeing and rowing represent a forward movement against the resistance of water, achieved through utilising that resistance. Push-off is not from a solid bottom or solid bodies, but from water. Since the muscles basically have to work against a similar resistance, the dynamic characteristic is also roughly the same for both forms of movement. As in swimming, a feel for water resistance is also necessary in human-propulsion water sports. It can therefore be concluded that the swimmer's feeling for water is disturbed less by such water sports than by other forms of athletics training' (Schnabel, 1973, p. 421).

There remains the question as to whether, in the context of similar muscular movement, the young swimmer should give preference to kayak (double-bladed paddle) or Canadian canoeing (single-bladed paddle). Cross-country skiing has proved to be excellent muscular endurance training, with 'herring-boning' and double-poling simply as dictated by the terrain. Sessions of pure armwork should be introduced, however, with alternate and double poling. When the legs are energetically used in herring-boning, because of the size of the muscle groups involved the emphasis of the training effect is shifted from muscular endurance to general endurance.

It should again be pointed out that the climatic advantages of the swimming-specific supplementary sports to the indoor swimmer are particularly highly rated. The muscular endurance exercises of cross-country skiing can, incidentally, also be performed without snow, using grass-skis or even roller-skates, but still using cross-country ski sticks. The drawback of this muscular endurance training is the fact that it is carried out on dry land, and it is increasingly difficult to estimate the extent to which the trained muscular endurance can be transferred to swimming. The only thing that is certain is that the 'transfer loss' is least if the special muscular endurance training has been carried out in the water.

Special muscular endurance training in water operates with a systematic increase of the passive resistance in the swimming direction, forcing the swimmer to use more effort to maintain a given speed. The training equipment for this purpose includes: an inflatable inner-tube for the legs (leg-tube), tee-shirt, a retarding belt with pockets or flaps, a partner to be towed, stocking, etc. In short, anything that retards the swimmer in his forward progress through the water will do.

In this connection we ought also to mention swimming with paddles, which admittedly do not retard forward propulsion but raise the speed for the same arm frequency. The hand area enlarged by the paddles demands greater force in the propulsive phases and in this way trains specific muscular endurance, since both the stressed muscles and the movement patterns are almost identical to those of swimming movements without paddles.

Water training for special muscular endurance can also include swimming against an elastic rope tied round the waist or against a weight pulling the swimmer back to the start via a system of ropes and pulleys. Also to be considered, particularly for the special muscular endurance of the leg muscles, are: kicking exercises against the resistance of a kicking board held vertical in the water; kicking with the body in a vertical posture, with additional weights which have to be held above the water; pushing a partner backwards.

It is important in all these special muscular endurance exercises in water that the apparatus used does not excessively change or prevent the execution of the movement compared with the swimming stroke. The body should simply be retarded in the swimming direction or be kept at the same spot. The apparatus should not, for example, pull the body under the surface.

This special muscular endurance training is only effective if the swimming speed or movement frequency (in paddle swimming) is correspondingly high. For example, gentle swimming with a rubber tube does not in itself constitute muscular endurance training.

It is not until an individual speed depending on the trained condition is maintained that there will be any improvement in special muscular endurance.

Because of the high load-intensity of muscular endurance training in water, it is divided into sets with intervening rests, e.g. 20 × 10 sec crawl kick in a vertical attitude (holding a half-filled bucket) with 20-sec rest intervals; 10 x 100 m crawl armpull with paddles and thick rubber tube with 30-sec rest intervals.

Besides stressing the propulsive muscles, race-specific muscular endurance training demands the greatest possible approximation to the swimming movement pattern and the movement frequency, at which the main competition distance will subsequently be swum. For this reason, the breaststroke swimmer and butterfly swimmer mainly pull simultaneously with both arms in their pull rhythm, whereas the crawl swimmer does so with alternate pulls. The backstroker trains for the most part lying on his back on a bench.

In order, in addition, to approximate as closely as possible to the force/time curve of swimming (cf. FIG. 151), only equipment offering a resistance similar to water resistance when swimming should be used for race-specific muscular endurance training, e.g. mini-gym, swimming bench, Exergenie, workhorse. Pulling apparatus which can only be pulled alternately with the right and left handles can be used in pairs by breaststroke and dolphin butterfly swimmers: the swimmers grasp the handles of two sets of apparatus and pull evenly against each other (FIG. 193, p. 186).

At the outset few swimmers can stand the load of muscular endurance training which has been specifically prepared for their race. For this reason the total number of movement cycles of the race distance being prepared for is broken down into sets of 20–25 movement repeats. Between the sets are rest intervals of about half a minute duration.

Should a swimmer prove to be incapable of maintaining the load intensity and frequency according to the race distance within the sets, the sets must first of all be shortened (low repetition numbers) and the rest intervals be extended. The aim of completing the whole series once remains. The rest intervals can, however, be gradually reduced until they disappear altogether. To compensate for this alleviation (with the exception of distance swimmers), the total number of movement repeats for the race distance is increased by 10 per cent. It is therefore initially a question of achieving 110 per cent with the help of the rest intervals.

The movement frequency and movement pattern should, however, largely correspond to the execution characteristics over the race distance. It is only with a gradually improved trained condition and with the interpolation of a rest interval of three to five minutes that it is possible to construct a repetition of the complete set in a similar manner: 110 per cent of the movements for the distance without a break and, after an interval of several minutes, 110 per cent again in sets of 25 with a rest interval of 30 sec between sets. Anything in excess of two repeats for the distance swimmer and five for the sprinter is not a good idea.

The greatest problem in race-specific strength endurance training is that of choosing the load intensity. According to past experience, it is between 50 and 70 per cent of the maximum force that can be applied in the respective strength exercise. The load intensity is naturally a function of the distance and swimming speed. Whereas, for example, the 100-m freestyler should execute around 110 arm pulls (55 per arm) at 70 per cent load, the target aimed at by the 400-m swimmer should be approx. 380 pulls (190 per arm) at 50 per cent intensity.

The values in TABLE 7 have been determined as a rough guide for absolute load intensities for arm pull and arm-stretching exercises.

For the reasons mentioned, race-specific muscular endurance training is best carried out in the water. Short distances of 25-50 m are swum several times in succession at the target race speed and frequency as a sort of broken swim.

The repeat distances should add up to the race distance and the rest intervals should be chosen so that the speed and frequency can be maintained in accordance with the objective. As in special aquatic muscular endurance training, the swimmer should be retarded while swimming.

TARGET SWIMMING SPEED	LOAD INTENSITY PER PULL/PUSH PHASE OF ONE ARM (in simulated crawl exercises)
2 m/sec	21 –24 kgf
1.9 m/sec	18 –21 kgf
1.8 m/sec	15.5–18 kgf
1.7 m/sec	13 –15.5 kgf
1.6 m/sec	11.5–13 kgf
1.5 m/sec	10 –11.5 kgf
1.4 m/sec	8.5–10 kgf
1.3 m/sec	7.5– 8.5 kgf
1.2 m/sec	6.5– 7.5 kgf
1.1 m/sec	5.5– 6.5 kgf
1 m/sec	5 – 5.5 kgf

TABLE 7 Recommended load intensities for race-specific muscular endurance training

The retarding effect must not of course be excessive, otherwise the race speed or the frequency cannot be maintained.

TABLE 8 gives the percentage increase or reduction of the passive drag when using various retarding devices, compared with the resistance without apparatus.

V (m/sec)	Training aid Pull-buoy	Leg tube	Tee-shirt	Resistance belt	Resistance trousers	Stockings	Bucket
0.8	– 15	3	7	32	24	2	25
1.0	– 8	14	13	41	30	9	44
1.2	– 5	21	11	40	30	9	52
1.4	– 3	23	13	40	27	9	57
1.6	– 1	19	17	43	29	9	62
1.8	– 1	12	14	38	26	8	52

TABLE 8 Percentage increase or reduction of drag when using retarding apparatus, as a function of speed. A minus sign in front of a number indicates a reduction in resistance. All the resistance increases and reductions relate to the drag without apparatus

From the table, a few conclusions can be drawn for training practice:

1 Swimming with a pull-buoy reduces the passive resistance. For the swimmer this means less work than in full-action swimming. Swimming with a pull-buoy is consequently not suitable for improving race-specific muscular endurance.

2 Swimming with an inflated leg tube round the ankles increases the (passive) resistance by about 20 per cent, compared with swimming without apparatus at the usual training speed of between 1.2 and 1.4 m/sec. The stimulus for improving muscular endurance should therefore be just right. Since the legs remain inactive in this exercise and the resistance increase is considerable, swimming with a leg tube is primarily suitable for stroke-specific muscular endurance training, rather than for race-specific strength endurance training.

3 For the same speed, swimming with a resistance belt, resistance trousers or with a bucket tied to the feet increases the resistance by between 30 and 60 per cent compared with swimming without apparatus. Such an increase in resistance makes it almost impossible, even for short distances, to swim at race speed. It is therefore recommended that the apparatus referred to be used to improve the special and not race-specific muscular endurance.

4 An armless tee-shirt and stockings are best for increasing the resistance to a certain extent (on average 10–12 per cent), which over short distances permits the maintenance both of race speed and race movement frequency. It is also important for race-specific muscular endurance training that the swimming stroke can be executed unimpeded. We thus arrive at load norms close to those for broken swimming (cf. p. 191). Apart from the use of apparatus, the difference is in the slightly longer rest intervals between the repeat distances.

	Explosive power	Maximum strength		Strength endurance		
	specific	general	specific	general	specific	race-specific
Methods						
Working mode of muscles	Overcoming resistance	a) contracting and overcoming resistance b) contracting and holding resistance c) attempting to contract, but lengthening against resistance		Overcoming resistance		
Contraction mode of muscles	Isotonic Isokinetic	In a) isotonic, isokinetic In b) isometric In c) eccentric		Isotonic Isokinetic		
Load norms						
Aim						
Number of repeats and sets	6–10/4–6	for a) 3–8/2–3 for b) 3–5 positions/3–5 for c) 2–4/3		8–30/ 2–4	15–∞/ 2–4	20 times up to 110% of race pull number/1–3
Duration of each repeat	Fastest possible	for a) 1–2 sec. for b) 6–10 sec. for c) 2–4 sec.		Briskly	Briskly (approx. 1 sec)	Same frequency as racing
Form of exercise	– Squat jump with/without extra weight – Simulated arm and leg movements of swimming stroke – Adduction (closing) legs – Leg extension	for a): general strength exercises with and without barbells/apparatus for b) Hold in stipulated angular position for c) Eccentric exercise	for a): strength exercises for swimming muscles, especially the propulsive muscles	Arbitrary	Propulsive swimming muscles	Strokes as used in racing on an isokinetic pulling apparatus
Intensity	30–60%	for a) 85% (70–100% pyramid) for b) greatest possible for c) greatest possible		50–70%	50–70%	Equivalent to the resistance to be overcome in race (see Table 7)
Rest interval between individual repeats and sets	–/1:30–3 min	for a) 1 breath/2–3 min. for b) 0:30–1/2:30 min for c) several breaths/ 2–3 min		–/0:30– 1:30 min	–/0:30– 1:30 min	–/0:30 min reducing to 0; after reaching race pull number 3–5 min

TABLE 9 Methods and load norms of swimming strength training

FORMS OF EXERCISE FOR INCREASING MAXIMUM-STRENGTH, EXPLOSIVE POWER AND MUSCULAR ENDURANCE

General strength training

Joint	Joint movement	Muscle/muscle-group	Apparatus preferred	Movement sequence
Head	Flexion	Palmar flexion 1 Flexor carpi radialis 2 Palmaris longus 3 Flexor digitorum superficialis 4 Flexor carpi ulnaris 5 Flexor digitorum profundus	Own weight	All exercises in which the hand joint is flexed, inverted or everted against a resistance
	Pronation (turning inwards)	6 Pronator teres 7 Pronator quadratus	Partner	
	Supination (turning outwards)	8 Supinator 9 Biceps brachii	Barbells	
Elbow	Flexion	9 Biceps brachii 10 Brachialis 11 Brachioradialis	Own weight, partner, weights/bar-bells, expanders/ stretch-cords, universal gym, mini-gym	All exercises in which the elbow joint is flexed against a resistance
	Stretching	12 Triceps brachii		All exercises in which the elbow joint is extended against a resistance

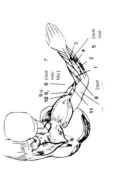

FIG. 152 Arm muscles used in swimming (according to Nemessuri 1963). The muscles in bold type can be strengthened by specific strength training

Joint	Joint movement	Muscle/muscle-group	Equipment preferred	Movement sequence
Shoulder	Abduction (sideways away from centre line)	13 Deltoid (total muscle, but mainly middle fibres) 14 Supraspinatus	Own weight, partner, weights/bar-bells, expanders/ stretch/cords, universal gym, mini-gym	All exercises in which the arm is moved away from the body against a resistance
	Adduction (bringing together)	13 Deltoid (middle fibres) 14 Pectoralis major 16 Latissimus dorsi 17 Teres major		All exercises in which the arm is brought towards the body against a resistance
	Arm flexion (swinging forward)	13 Deltoid (mainly anterior fibres) 15 Pectoralis major (clavicular and sternal portions) 9₁ Biceps – short head 14 Supraspinatus		All exercises in which the arm is swung forward against a resistance
	Arm extension (bringing back)	13 Deltoid (pars acromialis et spinalis deltoidei) 16 Latissimus dorsi 17 Teres major		All exercises in which the arm is taken back against a resistance
	Rotation (turning inwards)	13 Deltoid (anterior fibres) 18 Subscapularis 16 Latissimus dorsi 17 Teres major	Barbells, mini-gym	All exercises in which the upper arm is turned inwards against a resistance

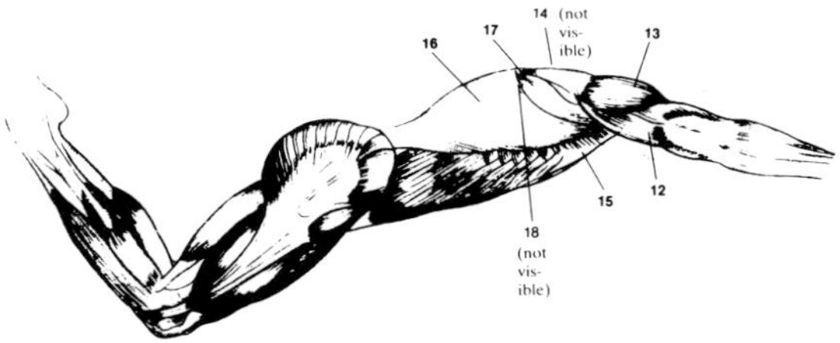

FIG. 153 Shoulder and arm muscles used in swimming (according to Nemessuri 1963). The muscles in bold type can be strengthened by specific training

Joint	Joint movement	Muscle/muscle-group	Apparatus preferred	Movement sequence
Spinal column	Flexion Lateral-flexion Rotation	19 Internal oblique muscle of abdomen 20 External oblique muscle of abdomen 21 Transversus abdominis 22 Rectus abdominis 23 Pyramidalis 24 Quadratus lumborum	Own weight, barbells, partner, expanders/ stretch-cords, universal gym, mini-gym.	All exercises in which, against a resistance, the body is raised upright from the supine position (4.1), raised from the side position (4.2), raised from the prone position (4.3) and raised to the vertical, with rotation, from a supine position (4.4).
	Stretching	25 Interspinales 26 Spinalis 27 Intertransversarii 28 Longissimus 29 Iliocostalis		
	Adduction	30 Pectineus 31 Adductor longus 32 Adductor brevis 33 Adductor magnus 34 Gracilis	Own weight, barbells, partner, expanders/ stretch cords, universal gym, mini-gym.	All exercises in which the leg is brought up to the body against a resistance.
Hips	Hip and knee flexion (bending)	35 Iliopsoas 36 Rectus femoris 37 Tensor fasciae latae 38 Sartorius		All exercises in which the leg is swung forward against a resistance.
	Hip and knee extension (straightening)	39 Gluteus maximus		All exercises in which the leg is taken back against a resistance.

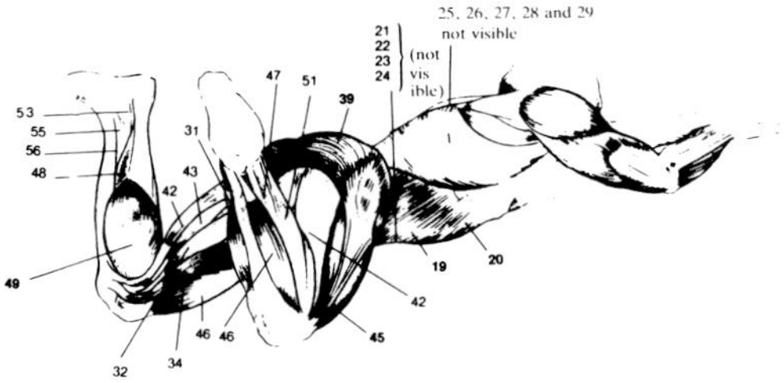

FIG. 154 Leg and trunk muscles involved in swimming (according to Nemessuri 1963). The muscles in bold type can be strengthened by specific strength training

TABLE 10

Joint	Joint movement	Muscle/muscle group	Apparatus preferred	Movement sequence
Hips	Rotation (inwards)	40 Gluteus medius 41 Gluteus minimus 33_1 Adductor magnus (lower portion)		All exercises in which the thigh is turned inwards against a resistance
Knee	Flexion	42 Biceps femoris 43 Semitendinosus 38 Sartorius 44 Semimembranosus	Own weight, barbells, partner, expanders/ stretch-cords, universal gym, mini-gym	All exercises in which the knee joint is extended against a resistance
	Extension	45 Quadriceps femoris		
Foot	Flexion (dorsiflexing)	46 Tibialis anterior 47 Extensor digitorum longus 48 Extensor hallucis longus	Own weight, barbells, partner, expanders/ stretch-cords, universal gym, mini-gym	All exercises in which the ankle joint is flexed or extended against a resistance
	Extension (plantar-flexing)	49 Gastrocnemius 50 Soleus 51 Peroneus longus et brevis 52 Flexor hallucis longus 53 Flexor digitorum longus 54 Tibialis posterior		

FIG. 155 Muscles at the front of the body that are most important in swimming (according to Nemessuri 1963). The muscles in bold type can be strengthened by specific training

PHASE STRUCTURE	APPARATUS	MOVEMENT PATTERN, EXERCISES
1 PULL PHASE (all strokes)	Mini gym, Workhorse or Exergenie, expanders/stretch-cords, roller bench, barbells.	All exercises standing or lying down, in which the movement pattern of the four swimming strokes can be performed against a resistance.
2 PULL-PUSH PHASE (crawl/back-stroke/butterfly)	Mini-gym, Workhorse or Exergenie, expanders/stretch-cords, roller bench, barbells.	All exercises standing or lying down, in which the movement pattern of the pull/push phase of the four strokes can be executed against a resistance.
3 ARM ADDUCTION (breaststroke/ butterfly)	Mini-gym, Workhorse or Exergenie, expanders/stretch-cords, barbells.	All exercises standing, lying down or seated, in which the arms can, against a resistance, be moved towards the body or be brought together in front of the body
4 OUT-OF-WATER RECOVERY PHASE (butterfly/crawl/in part backstroke)	Barbells, mini-gym, expanders/stretch-cords.	All exercises in which the arms are, against a resistance, raised above the head (when standing) or brought together behind the body.
5 ROTATION AT SHOULDER JOINT (all strokes)	Mini-gym, expanders/stretch-cords, barbells, partner.	All exercises in which the upper arm is turned inwards against a resistance.
6 LEG EXTENSION (all strokes)	Mini-gym, universal gym, barbells.	All exercises in which the flexed leg (at knee and hip joints) is extended against a resistance.
7 LEG ADDUCTION (breaststroke)	Mini-gym, expanders/stretch-cords, own bodyweight.	All exercises in which the splayed legs are brought together against a resistance.

Only indirectly important to propulsion: holding a straight body position:

8 BACK EXTENSORS (all strokes)	Own bodyweight, barbells.	All exercises in which the back is raised or extended against a resistance.
9 ABDOMINAL MUSCLES (all strokes)	Own body weight, barbells.	All exercises in which the upper body is bent to the legs or vice versa.

TABLE 11 Specific strength training

	APPARATUS	EXERCISES	EXERCISE CONDITIONS
ON DRY LAND	Mini-gym, swim-bench.	1. Crawl arm movement (alternate pull).	Prone position on bench.
		2. Backcrawl arm movement (alternate pull).	Supine position on bench or standing (pulling apparatus fixed vertically above swimmer).
		3. Breaststroke arm movement (simultaneous pull).	Prone position on bench or standing.
		4. Butterfly arm movement (simultaneous pull).	Prone position on bench or standing.
	Workhorse, Exergenie.	5. 6. Same as 1,2,3,4 7. 8.	
	Own bodyweight	9. Squat jumps (breaststroke)	Normal squat jumps from deep squat for same time as race time and at race frequency for the swing splits.
IN WATER	Tee-shirt, rubber tube, paddles, resistance board, drag suits, resistance flaps, stockings, leotards.	Complete action of all four strokes	Stroke count of race distance and at race frequency, initially divided into 2–4 sub-distances, similar to classical 'broken swimming' (see p. 191).

TABLE 12 Race-specific muscular endurance training

FIG. 156

FIG. 157

FIG. 156 Press-ups with hands wide apart. It is important that the body should remain straight and that it is lowered until it touches the floor.
Variations: a) hands shoulder-width apart b) hands one on top of the other with finger-tips pointing inwards c) with one arm, the other held behind back

FIG. 157 'Wrestler's bridge.' NB On a non-slip surface.
Variations: a) bending and stretching arms b) 'walking' as far as possible towards and away from hands

FIG. 158

FIG. 159

FIG. 158 'Jack-knife' with simultaneous twist of upper body. NB Extended legs should be raised from extended supine position.
Variations: a) without rotation, with hands touching feet b) with extended arms held at sides c) with hands interlocked behind neck

FIG. 159 Single-leg knee-bending: no support from hands; knee flexed until buttocks are touching heel, with free leg held outstretched.
Variations: a) with light extra weight b) with one hand behind back c) with arms folded on chest

FIG. 160   FIG. 161

FIG. 160 Knees are flexed without simultaneous bending at hips. The upper body is inclined backwards and turned so that one hand can touch opposite ankle. NB Thrust hips forward, rotating alternately to left and right

FIG. 161 Arms and legs are simultaneously raised from floor.
Variations: a) raising only one leg b) raising only one arm c) raising left arm and right leg simultaneously and vice versa d) rocking backwards and forwards with arms and legs raised

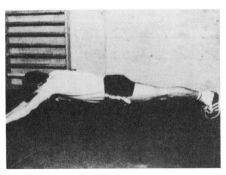

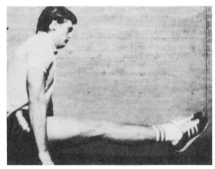

FIG. 162   FIG. 163

FIG. 162 Lying outstretched on floor. The slightly flexed arms are extended and the body raised from floor. NB Non-slip surface

FIG. 163 Half-lever press-up from floor. NB Legs should be extended.
Variations: a) supported on finger-tips b) feet moved as close to head as possible

FIG. 164   FIG. 165

FIG. 164 Reverse press-ups, supporting arms on a bench. NB Elbows should be flexed as far as possible, legs kept extended and feet placed as far from bench as possible

FIG. 165 'Handstand bends', flexing arms until tip of nose touches mat. NB Feet should be supported against a wall and a mat should be used.
Variations: a) with light extra weight b) rapid sequence of several half arm-movements

FIG. 166 'Dips'. Body is raised and lowered. NB Lower as far as possible.
Variations: a) with legs bent up to buttocks b) with extra weight

FIG. 167 From hanging position on wall-bars, legs are raised to above head. Variations: a) legs raised extended b) legs weighted down with additional load

FIG. 168 'Chinning'. NB Grip should be with backs of hands towards swimmer. Pull body up until chin is above level of bar.
Variations: a) with reverse grip b) with extra weight c) made easier by standing on expander cord whose handles are fixed to bar or made easier by standing on a raised surface so that arms are bent

FIG. 169 Overhead throwing of medicine ball to partner with both arms. NB One foot in front of the other, body slightly arched, arms only slightly bent. Variations: a) single-arm throwing b) throwing backwards c) throwing backwards through legs d) from the back throwing forwards over head with both arms e) sudden throw f) 'shot-putt'

FIG. 170   FIG. 171

FIG. 170 Arms are pulled forward and together simultaneously. NB One foot in front of the other, hands open, arms slightly bent, always pulling at shoulder height

FIG. 171 'Bench press-ups'. NB Lower barbell to chest.
Variations: a) gripping at one hand's width b) gripping at 1½ shoulder-width

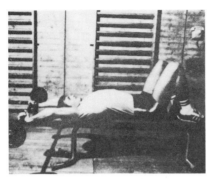

FIG. 172   FIG. 173

FIG. 172 Barbell is lowered from vertical to horizontal position behind head. NB Arms slightly bent, hands raised before elbows

FIG. 173 'Arm rotator.' NB Right-angle at elbow joint and at armpit (between upper arm and side of rib-cage), upper arm remaining in same position

FIG. 174   FIG. 175

FIG. 174 Arms are extended upwards. NB Elbows should be kept as close together as possible.
Variations: a) standing b) lying on a bench, with upper arms forming an angle of approx. 60° to bench

FIG. 175 Hand joints are flexed and passively hyperextended downwards. NB Always have forearms resting on thighs.
Variation: reverse grip

FIG. 176   FIG. 177

FIG. 176 Raise weight until elbows are fully bent. NB Forearms against trunk, keeping trunk steady.
Variation: sitting position

FIG. 177 Raise barbell or weight in front of body to shoulder level. NB Elbows out, gripping at a hand's width, upper body kept steady.
Variation: behind back

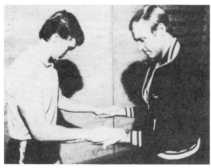

FIG. 178 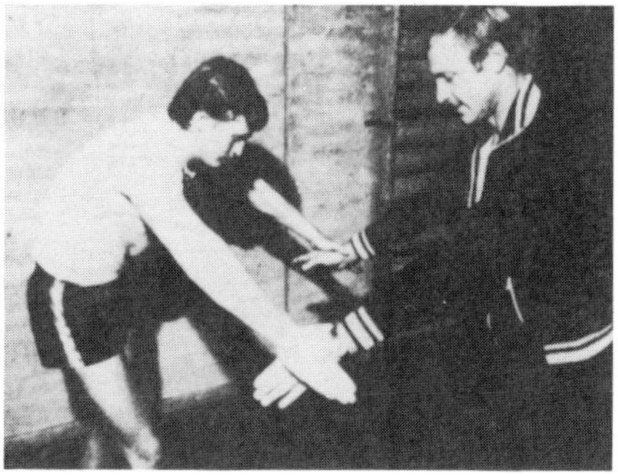   FIG. 179

FIG. 178 Isometric exercise: partner on left tries to extend his arms, while the other resists. NB Trunk held erect, with upper arms against trunk

FIG. 179 Isometric exercise: partner on left attempts to force his arms inwards, while the other resists. NB Elbows high, hands open, one foot in front of the other, trunk inclined slightly forwards

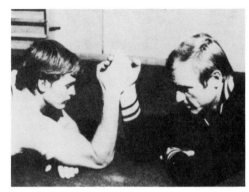

FIG. 180   FIG. 181

FIG. 180 Isometric exercise: partner on floor attempts to force his arms down to his hips while the other resists. NB Hands open, elbows slightly bent, elbows held high

FIG. 181 Isometric exercise: 'arm wrestling', alternately with left and right hands, supporting active arm with free hand

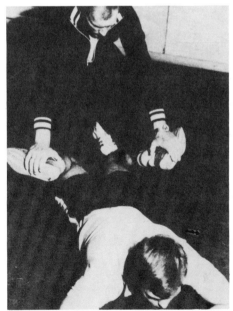

FIG. 182 Isometric exercise: 'breast-stroke leg stretching'. Partner on floor tries to extend his legs backwards and inwards; the other partner resists carefully

FIG. 183 Legs are extended from the breaststroke sitting position. NB Hold torso erect; soft floor covering

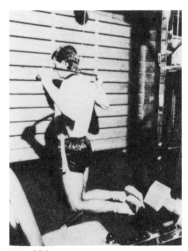

FIG. 184

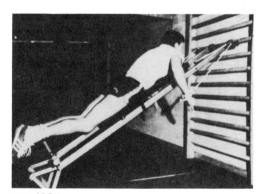

FIG. 185

FIG. 184 'Latissimus pull'. NB Keep upper body steady; legs may be weighted down if swimmer is capable of pulling more than his bodyweight.
Variations: a) pulling down infront of body b) alternately infront of and behind body

FIG. 185 Double-arm pull on roller bench. NB Hands open, elbows held high.
Variation: intensity and speed varied by changing angle of bench

FIG. 186   FIG. 187

FIG. 186 The arms are extended upwards. NB Elbows as close together as possible, upper arms and trunk held steady.
Variation: both ends of a stretch-cord on which the young swimmer is standing are pulled upwards

FIG. 187 Double-arm pull standing. NB Hands open, elbows held high throughout, one foot in front of the other, regular breathing

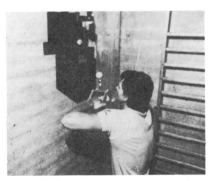 

FIG. 188   FIG. 189

FIG. 188 Double-arm pull standing, with double hand-grip. NB While pulling, the elbows should be directed upwards and outwards.
Variations: a) kneeling b) in straddle sitting position

FIG. 189 'Crawl arm-pull on swim-bench'. NB Hands open, elbows held high, pulling alternately, regular breathing

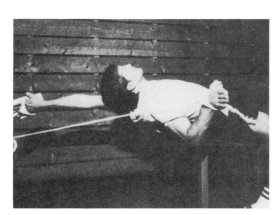

FIG. 190   FIG. 191

FIG. 190 'Backcrawl arm-pull on swim-bench'. NB Hands open, upper arms turned inwards, i.e. elbows pointing towards floor, alternate pulling, regular breathing

FIG. 191 'Breaststroke arm-pull on swim-bench'. NB Hands open, elbows held high, emphatic inward movement of arms at end of pulling phase, regular breathing. Variation: butterfly stroke arm action

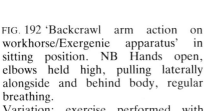

FIG. 192 'Backcrawl arm action on workhorse/Exergenie apparatus' in sitting position. NB Hands open, elbows held high, pulling laterally alongside and behind body, regular breathing.
Variation: exercise performed with hemp rope, the middle of which has been wrapped several times round a horizontal bar or rung of a ladder

FIG. 193 Inward movement of breast-stroke and butterfly arm-pull using two workhorses/Exergenies attached fairly high up to the side walls. One partner pulls inwards while the other gives way slowly. NB Hands open, elbows held high, one foot forward, trunk bent forward slightly and held steady

FIG. 194   FIG. 195

FIG. 194 'Backcrawl arm-pull' using expander in standing position. Middle of expander is fixed above swimmer. NB Hands open, elbows held high, regular breathing. Variation: arm movements in front of body down to thighs, possibly also using strong elastic rope (shock cord)

FIG. 195 'Elbow extensor with expander or stretch-cord'. The arms are extended downwards. NB Upper arms against body, no leaning forward or rocking, hands open, regular breathing

FIG. 196   FIG. 197

FIG. 196 'Swinging straddle in supine position' against an elastic rope. Assume supine position on bench or vaulting box. Rope is fixed behind swimmer at points about 1 m apart. NB Everted dorsiflexed feet

FIG. 197 Sitting on a bench or box, the legs are adducted (brought together) against the powerful resistance of an expander or stretch-cord, which is fixed behind the swimmer at points about 3 m apart. NB Knees flexed and feet dorsiflexed

14 Training for swimming speed endurance

In order to ensure that in a race a swimmer is able to utilise his anaerobic capacity to the full, his body must, as has already been mentioned, become used to very intensive loads. The swimmer has to be made capable, despite muscular pain and the discomfort of high blood lactate levels, of standing further loads and of reproducing the swimming action without loss of quality. This is achieved by speed endurance training.

For speed endurance training to prepare the swimmer most effectively for the demands of competitive swimming, the work duration should be chosen so that the mechanism of anaerobic energy provision is fully utilised. This calls for a work duration of not less than about 30 seconds and not more than two minutes. The intensity should be as high as is just possible (cf. TABLE 13 and FIG. 198).

Controlling effort and speed for speed endurance training presents the coach with fewer problems than basic endurance training. He must of course be able to motivate his charge to swim as fast as possible, which is not always easy.

There are three methods available for improving anaerobic capacity (cf. TABLE 13):

- repetition training;
- swimming the race distance in stages (broken swims);
- intensive or fast interval training.

The most effective method is repetition training. Distances of between 50 and 150 m satisfy the condition of the requisite load duration of between 30 and 120 sec. It is absolutely essential that they are swum at the greatest possible intensity.

Repetition training can be organised as follows to make it easier for the swimmer to satisfy this requirement:

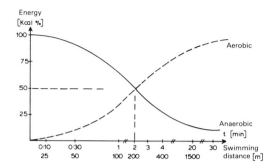

FIG. 198 Relationship between work duration/swimming distance and percentage contributions of aerobic and anaerobic processes in total energy provision (diagrammatic representation after Hollman/Hettinger 1976)

- The individual swimmer should be given enough space, i.e. if possible not having to swim on a 'conveyor belt'. If this is unavoidable, it should be with only a small number of swimmers per lane. In this way the individual is more likely to be stressed to the limit than if he has to watch out for a lot of other swimmers in the lane and swim in continual fear of collisions.

- Every distance should begin with a diving start from the blocks at a starting signal. This gives practice in starting, and each repeat is from the starting acceleration. In addition, the times swum can be directly compared with race times.

- Swimmers of equal speed should swim alongside each other every now and then. Handicap races can be arranged for team members who are not as fast as each other, so that they can not only swim against the clock but may be motivated to higher load limits by having opposition. This is particularly helpful when two or three repeats have already been swum and the swimmers with a high lactate accumulation have to attempt to maintain their speed during the next repeat.

Repetition training is thus suitable for simulating race conditions. This applies both to the mental attitude of the swimmers and to the external conditions.

After each stress phase the swimmers should swim rather more easily, climb out of the water, rub themselves down and prepare for the next repeat, as far as the rest interval allows.

It goes without saying that the coach should have recorded the exact swimming time of each swimmer and show it to him in the rest interval. At the same time he should discuss any errors in technique or tactics and give any important instructions for the next repeat.

Because of the high intensity, and despite the long rest intervals which can quite reasonably be allowed to last for up to 10 minutes (cf. TABLE 13), even a well-trained body can stand only a relatively small number of repeats:

8–12 repeats of 50 m;
4–6 repeats of 100 m;
3–4 repeats of 150 m.

In cases where there has been a clear drop in swimming speed, it is pointless for the swimmer to complete a planned set by forcing himself to the limit. Should the first repeats be swum too hard, an intolerable acidosis of the entire body will occur earlier than planned. Continuing the set at a considerably lower intensity can serve as nothing more than training will power. The desired physiological training effect is no longer obtained. It is important, however, that the coach should learn to distinguish between actual and feigned acidosis in his young charges.

Broken swims should be organised in the same way as repetition training. The coach and swimmer have to observe a similar procedure. In its original form, i.e. with rather longer rest intervals, the broken swim fulfils the same task in improving anaerobic capacity as repetition swimming.

It does, however, have a few other purposes. Originally the broken swim was used as a test of the target race speed. The race distance is divided into shorter distances, for example, the 100 m into 4 x 25 m or 2 x 50 m or 50 m plus 2 x 25 m (cf. TABLE 13). All the component distances should be swum at the prescribed race speed, and the interpolated rest intervals should be of 5 to 20 seconds.

It is important that the first sub-distance should begin with a diving start from the blocks at a starting signal and that the turns are taken into account in the timing. Consequently the watch should not be stopped when the swimmer's hand touches but when the feet touch the wall after a complete change of direction. If the watch is kept stopped during the rest intervals, the time obtained at the end is the pure swimming time which, bearing in mind the rest intervals, can be used as an acceptable forecast of possible competitive performance.

As a rule-of-thumb, the average time for two repeats of the race distance (with 10 seconds' pause between the sub-distances and 10 minutes' rest between the two race distances) can be achieved in competition. The broken swim should be repeated two or three times as a race test. The rest intervals between the tests should be about 10 minutes. Under certain circumstances they can be even longer.

Besides the physiological effect (improvement of anaerobic capacity), the broken swim helps to divide up the race distance correctly. It also contributes to the development of sensitivity to race speed. With this last objective in mind, the broken swim is of prime importance during the last weeks of training prior to important races.

It is recommended that broken swims are started three or four weeks before the main race. Since at this time the swimmer is still doing full training, it must not be expected that he can achieve the target race time with 10-sec rest intervals. 20-sec pauses can therefore be used initially, reducing them by 5 seconds each week. The shortest rest interval should not, however, be less than 5 seconds.

It should also be borne in mind that total distances of over 200 m (e.g. 4 × 50 m with 10-sec intervals) have less and less effect as the distance increases, as far as anaerobic stimulus is concerned (cf. repetition training). A 400-m-medley swimmer can in fact swim a broken 3 × 8 × 50 m with 10-sec and 10-min rest intervals to develop his breakdown of the race and his time sensitivity, but this is not so effective for anaerobic training. This is even more applicable to the 800-m female swimmer or the 1500-m freestyler: when they swim 8 × 100 m or 15 × 100 m with 10-sec rest intervals, it is evident from the total stress time of $\simeq$ 10 min and $\simeq$ 20 min that the physiological effect of such training is primarily to improve aerobic energy generation (cf. FIG. 198).

Regardless of the race distance, the sub-distances must not be too long if the aim is race speed. For 100 m and 200 m races the longest component distance is 50 m. In some cases it would be conceivable to have a split of 100 m plus 2 × 50 m for a 200 m swimmer. For 400 m and longer race distances, a sub-distance of 100 m should not be exceeded.

Like basic endurance training, intensive interval training can be organised on a chain swimming basis.

Since, particularly at the shorter sub-distances up to 100 m, the rest intervals are almost as long as the work duration (cf. TABLE 13), it is advisable to split up the training group. In this way only half the participants are swimming at one time, which means a larger and less choppy water area for the individual while the other half are resting, and vice versa. What is important is that the intensity should be well above that of basic endurance training. Be that as it may, each swimmer should endeavour to swim the sets at a constant speed or at least at only slightly slower times. The load intensity should demand a considerable proportion of (lactic acid) anaerobic energy provision. Ideally, this is equivalent to a lactate accumulation of 6–8 mmol/l, as

Load norms	Training methods		
	Repetition training	Broken swims	Intensive or fast interval training
A	Improving – local influencing factors, – central influencing factors. Stress: 80–90% anaerobic glycosis, and 10–20% aerobic depending on race distance.	Improving – local influencing factors, – central influencing factors. Stress: depending on race distance, 80–90% glycolytic (100–200 m) + 10–20% aerobic, up to 60–70% aerobic + 30–40% anaerobic glycosis (800 – 1500 m).	Improving – local influencing factors, – central influencing factors. Stress: 70–80% aerobic + 20–30% anaerobic glycosis at transition to basic-endurance training.
N	2–12 (possibly in several sets).	1–5	5–30, depending on distance (possibly in sets).
D	50–150 m	Sub-distances between 25–100 m. Total distance = race distance (100–1500 m).	25–200 m
F	At steady or slightly-increasing speed, in all strokes.	Race speed in all strokes to be swum in forthcoming competition.	At steady or increasing speed, in all strokes.
I	– At maximum speed possible for distance. – 100% race-speed or even above race-speed. – Lactate concentrations above 10–12 mmol/l.	At target race-speed.	As % of currently possible race-time over: 25 85% equivalent to 50 88% approx. 6 – 8 75 89% mmol/l 100 90% lactate 150 90% level 200 90% Pulse rate roughly maximum
R	2–10 min	5–20 sec. between sub-distances; 3–10 min. between total race-distances.	1 × to 2 × the stress time, max. 90 sec.

TABLE 13 Training methods and load norms for swimming speed endurance

shown in FIG. 147. Such an intensity can only be maintained with great will power. The coach must ensure that the set is not started too quickly, because this can lead to a 'collapse'. Instead, the quality of the set should be maintained until the very end.

Experience has shown that anaerobic capacity can be raised to the requisite level in four to six weeks, the level depending on the length of the race. This is assuming that a sprinter has at least carried out anaerobic training regularly throughout the year (cf. annual training plan on p. 204).

In speed endurance training there is a hidden danger of overtraining because of the high load intensity. The recovery times after intensive anaerobic stress vary between 12 and 72 hours.

The coach must therefore, by tests and observations, discover how his swimmer is standing up to the anaerobic stress. Only by so doing can he establish the individual frequency and extent per week.

	BASIC SWIMMING ENDURANCE	SWIMMING SPEED-ENDURANCE	BASIC SWIMMING SPEED
Sprints (10–25 m)	–	small	very great
Repetition training	very small	very great	moderate
Broken swims	small	great	small
Intensive (fast) interval training	moderate	moderate	very small
Extensive interval training	very great	–	–
Fartlek (speed-play)	great	small	–
Continuous swimming	very great	–	–

TABLE 14 Training methods in swimming and their effect in improving basic swimming endurance, speed endurance and basic speed

For the majority of swimmers one can start on the assumption that, over a period of four to six weeks, they can train anaerobically every second or third day.

In such cases it is most advantageous to conduct three training sessions a week to increase speed endurance. They are particularly relevant to the sprinter.

More frequent repeats lead inevitably to Basedow-type overtraining (cf. p. 279).

For this reason it is important to pay attention to not losing sight of the aim of anaerobic training. TABLE 14 summarises the training methods and their effect in improving basic endurance, speed endurance and basic speed.

15 The element of competition in the training schedule

One of the main aims of the long-term training schedule is the realisation of potential performance in the form of good competition results.

Even for the mature athlete, and particularly for the age-group swimmer, because of the nervous stress involved every race represents an exceptional human situation, generating feelings of anxiety to some degree. A certain amount of anxiety is of course desirable to keep the sportsman mentally and physically attuned to an extent sufficient to stimulate his efforts for above-average performances.

One of the aims of coaching is therefore to make the sportsman capable of competing, i.e. to make him able to stand the stress situation of competition and to cope with it successfully by applying well-trained abilities and behaviour patterns.

In most cases this calls for a multi-year sports education process, running in parallel with the training programme and introducing races into the schedule in a planned manner. This process gradually introduces the age-group swimmer to the actual difficulties of the competitive situation, so that there is no build-up of failures or of excessive anxiety experiences, leading to unfavourable motivation or panic prior to races.

The young person must learn, for one thing, how to tolerate the special mental tension of competition and to keep his excitement within bounds permitting sensible sporting behaviour. The fact that this is possible by systematic familiarisation with the competitive situation is borne out by the investigations of Drakič/Paranosic (in Vanek 1978). Using sportsmen (basketball players) properly prepared for competition, they established that their cerebral cortex responsible for movement is protected against overload by anxiety. In contrast to 'ordinary' people, the competitive sportsmen became not more but less conscious of their anxiety, which must be regarded as a neurovegetative protection process resulting from systematic competition training. There is no doubt, however, that this kind of competitiveness in swimming involves participation in about 50 to 80 races. Competition therefore implies the organisation of several races for the swimmer.

How can the path towards competitiveness be smoothed for the age-group swimmer?

This is best done initially by reducing the risks which the sportsman sees in competition:

– Regular performance comparison within the training group is less fraught than against unknown swimmers.
– Competition takes place first of all within the circle of the swimmer's own friends. Only gradually is the circle extended to other training groups in the same club, then to nearby clubs, and so on: exposure to the public is controlled in stages.
– By designing performance comparison as a combined competition, i.e. several races, the result does not hang on a single test. The young swimmer knows that he will be given other opportunities to make up for a poor performance.
– As soon as the first races outside the training group and the club come along, in the first few years the risk of failure should be borne by the group as a whole (relay, team race) and is thereby reduced for the individual.

The young swimmer also has to learn that the difficult task of competition can be coped with successfully if it is prepared for appropriately, i.e. through scientific training.

It has to be ensured that, for the young swimmer's first races, what is demanded of him and judged is what has been thoroughly learned during training and has been practised until mastered.

The question is bound to be asked as to what can be tested in a competitive manner during the years of basic instruction and basic training.

Since the first years of training are concerned primarily with acquiring and practising the competitive swimming strokes (cf. TABLE 1), the monitoring of the learning process should also embrace this aspect. Technique competitions are organised within the group, related to the quality of swimming technique, starts and turns, but also the mastery of swimming exercises which have already been worked through.

This includes measuring the glide after a push-off, backstroke start and dive start. It can be applied to mobility exercises and to selected gymnastics exercises, and be made into a combined competition. Judgment of underwater exercises and diving proper can also be included if they have figured in training previously. Even team games with a ball in water can be organised so that every member of the winning team receives a set number of points and each player on the losing team gets half that number of points.

If the previous week's training has included, say, a run in the woods, it is an obvious step to have a longer, timed run. The coach's greatest problem is to work out an evenly weighted points system for the very varied activities in such combined competitions.

As soon as basic swimming endurance appears in the training schedule, it too is included in the combined competition. This does not happen, of course, until after a few weeks of training, in the form of a timed 300-m to 500-m distance. Similar treatment can be given to basic swimming speed, but only distances of 10 to 20 m should be measured in the competitive evaluation. In a 25-m pool this could be a sprint race over half the pool, i.e. 12.5 m, according to time.

As technique training and conditioning proceeds, the more the combined competition shifts towards the special swimming disciplines. Thus, for example, in keeping with the biological development of the children and the objectives of basic training, these races are recommended:

- 400 m,
- 25 m,
- distances in minimum time with technique being judged.

These criteria suggest a swimming triathlon with points awarded: 25 m according to time (speed of movement/basic speed); 400 m according to time (basic endurance); 4 x 25-m medley with style judged ('style swimming'). Despite this appropriate shift of emphasis, we should guard against premature limitation of the general sporting movement requirements and even of their complete disappearance.

We should also bear in mind when planning participation in competition that the swimmer has to create and reinforce his own athletic basis at the start of his career and from time to time later.

It cannot be stressed enough that the age-group swimmer, during his first years of competition, ought to experience the relationship between careful preparation in training and success in competition. He also has to learn to recognise as success the *time* he does related to the amount of training he has done and not just the victory or being placed in a race. It is of course in the coach's power to enter him occasionally for races in which a good performance and a good finishing place will coincide. On no account should there be races calling for abilities which the young swimmer has not previously trained sufficiently.

Admittedly, as his 'training age' increases, i.e. at the latest by the elite stage, the swimmer takes part in races while in full training. Since these races are preceded neither by recovery nor tapering, outstanding performances should not be expected. This should be explained at a team talk, so that the swimmers involved do not raise their expectations too high: they are basically test swims under race conditions. But it is just because of these conditions that they contribute to the competition experience of the young swimmer and increase the number of stress situations coped with. What is more, every competition always constitutes a highly intensive stimulus to training.

The same applies to the minor races within the framework of a major meet. They raise the swimmer's race routine, even though their role in most cases is as a preliminary to a major race. It is therefore advisable, on the day prior to an important race, for an age-group

TRAINING YEAR	NUMBER OF COMPETITIONS PER YEAR	NATURE OF COMPETITIONS
1st	2–3	Combined competition within training group
2nd	4–6	Individual comparison within training group, combined competition and group competition within club
3rd	6–8	Relay races and combined competitions against local clubs
4th	8–12	Relay races and team competitions, club competitions
5th	10–14	Team and relay races, individual races
6th	12–16	Individual races, relay and team races, races with home coach not present
7th	14–20	
8th	16–26	

TABLE 15 Competitions and races in the training schedule

swimmer to be made wherever possible to swim in a less important race (but naturally not a long-distance race).

For the older swimmer, the significance of the subsidiary competitions and races is to gain experience if he or she has not raced competitively for a long time or is excessively nervous.

16 Dividing up the training year

Everyone knows that top form cannot be maintained all the time. Further, if the performance improvement gradient were known and straight with no possibility of further improvement, this would in most cases not be at all desirable either.

Performance does not, however, improve steadily and continuously.

To achieve an improved performance in the course of a year taken as a whole, for this to be a better performance than in the previous year, and for it to be achieved at the right time, demands that training be divided into periods of different stress.

These are:

1 periods of heavy and light training loads;
2 periods of high and low performance;
3 periods of general, swimming specific and race specific training;
4 periods of rest and recovery.

Although the extent and intensity of the training load will increase considerably in the course of the training year as a whole, and although the training methods and forms become more specialised and more race specific as 'training age' increases, the fundamental training structures are repeated within certain time units because of their peculiar biological and psychological modes of action.

On the basis of the 'cyclical' repetition of training periods, these time units are referred to as training cycles. The largest time unit of such repetition is a macro-cycle and the smallest a micro-cycle, with a meso-cycle between the two. The duration of the various cycles depends on the requirements and conditions of the sport concerned. They can sometimes deviate appreciably from the concepts of general training theory (cf. FIG. 199).

Since a three-stage training period has become the established norm in swimming, the training year is divided into three macro-cycles. A macro-cycle is between 10 and 14 weeks in length. The micro-cycle, lasting one week, does not occur until the high-pressure (or elite)

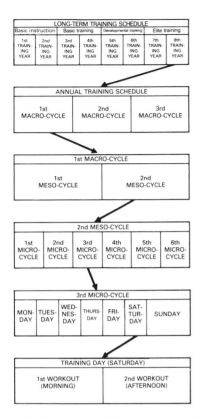

LONG-TERM TRAINING SCHEDULE							
Basic instruction	Basic training		Developmental training		Elite training		
1st TRAIN-ING YEAR	2nd TRAIN-ING YEAR	3rd TRAIN-ING YEAR	4th TRAIN-ING YEAR	5th TRAIN-ING YEAR	6th TRAIN-ING YEAR	7th TRAIN-ING YEAR	8th TRAIN-ING YEAR

ANNUAL TRAINING SCHEDULE		
1st MACRO-CYCLE	2nd MACRO-CYCLE	3rd MACRO-CYCLE

1st MACRO-CYCLE	
1st MESO-CYCLE	2nd MESO-CYCLE

2nd MESO-CYCLE					
1st MICRO-CYCLE	2nd MICRO-CYCLE	3rd MICRO-CYCLE	4th MICRO-CYCLE	5th MICRO-CYCLE	6th MICRO-CYCLE

3rd MICRO-CYCLE						
MON-DAY	TUES-DAY	WED-NES-DAY	THURS-DAY	FRI-DAY	SAT-TUR-DAY	SUNDAY

TRAINING DAY (SATURDAY)	
1st WORKOUT (MORNING)	2nd WORKOUT (AFTERNOON)

FIG. 199 Relative location of a day's training in the overall arrangement of cycles, years and long-term training schedule (example)

training stage. The meso-cycle lasts from five to eight weeks both in developmental training and elite training. By virtue of the increased number of workouts at the elite stage, a meso-cycle embraces about a third more workouts than at the developmental training stage (cf. FIG. 200).

Training in cycles includes repetition of the objective emphasised in each cycle, e.g. increasing basic swimming endurance in each micro-cycle. This can be achieved by different forms of training and sometimes even by alternating methods, e.g. mainly by the continuous method one week and more by the interval method the next.

Amongst other things, sub-division into micro-cycles permits a weekly check on performance development, with immediate modification of the training schedule if the results achieved deviate from those planned. The same applies to the meso-cycle, which normally concludes with a competitive test. Two meso-cycles form a macro-cycle. The second meso-cycle ends with a major competition: team championships, an international match, national championships. If the

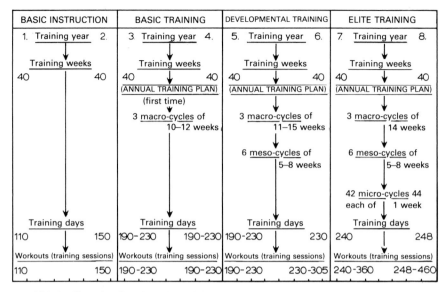

BASIC INSTRUCTION	BASIC TRAINING	DEVELOPMENTAL TRAINING	ELITE TRAINING
1. Training year 2.	3. Training year 4.	5. Training year 6.	7. Training year 8.
Training weeks	Training weeks	Training weeks	Training weeks
40 40	40 40	40 40	40 40
	(ANNUAL TRAINING PLAN) (first time)	(ANNUAL TRAINING PLAN)	(ANNUAL TRAINING PLAN)
	3 macro-cycles of 10–12 weeks	3 macro-cycles of 11–15 weeks	3 macro-cycles of 14 weeks
		6 meso-cycles of 5–8 weeks	6 meso-cycles of 5–8 weeks
			42 micro-cycles 44 each of 1 week
Training days	Training days	Training days	Training days
110 150	190-230 190-230	190-230 230	240 248
Workouts (training sessions)	Workouts (training sessions)	Workouts (training sessions)	Workouts (training sessions)
110 150	190-230 190-230	190-230 230-305	240-360 248-460

FIG. 200 Outline plan for the sub-division of the training year within the framework of the long-term training schedule

results at the end of the first cycle are not as anticipated, the objectives as a whole are retained but the training forms and possibly also the methods have to be changed in order to prepare with any degree of promise for the major competition (cf. training control).

The macro-cycles are similar with regard to objectives and structure. These too end with an important competition, since their ending coincides with that of the second meso-cycle.

Making the training cyclical right down to the weekly work of the micro-cycles only becomes necessary after the young swimmer has six or seven years of systematic training behind him. There are three reasons for this:

1 Only after six or seven years can one reckon on the swimmer being willing and able to train throughout the year with only a few weeks' break.
2 After the break in training at the end of the competition season, it takes only a few weeks to reach the trained condition of the previous year.
3 The swimmer's body then needs a more frequent alternation of training stimuli, and in some cases greater stimuli, to improve performance. Long periods of identical training methods and forms in most cases produce stagnation and represent a pointless training effort.

Because the training patterns are repeated in cycles the coach must not be drawn into using the same length and intensity of work i.e. he must not keep the total load the same.

Both within the micro-cycle and in the meso- and macro-cycles, the total load varies in the shape of a wave, or, if the essential recovery phases with a lower load are not observed, in a stepped form. It challenges the athlete's body, and also his mental and emotional attitude, with the task of fresh adaptation and achievement.

For this purpose, not only does the total load vary in a wave or stepped shape, but there is also a variation in the basic amounts and intensities. These behave fundamentally in a contrary manner, i.e. the intensity peak coincides with a trough in the amount of training and vice versa (FIGS. 201–5).

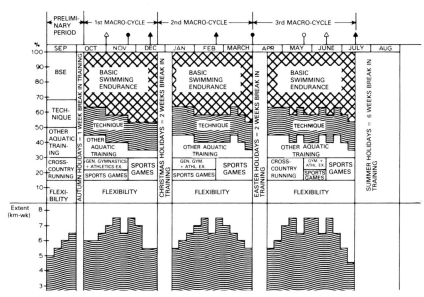

△ = competition with judging of technique, 0 = relay races, ▲ = individual competitions within the framework of club competitions, ● = competition combining dry-land activities (e.g. cross-country running), water activities (e.g. diving or plunging exercises), swimming 25 m and 400 m or more, judging technique.

FIG. 201 Cycles in the third training year (example)

Nonetheless, this ratio of load intensity has to change as the training age of the young swimmer increases, in order to produce improved adaptation and thereby improved performance. The load peaks of amount and intensity move closer together for a time, thereby raising the total load. The long waves of the early training years suddenly give

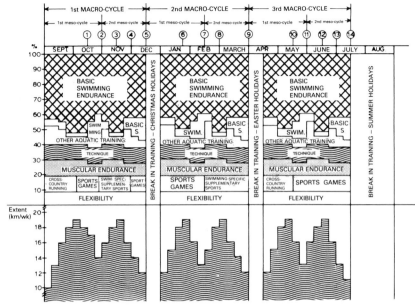

FIG. 202 Cycles in the fifth training year (example)

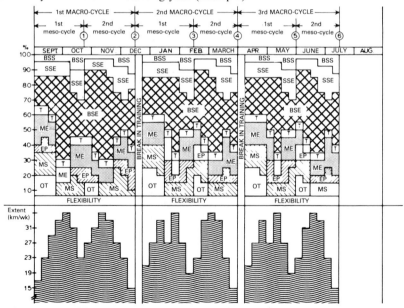

FIG. 203 Cycles in the eighth year of a sprinter (example)

Abbreviations for Figs. 201–205:

BSS	= basic swimming speed	MS	= maximum strength
BSE	= basic swimming endurance	EP	= explosive power
SSE	= swimming speed-endurance	OT	= other training (in water)
T	= technique (training)	OTL	= other training (dry land)
ME	= muscular endurance	②④⑥	= main competitions at end of macro-cycles
		①③⑤	= important competitions at end of first meso-cycle

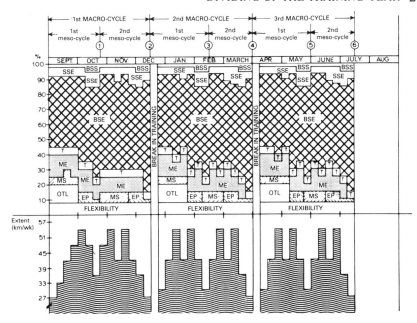

FIG. 204 Cycles in the eighth training year of a middle-distance swimmer (example)

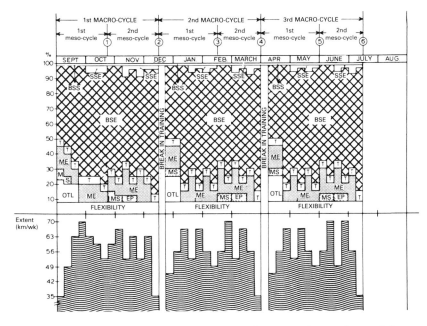

FIG. 205 Cycles in the eighth training year of a distance swimmer (example)

way to a larger load wave shape in the seventh and eighth years of training. After a training build-up of about six years, the increased physical capability, greater mental hardness in the face of training load demands and greater determination influenced by experience and understanding seem to justify such training cycles.

It is also important to remember in this connection that the effectiveness of the same training methods and loads decreases with increasing years of training. Despite the high intensity, the athlete is no longer capable of reacting to the same or similar stimulus with worthwhile adaptation. Besides the wave shape of the load, it is also necessary to alternate cyclically the training aims of conditioning, such as maximum strength, strength endurance etc.

After phases of very specific swimming training it is necessary, using general forms of training, to reproduce and consolidate the general overall athletic performance level.

The training cycle is thus given a time-and-content significance in the planning and periodisation of training for the age-group swimmer. It will also be apparent that the large time units of the early training years, together with their protracted similar or only gradually increasing stimuli are divided into smaller units (meso-cycles and micro-cycles) as training years increase and performance improves.

While the initial basic teaching period should be completely free from the influence of any competitive peaks, the macro-cycles in the following periods of training are increasingly arranged in three-peak cycles instead of the two-peak cycle more common in other sports. This requires the planning of three macro-cycles, each of which should always conclude with some form of check on learning and training. In the early years this consists of a test within the group of what has been learned and practised with regard to swimming technique in the preceding period, or on which emphasis has been placed in training, e.g. on basic endurance or basic speed. Each macro-cycle leads to tests of what has been learned and grooved; it does not lead to a competition peak.

Only in later years does each macro-cycle eventually lead up to a formal competitive high point: major team competition, winter championships and summer championships, at a local or regional level, i.e. at a performance level corresponding to the age-group swimmer's current ability.

One essential factor in favour of the three-part cycle is the rapid alternation of training loads and methods under the criterion of effective training organisation. From the teaching theory point-of-view, the easier grasp of the shorter period, at the end of which the young person is to receive confirmation or correction for his or her efforts, is important for serious and full cooperation and concentration.

Another factor which favours division into three macro-cycles to an even greater extent is the sub-division of the school year or academic year with which the training schedule has to be integrated. Each macro-cycle is followed by a short (in the summer a long) break in training (cf. FIG. 201). This should be devoted to recovery, against a background of family activities. During developmental training, and certainly during elite training, a proportion of this time will of course be spent on individual or team activities: in the sporting area, short training camps for swimming-specific supplementary sports; trips for a change of climate and for 'social' experience.

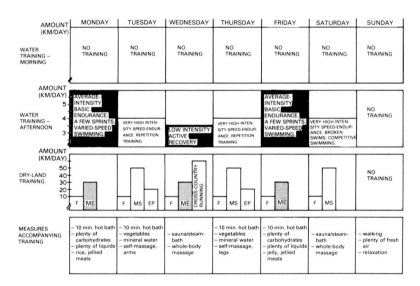

FIG. 206 Example of a micro-cycle (8th training year, 1st macro-cycle, 2nd meso-cycle, 5th micro-cycle) for a sprinter

In addition to this, an annual family holiday and time at home with the family should also be written-in, at least for the main holidays. Experience so far has shown that three-peak planning goes a long way towards meeting these requirements.

It has been recommended that from the seventh or eighth year of training, the smallest unit in the schedule should be a micro-cycle of one week's duration (cf. FIGS. 207, 208). This has proved effective in top-class swimming (Sweetenham 1980).

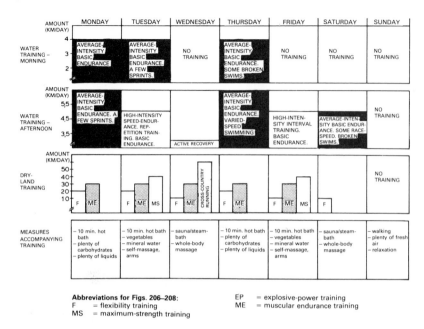

FIG. 207 Example of a micro-cycle (8th training year, 1st macro-cycle, 2nd meso-cycle, 3rd micro-cycle) for a middle-distance swimmer. (F = flexibility, ME = muscular endurance, MS = maximum strength)

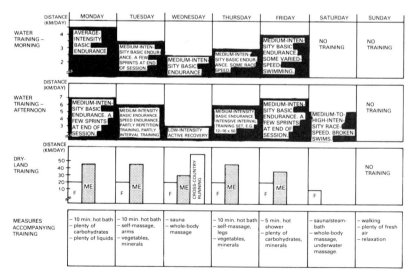

FIG. 208 Example of a micro-cycle for a distance swimmer (8th training year, 1st macro-cycle, 2nd meso-cycle, 5th micro-cycle)

The high/low nature of the training load is naturally encountered again in the micro-cycle, e.g. as hard and easy training days or as contrast between great distance and high speed from one workout to another. The one-week micro-cycle is also suitable for the 'form training' between races and for 'peaking' (tapering, cf. p. 271). 'The individual aims and contents of a micro-cycle should be arranged so that technique exercises, speed, explosive power and maximum-strength loads are carried out as far as possible in periods of high performance, whereas basic endurance, muscular endurance and speed endurance performances may take place in a state of incomplete regeneration' (Martin 1980, p. 115).

It is thus recommended, for example, that there should be no sprinting requirements or difficult swimming technique exercises on a Monday morning. Experience has shown that this is not a favourable time for demands for great concentration or application of will power, because the preceding Sunday, either as a race day or as a recovery day, has not keyed up the swimmer ready to perform, i.e. to a state favourable for sports exercises involving great demands on his nervous system and on his preparedness to make an effort. On a Monday morning a swimmer has to 'swim himself' in for such demands.

In addition to the short-term load variation, the one-week micro-cycle offers the opportunity of determining the young swimmer's performance and training progress from time to time from his reaction to the repetition of the same training cycles.

On the basis of the individual and average times swum, of the recovery pulse rates and of the subjective recovery from one workout to the next, the swimmer's general condition can be determined by comparison with previous results.

FIG. 199 illustrates the relationship between the 'Outline plan for the sub-division of the training year within the framework of the long-term training schedule' (FIG. 200) and the examples of division into cycles (FIGS. 201–5) and micro-cycles (FIGS. 206–8). An example is given of a week's schedule for a middle-distance swimmer in his eighth year of training (FIG. 207). In FIG. 199 this week's schedule (3rd micro-cycle) is in the second box from the bottom and is linked by an arrow to the 2nd meso-cycle (3rd box) of the 1st macro-cycle (4th box) in the eighth training year (5th box).

The cyclical examples indicate both the intensity and extent of training. The intensity is apparent from the listing of the conditioning exercises or capabilities being trained for and from the illustrated percentage involvement of these exercises or capabilities in the week's training as a whole. In the annual schedules (= division of the training year into cycles) this information is in the top half.

Thus, for example, the third week in October (= 7th micro-cycle in 1st meso-cycle) for a sprinter in his eighth training year is at very high intensity, because the swimmer is heavily loaded energy-wise by around 30 per cent of training for basic swimming speed and speed endurance, coupled with around 33 per cent of strength training.

The distance of 23 km in the swimming programme for this week is quite small, as can be seen from the bottom part of the diagram. If this week is compared with the first week in October (= 5th micro-cycle in 1st meso-cycle), the inversion of the ratio of intensity to amount will be evident.

The same applies to the individual days of the week in the micro-cycle schedule examples. The top part shows the conditioning training objectives with the corresponding intensity details for morning and afternoon workouts. At the left-hand edge of the diagram the suggested training extent can be read off from the kilometre scale for the swimming programme and from the minutes scale for dry-land training.

17 Hints on training methods for the individual training years, distances and composition of training

HINTS FOR THE FIRST YEAR OF TRAINING

The first year of training is used for basic technique development. The year is planned so that the movement patterns to be learned in the water and on dry land, as well as the times of acquisition of sporting knowledge, are well distributed over the time available. Formal planning is not relevant. The distribution of the three 'training days' through the week should be as even as possible (cf. FIG. 211, p. 246), in order to avoid an excessive density of similar stresses for the children.

Since the small number of competitions are conducted as comparisons within the group and are timed by the coach himself, no external yardsticks have to be met. The competitions within the group arise from and test skills and training aims which have been thoroughly learned and practised in the period immediately prior to the test.

During the school holidays regular training is not essential at first. Instead, it is highly desirable that the children participate in sporting activities other than swimming. Other sports should, in general, be practised as far as time and school commitments allow. In particular, gymnastics, athletics and ball games – at least within the framework of school sports – can be used as additional training stimuli to develop the general performance of the young body as a whole, and to cover a wide range of sporting-action experience.

The first training objective, which is maintained and systematically pursued from the very first year of training, is increased flexibility. For this the children learn ten to twelve standard exercises, which they perform at the start of every training session, at first with supervision and later without. At the technique learning stage visual aids can be used, such as films, slides, videos, diagrams and drawings. Such methods also enhance the teaching of the competitive strokes frontcrawl and backcrawl, together with their associated starts and turns. The correct technical terminology should be introduced during the visual presentation of the movement patterns.

Besides learning the strokes mentioned, plunging and diving from the side of the pool, from a platform or board and ball games in the water should on no account be neglected. The children will look forward more eagerly to the next lesson.

They should be able to move about in the water with the greatest dexterity and versatility. In this way, they will learn the first two strokes and also the subsequent ones, especially the butterfly, with a high-quality technique. The variety of exercises in the water does not of course rule out parts of the lesson being devoted to very concentrated work on the strokes. On the whole, the essential aim of the first training year is for the children to obtain pleasure and enjoyment from movement in the water and for them to feel drawn into their group. If this is achieved, it will not be difficult for them to get used to regular disciplined participation in training sessions. Apart from this basic attitude, the young swimmer must naturally assimilate the major principles of sound hygiene:

- thoroughly drying hair and ears;
- wearing head-covering and warm clothing after training in cold weather;
- wearing bathing slippers;
- taking showers;
- disinfecting feet, etc.

Special nutritional supplements or treatment to promote recovery after physical stress, e.g. massage, are not needed. On the other hand, examination by a sports doctor at least once a year is highly advisable.

At the end of the first year of training what should the young swimmer know, be capable of and demonstrate by his behaviour?

- turn up regularly and punctually for training sessions;
- be able to swim a crude front and backcrawl;

- execute grab start and backstroke start;
- do the flip turn during the crawl;
- do the backstroke tumble turn;
- master the relay takeover with grab start and backstroke start;
- use and explain the technical terms of the swimming strokes mentioned;
- perform ten to twelve mobility exercises independently;
- participate intensively in all school sports;
- do gymnastics or athletics at least once a week;
- use simple hygienic measures regularly.

| TRAINING YEAR | Amount of training | | | | |
	NUMBER OF TRAINING SESSIONS PER WEEK	DURATION OF TRAINING SESSION IN MINUTES	NUMBER OF TRAINING SESSIONS AND WEEKS PER YEAR	DISTANCE OF TRAINING PER SESSION AND TRAINING YEAR	NUMBER OF COMPETITIONS PER YEAR
1st	3	65	110 40	500 M 55 km	2–3 within training group
2nd	4	65	150 40	900 M 135 km	4–6 within group and club

| TRAINING YEAR | Content per week (in the water) | | | | |
	TECHNIQUE	BASIC SWIMMING ENDURANCE	BASIC SWIMMING SPEED	SWIMMING SPEED-ENDURANCE	OTHER TRAINING OR PRACTICE
1st	38,5% = 3 × 25 min	—	—	—	23% = 3 × 15 min
2nd	46% = 4 × 30 min	15,5% = 4 × 10 min	—	—	11,5% = 2 × 15 min

| TRAINING YEAR | Content per week (dry land) | | | | |
	MOBILITY (FLEXIBILITY)	MUSCULAR ENDURANCE	EXPLOSIVE POWER	MAXIMUM STRENGTH	OTHER TRAINING
1st	15,5% = 3 × 10 min	—	—	—	23% = 3 × 15 min
2nd	15,5% = 4 × 10 min	—	—	—	11,5% = 2 × 15 min

TABLE 16 Amount and content distribution of training during technique learning period

HINTS FOR THE SECOND YEAR OF TRAINING

In addition to learning breaststroke and butterfly, emphasis is laid on practising the strokes learned in the first year: the frontcrawl and backcrawl are repeated frequently and practised in a variety of situations.

Plunging and diving into the water and playing in the water offer variety and enjoyment, but at the same time extend the range of aquatic movement patterns and experience of movement. By the end of the second training year the children should thus possess considerable agility in the water. This is usually expressed not only in the grace and style of the swimming movements practised, but also in the quick and correct learning of new tasks in the water.

The quality and style of the swimming technique depend not only on the series of exercises, but also to a great extent on the degree of flexibility. The obligatory programme of every age-group swimmer must therefore include regular flexibility training with no long breaks. In the second year some ten new exercises are introduced, particularly for the flexibility of shoulder, hip and ankle joints, as well as the spinal column. These are mainly slow exercises, in which the swimmer's own bodyweight is used for stretching (type-A exercises) and swinging-type exercises for suppleness (C exercises).

A new training aim is the improvement of basic swimming endurance. An improvement can be achieved by:

- the continuous method;
- the interval method, to a substantial extent using short-rest sub-maximal interval training;
- a combination of continuous and interval method.

The initially limited ability of children to swim long distances and their age-related desire for a rapid change in activity is met by sub-maximal quantity interval training. This could, for example, be in the form of 10 x 25 m at an average swimming speed with rest intervals of 10 to 15 sec, or 8 x 50 m with rests of 15 to 20 sec. In the continuous method, longer distances are swum at a uniform pace, which is below that of the above example. The distance can be 100 m to 200 m to start with. By the end of the year it should have risen to about 600 m.

The second half of the year sees the introduction of fartlek (speed-play), which is a combination of the continuous and interval methods. An example of the application of fartlek would be to swim 300 m with 50 m at a gentle pace, 25 m more quickly, and so on.

Basic swimming endurance is improved by training only in the strokes which have been reliably mastered. Butterfly is not used at all because, as fatigue increased, its movement patterns would be 'grooved' with too poor a quality. Extensive or quantity interval training can also be carried out with an alternation of swimming strokes, e.g. as a medley minus the butterfly.

In the same way as there has up to this point been basically no difference between boys and girls in their swimming development, there is also no need for such a differentiation for endurance training. Research has produced no differences between the sexes for endurance training at the age of 8 to 10 years (Gerhardus 1980). Other training stimuli, e.g. the development of speed or strength, should at first be presented in a wide range of activities, e.g. by variety in games on dry land and in the water, in gymnastics and athletics movements and in gymnastics with and without hand apparatus. The activity range is extended by diving and plunging and by aquatic ball games. Since hardly any competitions are organised outside the club in the second year of training, an annual training schedule should only be drawn up if it ensures a systematic alternation of stress and recovery.

The young swimmer should, in addition, take part once or twice a week in an athletics or gymnastics session.

With the mastery of the four swimming strokes, the most important competition rules should be learned and applied in competitions within the club.

Care should be taken in training that swimming technique, and particularly the turns and push-offs, is practised regularly. This also applies to the endurance training periods. From the training group, several equal-sized teams can be formed which compete against each other on a points system over a protracted period in the execution of turns, attendance at training sessions, and so on.

At the end of the second year of training, what should the age-grouper know and be capable of?

- steady pace in crawl, backcrawl and breaststroke from a start;
- crude form of butterfly for 25 m;
- use flip turn in all swimming strokes;
- do 100-m medley;
- perform all the relay takeovers in accordance with the rules;
- explain all the competition rules for the various strokes;
- dive head-first and feet-first from the 3-m board;
- organise aquatic ball games with 5 to 8 fellow-swimmers;
- submerge head-first and feet-first from the surface of the water;
- coordination exercises under water in pairs or groups;

– execute about 20 static and dynamic flexibility exercises for the whole body, the shoulders, arms and feet;
– swim 600 m steadily without a break;
– swim up to 8 x 50 m in the alternating-pull strokes (quantity short-rest interval training);
– swim 300 m in fartlek manner.

HINTS FOR THE THIRD TRAINING YEAR

The third year of training shows for the first time an annual programme that is divided into three large cycles (macro-cycles). The young swimmer gradually takes part in competitions outside the club, even if they are mainly in the form of team competitions. In this way he becomes accustomed at an early stage to the three-peak cycle which at present predominates in competitions.

What is more important, however, is that the division into three main training cycles leads to an earlier variation of training exercises and methods and has a far less tiring effect on children than protracted identical training periods. When the four competitive swimming strokes have been mastered and the amount of basic endurance training increases sharply, there is a danger that a comparatively slow stroke tempo will be too firmly implanted in the swimmer by these training methods and will be difficult to change. This can be systematically countered by short accelerating swimming for 8–12 m, by increasing the movement frequency (or tempo) while swimming (cf. p. 10 f.) and by swimming technique drills, especially by special technique drills for crawl, backcrawl, butterfly and breaststroke (cf. pp. 65–70).

Flexibility training also plays an important role. At first it consists of simple slowly executed exercises with a partner (type-B exercises). These are initially performed under the watchful eye of the coach in order to prevent injuries (torn muscle etc.). For the first eight to ten times the pairs should be formed from the same children if possible. During this period the coach should explain to the young sportsmen the concept of responsibility and respect for one's partner.

General strengthening can also be organised as pairs exercises: if possible these should be arranged immediately after the stretching. It may take the form, for example, of strength exercises against partner resistance (isometric exercises). Another form, which is simple and safe, employs the swimmer's own bodyweight. Examples of this include: front support position and rear support position bends, swing-up to handstand, half-lever support, front and reverse bridge. Two-arm medicine ball throwing (drawn well back over the head) and ball-over-the-rope with a medicine ball combine strengthening with the excitement of a game.

Apart from this, the play-needs of the swimmers and their desire for social acceptance are satisfied by games. Speed of reaction is also stressed by games such as basketball, volleyball, mini-hockey, hand-ball and by continuing with water ball games.

When it is introduced, cross-country running must not be allowed to scare off the young swimmer by the pace being too fast. The swimmer will have a vital need of it in subsequent years as an outdoor stimulus and as a source of fresh air to offset increased indoor training. Because of these objectives there can be no question of running fast; it is rather a question of partial transfer of the cardiovascular training into the fresh air and sunshine. This makes it possible to create variety and to strengthen the swimmer in a healthy environment. The emphasis in the longer runs will consequently be on extremely varied terrain. The running speed is sufficient if the runners can enjoy themselves and talk to each other while running.

Whenever possible, running should be organised in groups. The young swimmer should feel at one with the group and be drawn along by it, especially at times when, if he had been on his own, he would have given up out of fatigue or simply because he didn't feel like carrying on. It is through such experiences of 'community' and group feeling that the team-related behaviour, or team spirit, can be reinforced.

Team spirit should also provide support in the first competitions outside the club. The stress of performing under the critical eye of spectators should not be experienced initially as an individual competition. While success or failure ought to make a deep impression on the young swimmer, it must not be allowed to shatter him. In general, a team victory is a positive experience for a young sportsman, while defeat as a group can be coped with more easily than failure in an individual competition.

As far as acquisition of knowledge is concerned, major attention is paid to the rules of a healthy lifestyle: the ratio of sleeping time to time awake, sensible eating and drinking habits, precautions against illness and injury, avoidance of alcohol, smoking and drugs. The swimmers are also encouraged to observe their physical behaviour before and after competitions: sleep, in particular, has to be monitored. In cases of sleeplessness the swimmer should be aware of diversionary measures such as reading, doing crosswords or watching films.

	Amount of training				
TRAINING YEAR	NUMBER OF TRAINING SESSIONS PER WEEK	DURATION OF TRAIN- ING SESSION IN MINUTES	NUMBER OF TRAINING SESSIONS AND WEEKS PER YEAR	DISTANCE OF TRAINING PER WORKOUT AND TRAINING YEAR	NUMBER OF COMPE- TITIONS PER YEAR
3rd	5 (or 6)	65	190 to 230 40	1300 M 247(—300km)	6–8 relay races
4th	5 (or 6)	90	190 to 230 40	1900 M 360(—437km)	8–12 relay and team races

	Training content per week (in the water)				
TRAINING YEAR	TECHNIQUE	BASIC SWIMMING ENDURANCE	BASIC SWIMMING SPEED	SWIMMING SPEED- ENDURANCE	OTHER TRAINING OR PRACTICE
3rd	18,5% = 3 × 20 min	38,5% = 5 × 25 min	—	—	12% = 2 × 20 min
4th	13% = 3 × 20 min	45% = 5 × 40 min	—	—	11% = 2 × 25 min

	Content per week (dry land)				
TRAINING YEAR	MOBILITY (FLEXIBILITY)	MUSCULAR ENDURANCE	EXPLOSIVE POWER	MAXIMUM STRENGTH	OTHER TRAINING
3rd	15,5% = 5 × 10 min	—	—	—	15,5% = 2 × 25 min
4th	11% = 5 × 10 min	9% = 2 × 20 min	—	—	11% = 2 × 24 min

TABLE 17 Amount and content distribution of training during basic training

At the end of the third year of training, what ought the age-group swimmer to know and be capable of?

- swim all four competitive strokes correctly;
- accelerate over short distances and swim on at a steady pace;
- perform at least three drills per stroke from memory;
- swim 800-1000 m frontcrawl continuously;
- run gently for up to half an hour in the woods or open country;
- together with a partner, perform 5–8 flexibility exercises and a similar number of isometric strength exercises;
- execute long two-handed medicine ball throws after taking the ball well back over the head;

- support his own bodyweight in front-support position, half-lever position, bridge and handstand against a wall;
- take part in a sports game for its full duration;
- throw, catch and pick up a water polo ball one-handed;
- behave appropriately before and during a team competition: warm up, keep warm, stay with team, cheer on fellow-swimmers.

HINTS FOR THE FOURTH TRAINING YEAR

The new training objective introduced in this year is improvement of general muscular endurance (cf. pp. 160 ff.). This can be improved by other sports, such as athletics, apparatus and floor exercises, games (e.g. badminton), or cycling. It can also be developed at circuit training stations, with the alternate loading of arms, legs, front trunk and back.

Despite the general nature of muscular endurance training, the muscles of the arms, shoulders and trunk should be stressed more frequently. This is done initially with exercises using one's own bodyweight, e.g. 'easy' press-ups (arms on a bench), with expanders and with a medicine ball, e.g. throwing it up and catching it.

Stretch cords and dumb-bells can also be used for this objective. For example, the ends of a stretch cord can be pulled upwards at the sides, with the swimmer standing on the cord with both feet. The dumb-bells can, for example, be raised from and lowered to the side, in front of and behind the body.

The swimming actions do not figure at all in general muscular endurance training: it is carried out in sets containing as many repetitions as possible, against a small resistance. Because of the alternation of muscle groups, muscular strain does not occur as a result of muscular endurance training. These problems occur because the start of the season has been too vigorous, after a long break in training or after an extra big increase in intensity. It can be rectified by gentle continuous swimming, hot baths, 'alternate' showers and by self-massage (cf. TABLE 25).

In the fourth year of training the repertoire of swimming drills is extended by contrast exercises (pp. 99–102) to sharpen up the young swimmer's pressure-sensitivity for efficient use of the hand and foot-surfaces in the swimming strokes (the 'feel'). The contrast exercises are arranged after the warm-up swim within a training session, but before the speed training (frequent speed variations) or before the training for basic swimming endurance. They should always be performed before fatigue sets in.

Coordination exercises, on the other hand, are used as a warm-up swim. Provided they are not too strenuous, they can even be included in the short-rest interval training, e.g. as breaststroke pull + crawl kick.

The distance of the sets of basic endurance training are now approaching the 2000-m mark. As previously, they are swum alternating with the fast-interval, continuous and fartlek (speed-play) methods. Within the framework of continuous swimming, simple race splits are set and tested: even-pace times, quicker first half, faster second half, faster middle part, etc.

To avoid boredom, the basic endurance programme should be constantly varied. Two or three programmes should, however, be repeated at intervals so that the times swum and the rest intervals can be compared and conclusions drawn for further training (cf. p. 131).

The monotony of protracted training programmes to improve basic swimming endurance can be broken by games of water polo. A game of water polo at the end of a workout is an additional training stimulus for endurance and speed. It can therefore be used twice a week for about 15 minutes to round off a training session. The conditions and rules are simplified for the games:

- wastepaper baskets or buckets instead of goals;
- no goalkeeper;
- no off-side rule;
- no 4-m or 2-m area;
- minimum number of passes by attacking team before shooting.

In diving, the range of dives should be increased with a few new dives and combination dives to be assimilated. Occasional swimming with flippers also produces variety. This can be applied both to the alternate leg-kicks and also to the dolphin kick in every body position. Flipper swimming can be combined with different arm actions. It can also be performed on and under the surface without moving the arms. Swimming with flippers in this way makes it possible to increase the muscular endurance of the thigh muscles and also increase the basic swimming endurance, depending on distances, swimming speed and rest intervals.

Since the amount and intensity of the workload are increased considerably in this training year, recovery measures become more important. This involves the age-group swimmer in learning and applying simple self-massage concepts.

Other recovery measures to be considered include: 'alternate' showers, hot baths and saunas (cf. p. 282).

In the fourth year of training it is fine to introduce the young swimmer to team competitions, e.g. club competitions with points awarded. This kind of team competition demands that the individual swimmer produces his best performance in the form of an individual race. Nevertheless, his personal result does not yet constitute a personal victory or defeat, but is included in the team effort. This means that the individual swimmer is given opportunities for showing how well he can do without having to carry the total risk on his own in front of others.

The warm-up programme and pre-race behaviour should be discussed and inculcated in all participants. The group feeling demands that he prepares to the best of his ability out of a sense of responsibility towards the team. The team spirit can be further strengthened by occasional non-sporting social activities of a cultural nature, such as concerts, cinema, theatre, etc. Other communal pastimes, such as cycle-touring, ten-pin bowling, trips to other sporting events, should be encouraged.

At the end of the fourth year of training, what should the age-group swimmer know and be capable of?

- swim a two-beat and six-beat crawl;
- swim a steady 200-m medley with correct turns;
- do frontcrawl for 1000 m to 1500 m at an even pace and with a faster second half (negative split);
- carry out extended short-rest interval training, e.g. 8 x 200 m with 30-sec rest intervals;
- swim 600 m to 800 m at varied pace (fartlek);
- perform five contrast exercises and five coordination exercises;
- using flippers, swim underwater and do leg-kick and coordination exercises;
- perform at least three different dives, two of them head-first from the 3-m board;
- diving start from blocks with 10-m glide, push-off from wall with 7-m glide;
- take part in a game of water polo under simplified conditions;
- support his own bodyweight in a handstand for, say, 5 to 8 seconds, or walk on his hands for a few metres;
- from a supine position with his legs held down, raise the trunk to the vertical 15 times (hands interlocked behind neck);
- do at least two consecutive circuits with 8 to 10 simple whole-body exercises and a work/rest interval ratio of 30 sec to 30 sec;
- run gently for 30 to 45 minutes in the woods or open country;

- lightly massage his own arms, legs and shoulders;
- make up and carry out a warm-up programme before the first race;
- explain and apply the competition rules relating to starts, false starts, turns and swimming strokes;
- before each competition know the race programme for individual events and team races as well as the system of points scoring or team judging.

HINTS FOR THE FIFTH TRAINING YEAR

A new training objective in the fifth year is improving basic speed (cf. pp. 138–47). Besides speed of movement, this also calls for the necessary power and coordination.

The recommended forms of training to improve basic swimming speed are sprints from a diving start, from a push-off against the wall or from a stationary position in the water. It is important that the distances swum at maximum speed do not exceed 12–15m (anaerobic-alactacid phase). Only in this way, that is before the onset of muscular fatigue (the build-up of lactic acid) can the conditioning of the neuromuscular coordination of acceleration be effective.

To be performed to the best of the swimmer's ability, sprinting calls for thorough warming-up, concentration and mastery of swimming technique. It is advisable to limit the number of sprints per session to 6–8 and to ensure that there are suitable rest intervals of one minute up to several minutes. Such sprint training should be carried out at the most every other day.

Exercises for 'feel for the water' (cf. pp. 93–9) are similarly stressful. It is therefore recommended that only one of the two objectives should be trained for in any one day, i.e. either basic speed or feel for the water. This should be followed by a long period of basic endurance training, amounting to about 2500 m. In addition, in every second or third workout there should be a short period of muscular endurance training (cf. p. 164) in the water. For example, 2 x 200 m arm action with paddles and pull-buoys or with a towed partner who is doing only a leg-kick.

By far the greater part of muscular endurance stress is executed in the form of specific muscular endurance training (cf. p. 162 f.) on dry land: the sets are performed with dumb-bells, barbells (or wall-bars as a substitute), stretch cords and simple pulling apparatus, allowing the three-dimensional patterns of the swimming movements to be simulated. Such pulling exercises can be performed standing with the trunk inclined forwards, seated with the cord attached behind, in a prone or supine position, on an inclined bench or on a raised horizontal surface.

For the pulling exercises in a standing position with the upper body inclined forwards, the attitude adopted should be with one foot forward, knees slightly bent and back extended. It is also an advantage to attach the pulling apparatus to the ceiling for the sitting and kneeling exercises. The exercises stress mainly the propulsive muscles (cf. p. 169 f.). Specific muscular endurance training is conducted in several sets of exercise repeats, with recovery intervals between (cf. TABLE 9). Increased loading (progression) is achieved by increasing each individual set (greater number of repeats), by increasing the total number of sets, or by slightly increasing the pull resistance.

Occasionally playing water polo and underwater swimming with equipment can also be used as mental relaxation (because they involve variety and enjoyment) but these act at the same time as an additional physical training stimulus.

Because of the attendant dangers, swimming underwater with flippers, snorkel, mask (ABC equipment) or with any apparatus at all calls for intellectual challenge with the physical properties of water. There should therefore be theoretical instruction on underwater swimming. Its content should contribute to a deeper knowledge of swimming mechanics.

With a view to understanding future training measures, teaching the essential biological fundamentals for sporting exercise and performance should be stepped up. This will provide extra illustration of the biology instruction received in school. We are thinking in particular of the processes of breathing and muscle contraction, and energy release as a result of the duration and intensity of muscular stress.

The fifth year of training naturally brings with it an increase in basic swimming endurance training.

Since the number of training sessions is not increased compared with previous years and the duration of each session only increases by about half an hour, the greater total metres per workout is achieved mainly by raising the swimming speed (even at longer distances).

This is also in line with the gradual increase in performance as a result of several years of training development.

With normal development of the swimmer and assuming a good race condition, individual competitions can now be tackled. Despite the great mental excitement, these can be suitably coped with, i.e. be experienced as being 'achievable'. In view of girls' earlier maturation the beginning of individual competitions is more important for them than it is for boys. As a basic rule, the longer race distances from 400 m upwards are preferable because they correspond more closely to the natural capacity and previous training schedule than do the 100 m and 200 m. What is more, in the course of the race they offer the younger swimmer a longer period in which to apply what has been learned and practised.

The experienced coach will see to it that the swimmer's expectations are not raised too high, in order to avoid over-stimulation and probable disappointment. He should also ensure that individual competitions alternate with relay and team competitions.

TRAINING YEAR	Amount of training				
	NUMBER OF TRAINING SESSIONS PER WEEK	DURATION OF TRAIN-ING SESSION IN MINUTES	NUMBER OF TRAINING SESSIONS AND WEEKS PER YEAR	AMOUNT OF TRAINING PER SESSION AND PER TRAINING YEAR	NUMBER OF COMPE-TITIONS PER YEAR
5th	5 (or 6)	5 (or 6) × 120	190 to 230 40	1300 M 590–713 km	10—14
6th	SPR.: 6 MD/DS: 8	SPR.: 6 × 120 MD/DS: 8 × 120	230—305 40	3200/736 4500/1370	12—16

TRAINING YEAR	Training content per week (water)				
	TECHNIQUE	BASIC SWIMMING ENDURANCE	BASIC SWIMMING SPEED	SWIMMING SPEED-ENDURANCE	OTHER TRAINING OR PRACTICE
5th	10% = 3 × 20 min	46% = 5 × 55 min	7,5% = 3 × 15 min	—	8% = 2 × 25 min
6th	8,5% = 3 × 20 6% = 3 × 20	41,5% = 6 × 50 58% = 8 × 60	8,5% = 3 × 20 3% = 3 × 10	—	8,5% = 2 × 30 6% = 2 × 30

TRAINING YEAR	Content per week (dry land)				
	MOBILITY (FLEXIBILITY)	MUSCULAR ENDURANCE	POWER	MAXIMUM STRENGTH	OTHER TRAINING
5th	8,5% = 5 × 10 min	10% = 3 × 20 general and special	—	—	10% = 2 × 30 min sports games and cross-country running
6th	8,5% = 6 × 10 8% = 8 × 10	12% = 3 × 30 12% = 4 × 30 general and special	4% = 2 × 15 1% = 1 × 10 general and special	—	8,5% = 2 × 30 6% = 2 × 30 sports games and cross-country running

TABLE 18 Amount and content distribution of training during the period of developmental training

At the end of the fifth year of training, what should the young swimmer know and be capable of?

- swim the front crawl continuously at a constant speed for 1500 m;
- swim short sprints without changing or, in particular, lowering the quality of his swimming technique;
- swim middle distances and sets of repeats with paddles and pull-buoys;
- compete in individual races of 400 m and above and maintain rough splits while doing so;
- perform exercises for 'feel for the water' and incorporate them in the warm-up programme;
- train using muscular endurance sets on dry land on at least two different items of apparatus in the actions of all four competitive strokes;
- swim underwater with compressed-air apparatus or ABC equipment;
- explain water pressure, immersion processes and proper underwater conduct and safety;
- describe and demonstrate the movement patterns of the strokes;
- explain the energy release and mechanism of simple muscle contractions;
- take regular measurements of his own bodyweight, pulse at rest and while working, and make a note of these together with training performances.

HINTS FOR THE SIXTH TRAINING YEAR

In the sixth year the rough classification as sprinter or non-sprinter (cf. p. 238) (= middle-distance and distance swimmer) can be made for the first time. Power training is also introduced (cf. p. 159 f.). This is more important for sprinters than for other swimmers (cf. FIG. 150). On the other hand, the middle-distance and distance swimmers should increase the amount of water training, especially basic endurance training.

Towards the end of the sixth year, maximum-strength training (cf. pp. 153–59) is gradually begun. Power and maximum-strength training take place basically on dry land. They are reduced to zero shortly before important competitions (cf. tapering, pp. 275–77).

General multi-station strength-training apparatus or machines facilitate a successful and injury-free start to training. The young swimmer's movements are guided by the apparatus. The swimmer can concentrate on overcoming as large resistances as possible (for maximum strength) and lesser resistances at maximum speed (for power).

Training with free weights, on the other hand, calls not only for concentration on the strength exercise, but also in addition greater attention to the direction in which the weight has to be moved, where it is to be set down and how it is to be made safe. In particular, before maximum-strength training with barbells, the swimmers must be instructed on the dangers and correct handling of weights.

Training is initially only done lying or sitting down. A partner or 'spotter' assists the training swimmer. It should be explained, before the decision in favour of weight training is made, that exercises using one's own bodyweight, e.g. chin-ups and press-ups under more severe conditions, in themselves constitute maximum-strength training. These should be used first, so that subsequent barbell work produces fresh training stimuli. Muscular endurance occupies more training time than maximum strength and power. On dry land frictional resistance apparatus (workhorse, Exergenie) should primarily be used. Muscular endurance training is easiest to organise in the form of stations, as in circuit training. For example, the arm and shoulder muscles can be stressed at every other station. Only the breaststroke swimmer should stress his leg extensor muscles and the muscles which bring the legs together (adductors, cf. TABLE 106).

In the sixth year of training the swimmer should also increase specific muscular endurance by swimming with paddles and an inflated leg-tube at the same time. Here, again, the breaststroke swimmer is an exception in that he executes fewer arm movements and instead performs his leg action frequently against a resistance board (kick-board) held vertical in the water. He is thus doing the specific muscular endurance training for his legs (cf. p. 164).

The amount of training, which has been increased overall, and the considerable proportion of land training demand that the load be reduced before important competitions. This is a form of tapering, which is taken into consideration for the first time in the sixth training year when planning the total amount of training for the year. The reduced amount of training produced because of the taper is compensated for at other times.

Such planning principles should be explained to the swimmer so that he can understand the reasons and assist in planning. If the training plan is fully understood it is most likely that the young person will accept it and adhere carefully to it.

The swimmer should also learn to monitor himself to an increasing extent and to keep a written record. Weight and pulse checks have so far been entered in the training diary, which should be obligatory for every age-group swimmer. To these are now added entries of sleeping times and working times, as well as observations of significant reactions of the body and mind to training, competition and special events. The records of the amount of training, performances and tests are self-explanatory.

Comments should also be made about the swimming technique, performance strengths and weaknesses and sporting behaviour of other top-level swimmers. Attention should be directed not so much to a comparison of the swimmer's own performances with those of the 'outstanding swimmer', but rather to comparing methods of racing and tactics. To what extent does his swimming speed fall in the 400 m and 1500 m? What is the relationship between the average speeds over 50 m and 400 m? Does he swim long distances at an even or varied pace? In how many strokes is he good or outstanding? How do these relate to my own swimming?

When it concerns top swimmers, worthwhile conclusions can be drawn from such observations and comparisons. It would be desirable for any weaknesses in previous training to be corrected, instead of continually reinforcing existing strengths. This aim can also be applied to the adoption of new swimming technique exercises, and especially coordination drills as well as exercises for feel for the water and for swimming rhythm. For the same reason at least a third of competitions should be in the secondary swimming strokes.

A kind of underwater rugby can be introduced as a variation of training. This can be played with and without flippers and can be used to round off two or three workouts in the week.

After the sixth year of training, what should the age-group swimmer know and be capable of?

- compete in individual competitions in at least three different disciplines between 50 m and 400 m or between 200 m and 1500 m (800 m);
- swim relay races in at least two different disciplines;
- perform at least six different muscular endurance sets using his own bodyweight and with pulling apparatus or strength training machines;
- perform a series of at least 60 double arm-pulls against a slight resistance without a break;
- perform six different swimming drills for 'feel for the water' and six coordination exercises;

- swim a 400-m medley with all techniques perfect and with competence;
- swim 300-m crawl with paddles and inflated leg-tube;
- understand and explain the methods of training he uses most often and experimentally plan a few sessions himself;
- keep a training diary properly and regularly, including details of self-observation;
- make a realistic forecast of his performance and results in his own competition on the basis of performances in training, and compare it with the actual result;
- in the event of there being a great discrepancy between the predicted result and the actual result, examine the way the race was swum, at what point and why the race was swum differently from the way predicted;
- in consultation with the coach, establish the emphasis for sprinting or middle-distance/distance swimming in the next season;
- know the current world record, national record and his own performance.

HINTS FOR THE SEVENTH TRAINING YEAR

The essential difference in training compared with previous years is the systematic stressing of swimming speed endurance (anaerobic lactic acid phase). It should be borne in mind that training to increase speed endurance, even assuming the very highest levels of basic speed and even more so the highest levels of basic endurance, constitutes physically and mentally the hardest load in swimming training. Because of the recovery period of up to 72 hours after speed endurance training (cf. p. 193) the methods of repetition training can only be used twice a week, preferably every other day. Naturally middle-distance swimmers, and sprinters in particular, need a higher degree of speed endurance than distance swimmers do. However because of the necessity for a greater basic endurance capacity, the latter have to cover appreciably greater distances (see p. 230). It therefore becomes necessary to split team training into three groups: sprint, middle distance and distance.

The distance swimmer swims about 50 per cent more units and roughly twice as many metres as the sprinter. These principles alone favour further specialisation depending on main race distances and swimming strokes.

The coach will nevertheless endeavour to arrange as many training sessions for the full group as possible. For one thing, he is obliged to make use of the available water time and training time as economically as possible. Secondly, he would in most cases wish to reinforce the spirit or *esprit de corps* between the individual and the team and make him feel that he is training with his team.

Maximum strength training and muscular endurance training on apparatus (incl. lat. machine), barbells, on the mini-gym and other apparatus, are usually done together in the strength-training room or gymnasium (cf. p. 160 ff.), anyway. On the other hand, because of their different training schedules (cf. p. 166), the periods of muscular endurance training in the water in most cases run consecutively for short-distance and long-distance swimmers.

The distance swimmer needs a greater proportion of total stroke swimming and must accordingly begin this very early in the training session, while the middle-distance swimmer and the sprinter start sets with paddles, leg tubes, resistance trousers, boards etc., for their arm and leg movements.

The suggested training programme for the seventh year includes six total team workouts, i.e. on every afternoon except Sunday. The distance swimmer swims his three extra sessions early in the morning, the middle-distance swimmer doing the same with his two additional workouts (cf. TABLE 19).

In any case, training camps should be organised for all the team during part of the school holidays (Christmas, Easter or Summer). A few of the actual holiday days are left free for family activities. Swimming-specific supplementary sports, such as canoeing, cross-country skiing or rowing, and also cross-country running, can be done together.

Since most of these sports can rarely be indulged in at home, it is convenient to include them in training camp activities. This is supported by the physiological necessity, after heavy swimming stresses, of working on an appropriate general training routine in a different environment. In addition, new undertakings, such as rock-climbing, skiing, a long cycling tour, survival training at a scout camp etc., promote team unity. If after the last competition of the season none of these extra activities have been arranged within the frame-work of a club programme, part of the summer holidays should be used for this purpose.

It seems appropriate to the age and level of dedication to do theoretical work with the young swimmer on the knowledge of special training effects and methods. This includes knowledge of proper sports nutrition and physiotherapeutic recovery measures, such as sauna,

	Amount of training				
TRAINING YEAR	NUMBER OF TRAINING SESSIONS PER WEEK	DURATION OF TRAINING SESSION IN MINUTES	NUMBER OF TRAINING SESSIONS AND WEEKS PER YEAR	AMOUNT OF TRAINING PER SESSION AND PER TRAINING YEAR	NUMBER OF COMPETITIONS PER YEAR
7th	SPR: 6 MDS: 8 DS: 9	SPR: 6 × 140 MDS: 6 × 140 2 × 90 DS: 6 × 140 3 × 90	240 320 42 360	4,200/1000 4,600/1472 5,100/1836	14—20
8th	SPR: 6 MDS: 9 DS: 11	SPR: 6 × 160 MDS: 6 × 145 3 × 90 DS: 6 × 140 3 × 90	248 375 44 460	4,600/1140 4,800/1800 5,200/2400	16—26

	Training content per week (water)				
TRAINING YEAR	TECHNIQUE	BASIC SWIMMING ENDURANCE	BASIC SWIMMING SPEED	SWIMMING SPEED-ENDURANCE	OTHER TRAINING OR PRACTICE
7th	7% = 3 × 20 6% = 3 × 20 5% = 3 × 20	35,5% = 6 × 50 49% = 2 × 70 + 6 × 60 59% = 3 × 75 + 6 × 70	7% = 3 × 20 4% = 2 × 30 2% = 2 × 10	9,5% = 2 × 40 6% = 2 × 30 3% = 1 × 30	—
8th	6% = 3 × 20 5% = 3 × 20 5% = 3 × 20	31% = 6 × 50 50% = 3 × 70 + 6 × 60 60% = 11 × 70	6% = 3 × 20 3% = 2 × 15 1,5% = 2 × 10	13% = 3 × 40 7% = 2 × 40 5% = 2 × 30	—

	Content per week (dry land)				
TRAINING YEAR	MOBILITY (FLEXIBILITY)	MUSCULAR ENDURANCE	POWER	MAXIMUM STRENGTH	OTHER TRAINING
7th	7% = 6 × 10 8% = 8 × 10 8% = 9 × 10	11% = 3 × 30 11% = 4 × 30 13% = 5 × 30 general special specific	5% = 2 × 20 4% = 2 × 20 2% = 1 × 20 general special	11% = 3 × 30 6% = 2 × 30 3% = 1 × 30 general special	7% = 1 × 60 6% = 1 × 60 5% = 1 × 60 sports games cross-country runs
8th	6% = 6 × 10 8% = 9 × 10 8% = 11 × 10	13% = 3 × 40 13% = 5 × 30 11% = 5 × 30 general special specific	6% = 2 × 30 2% = 1 × 20 1,5% = 1 × 20 general special	13% = 3 × 40 7% = 2 × 40 3% = 1 × 40 general special	6% = 1 × 60 5% = 1 × 60 5% = 1 × 60 sports games cross-country runs

TABLE 19 Amount and content distribution of training during elite training period

baths, massage, self-massage, systematic balanced exercises and suitable recovery intervals after hard training loads.

The young swimmer must be fully conversant with the safety rules for maximum strength training, e.g. the use of secure footwear, no lifting of weights with a round back, preliminary warm-up and stretching, clothed upper body, partner 'spotting' when working with free weights, and so on. Since specialisation on the basis of certain criteria (cf. TABLES 21 and 22) and competition performances and training tests provides a series of key data, the swimmer is from now on required to declare his personal targets before each competition season. To this end, he needs to know his opponents, their performance development and the competition calender. The coach ensures that the targets are high but realistic. Such target performances and competition dates should be integrated in the development of the team as a whole. For female distance and middle-distance swimmers, the seventh year of training should produce performances at a national level.

Good motivation and the educational influence of the coach can mean that the young swimmer identifies strongly with the training plans. In conjunction with technical knowledge, this identification generally leads gradually to the swimmer's independence. For this reason, at least at the beginning of the season, the swimmer plans one training session a week himself, the plan being checked by the coach. It is a good sign of growing personal responsibility if the swimmer spends part of his pocket-money on his own training apparatus: paddles, leg-tube, tee-shirts, kickboard, retarding pockets, stretch cord or workhorse/Exergenie equipment, swimming goggles or pull-buoy.

At the end of the seventh year of training, what should the age-group swimmer know and be capable of?

- swim sets of fast interval and repetition training;
- perform at least five different maximum-strength exercises with barbells, lying and seated;
- perform at least five more maximum-strength exercises on fixed apparatus;
- take part in competition at national level as a distance swimmer or middle-distance swimmer;
- if not at national level, swim individual and relay races at regional level;
- (in consultation with the coach) plan, swim and afterwards analyse all main competitions tactically in relation to opponents;

- in a few race-specific dry-land muscular endurance exercises, manage up to 100 repeats without a break;
- during the summer holidays do hard training in swimming-specific supplementary sports (in the open air);
- take part in at least two training camps organised on a team basis;
- observe and analyse the swimming techniques of other swimmers;
- explain and apply training methods and their effect in improving maximum strength and basic endurance;
- plan individual training sessions and amend them in consultation with the coach;
- draw up appropriate menus for meals before races and long training sessions;
- list rivals and their potential performances;
- make realistic forecasts of personal performances for the next season and predict the competition possibilities for the team;
- plan the training 'peaks' and schoolwork, and distribute them over a calendar year.

HINTS FOR THE EIGHTH TRAINING YEAR

Unlike the preceding years, there are no new training objectives in the eighth year. Emphasis is on increasing the training load with regard to:

1 duration: two more hours a week for sprinters and middle-distance swimmers, three for distance swimmers;
2 distance: 140 km more for sprinters, approx. 330 km more for middle-distance swimmers and around 660 km more for distance swimmers, over the year;
3 intensity.

The distance swimmer manages this by training twice a day.

This considerable increase in load coincides with the trained physical condition and physical maturation of the swimmer (cf. FIGS. 3 and 4; TABLE 1). This is why, in particular, the increase in maximum strength and explosive power is arranged at this stage.

It should, of course, be again pointed out that it is the individual degree of development and maturity of each individual swimmer that govern the decision as to whether he should still be on developmental training or be transferred to high-pressure (elite) training. It should also be remembered that girls' development makes great surges in swimming performance less likely after their seventeenth year without heavy training loads. In the eighth year of training the female sprinter should accordingly be producing results of a national performance level. On the other hand, the later and slower maturation of boys means that the coach can expect the first top-class performances from middle-distance and distance swimmers towards the end of this year.

Depending upon sporting experience, the level of intellectual reasoning, maturity and, in cases of good initial instruction, sports knowledge, the swimmer will be ready to discuss his training schedules with the coach more and more often. After discussion, the plans can be modified if this seems necessary. In the first place, the results of the swimming tests carried out periodically (cf. pp. 262–70) can be used as data for planning. Secondly, within the framework of a plan for the swimmer's early life, the competitive swimming and educational/ professional objectives, together with their time scale and position in the plan should form the background for the individual training schedule produced in consultation with the coach.

It is also time to introduce the swimmer to simple methods of mental training, especially for the period prior to competition. This involves relaxation and concentration techniques, autogenic and mental training. The coach often employs a physiotherapist or psychology expert for this purpose. In particular, the stressful emotional condition before the start of an important race, after a defeat and when alone, can be countered by mastering one or other of the control techniques.

The desired inculcation of sporting independence (in planning and execution) and of self-control is directed towards developing mental strength and stability in competitive situations. It also contributes to a large degree to freedom from dependence on the coach in competitions abroad and in selected teams. It thus directly helps in sporting performance.

It should not be overlooked that sports-oriented education has value beyond its obvious direct usefulness in top-class swimming; it contributes to the independence and stability of the young swimmer's personality as a whole.

With regard to water training, the ever-wider endurance base permits hypoxic training. The length of time the breath is held should, however, only be increased gradually. According to the present state of our knowledge, hypoxic training can in no way replace speed endurance training. It is simply a way of getting the swimmer used to suppressing his need to breathe. Also because there are none of the movements of the breathing action, 'stream lining' (minimum resistance) is maintained as fatigue increases during a race (cf. p. 188).

The coach should always ensure that none of the young swimmers suffers from headaches or vertigo after hypoxic training. If they do, their hypoxic training should be cut out and started again slowly after a long period of basic endurance training.

In the eighth year training should emphasise all the techniques of endurance training are completely given over to specific swimming exercises and pulling apparatus. The roller bench or 'sledge' apparatus is therefore adopted for strength training. General strengthening and muscular endurance move to the transition period or to short sessions at the beginning of the macro-cycles. The same goes for cross-country running, cycling, cross-country skiing, rowing, canoeing, etc. These are concentrated into short sessions during the holidays or the transition periods and, by virtue of the changed environment and the different type of exercise, they constitute contrast programmes (cf. FIGS. 203–5).

In addition to maximum strength training, the emphasis from now on is on training for race-specific muscular endurance. The magnitude of resistance or weight and number of repeats should be specific to the main race distance (cf. p. 166).

In view of the great amount of strength training, flexibility plays an important role in preventing the swimmer having to pay for the increased swimming power and muscular endurance by a reduction in the quality of swimming technique.

It should again be pointed out that boys normally have to do flexibility exercises more frequently than girls.

In the eighth year training should emphasise all the techniques of importance in swimming, and it becomes very complex. The amount and intensity have also increased steadily. Reduced training loads and active rests before important competitions are thus physiologically essential in order to recover, to top up the energy stores and to peak at the best performance (tapering, cf. p. 271 ff.). In which way and for how long tapering is most successful has to be determined through trial and error by each swimmer in consultation with his coach. Tapering is, however, never synonymous with complete inactivity.

On the basis of a systematic training build-up over eight years, successful competition results would normally be expected in top-class national swimming. Consequently they offer the chance of taking part in international competitions.

Depending on the personal stage of training and the maturity of the young swimmer, this point may occur earlier or later. It is basically a year or two earlier with girls than it is with boys. Distance swimmers are 18 months or so in advance of sprinters. This means that sprinting performances of national significance can only be expected from a male swimmer after his seventeenth year, i.e. after the completion of his 8-year training build-up.

Nevertheless, on the basis of the development of performances, even for male sprinters, it is possible to reckon on further improvements in competitive performance. Up to this point, with precise planning of the daily schedule, it has been possible to combine sports and school instruction – admittedly with occasional difficulties.

The point has now been reached at which a decision has to be made, by consultation between the swimmer, his parents and coach, as to whether the further increase in the amount and intensity of training with a view to an international swimming career seems promising or whether he should continue to swim but with a reduced training input.

A decision to make swimming the focus of the following years in some circumstances involves a temporary limitation of plans for schooling or professional training.

Continuing swimming as just one area of one's life amongst others does not mean dropping out of the competitive arena altogether but merely reducing the demands. Among sprinters there have been numerous instances of swimmers who, after a thorough long-term build-up, have been able to maintain their performances over a number of years with considerably less training, and some who have even improved their performances. Especially in the framework of team and relay competitions, these swimmers have been able to harvest the fruits of their years of training in the form of sporting success, with the bonus of long trips to competitions and with the social experience of team membership.

At the end of his eighth year of training, what should the age-group swimmer know and be capable of?

- swim hard sets in the form of broken race distances and of a 'simulator' (cf. p. 191 f.);
- perform at least 15 different maximum-strength exercises with pulling apparatus, roller bench and barbells (cf. p. 173);
- step up the number of exercise repeats in the race-specific muscular endurance sets to the number of movements in his main race;
- match the intensity of flexibility exercises to the increased strength training;
- swim short-rest sub-maximal interval training sets, breathing at every sixth to eighth pull (hypoxic training);
- achieve the qualifying times for at least two individual races in the national championships;

- incorporate concentrated periods of several days of swimming-specific supplementary sports and cross-country running in his training;
- explain and apply at least one simple mental self-control technique;
- plan and carry out a micro-cycle, plan a macro-cycle and in consultation with the coach partly execute it on his own;
- deliberately compete in a few races without his coach present;
- discover and make a note of the most successful nature and duration of tapering by trial and error in subsidiary competitions;
- analyse his own competition prospects on the basis of observation of his own performance development over several years, together with that of his rivals;
- compare his own performance development with that of top-class national and international swimmers;
- put down in writing his ideas concerning a multi-year distribution of effort between professional training or education and swimming commitment, as a basis for joint consideration by parents and coach.

18 Criteria for classification into different training groups

Anyone wishing to participate in top-class swimming at a national or international level must, according to his level, i.e. according to his mental and especially physical capabilities, specialise in a main competitive stroke and on a particular distance. His training must be organised accordingly. This does not in any way imply that the three other strokes are no longer used or that no other distances are swum. They increasingly assume a supporting function, pushing the main competitive discipline to the fore. They enhance the wider skill and overall physical condition of the male or female swimmer.

To meet the requirements ideally, each swimmer should from this point onwards be given his own personal training programme, corresponding precisely to the stroke and distance of his specific discipline, to his current performance and to his potential and so on.

In the context of usual training facilities with several swimmers involved, this ideal is hardly practicable, either from the point of view of the extra work for the coach or for reasons of logistics.

To prevent indulging in unnecessary peripheral training, while ensuring at the same time that every swimmer develops all the skills and capabilities needed for his stroke and distance as well as possible through training, an initial classification into specialist training groups should be made from the sixth training year onwards.

There are normally natural limits to sub-division into a large number of training groups. The division depends itself on the other work of the coach and especially on the water space and training time available.

On the basis of knowledge of training physiology and for the reasons of specialisation given above, there should at least be a split into two training groups, each swimming its own training programme: a group of sprinters and a group of non-sprinters. Average race duration for the events provides the basis for this sub-division or grouping of events. In this way, the aerobic and anaerobic capacity can be improved in accordance with competition requirements. This primarily affects energy provision and therefore training can be undertaken largely on strokes other than the specialist stroke.

At the latest a year to 18 months later, i.e. roughly in the seventh training year, the non-sprinters should again be split up into a group of middle-distance swimmers and another group of distance swimmers (cf. TABLE 19). This implies, amongst other things, that at least one lane per group, i.e. a minimum of three lanes, has to be available. The classification is consequently as follows:

	MAIN RACE DISTANCE	RACE DURATION
Sprinters	100 m in all four strokes	Up to approx. 80 sec
Middle-distance swimmers	200 m in all strokes, 200 m medley, 400 m crawl as upper limit	Between around 2 and 5 min
Distance swimmers	800/1500 m crawl, 400 m medley, 400 m crawl as lower limit	Between around 4 and 18 min

TABLE 20 Classification of training groups according to race duration

The strokes which achieve the best results in competition can only be acquired through systematic training which is based on race duration. They are consequently of major importance in the coach's decision in allocating the swimmer to the relevant group. The coach should be capable not only of recognising and promoting the stroke suitable for each swimmer, but also of correctly estimating the race distance most favourable for each individual.

Decisions are still being made through which the sport of swimming annually loses swimmers of both sexes as a result of incorrect estimates or the complete absence of classification procedures. For the swimmers concerned this means great disappointment over the wasted time and effort put into training. In a few blatant cases the swimmer has not achieved his potential personal best performance because he has been swimming the 'wrong' stroke or the 'wrong' distance.

What method does the coach use in practice, after about five years of training, to recognise the stroke and distance in which each individual swimmer will produce his or her best performance in competition?

From certain characteristics or criteria, the coach can systematically obtain indications as to whether someone will achieve better performances over long distances or the sprint distances, using frontcrawl or breaststroke.

There are two different groups of characteristics:

1 Characteristics of competitive swimming stroke;
2 Characteristics of race distance.

ASSESSMENT OF THE COMPETITIVE STROKE

If all four strokes have been thoroughly practised during the first five years of training, the coach is in possession of empirical values for his young charges (see TABLE 21):

1 Degree of mastery of individual strokes.
2 Competition results in all strokes.
3 Preference for a particular stroke on the part of the young swimmer or an inclination towards all four strokes (medley).
4 Performance of rivals in age-groups and open classes at local, regional and possibly national level.

NAME	MASTERY OF STROKE	COMPETITION RESULTS	MOTIVATION	PERFORMANCE OF OPPOSITION
Butterfly				
Backstroke				
Breaststroke				
Crawl				
Medley				

Possible gradings:
++ = excellent   − = poor
+ = good   − − = extremely poor
o = moderate

TABLE 21 Decision criteria chart for choosing swimming stroke

On the basis of these criteria the coach should decide, in consultation with the swimmer, in which area the relatively best competition results are being obtained. For example, in a case of competent mastery of all four strokes, and despite a personal preference for the breaststroke, the decision may go in favour of the medley if the opposition is weaker at a local and regional level. Such a decision also has the advantage that the medley combines all four strokes and is frequently won on the breaststroke stage.

The above table can be used to take the various influencing factors into account, to make them clearer and to facilitate the decision in favour of a particular swimming stroke. The coach should, for each swimmer, enter the four empirical values as objectively as possible in the table and then, in consultation with the swimmer, reach a decision concerning a main stroke. If the coach does not feel capable of filling in all four columns straight off, he should pay particular attention to the areas of uncertainty for a time.

ASSESSMENT OF THE RACE DISTANCE

The question to be answered is: Is the young swimmer a 'typical' sprinter, is he more inclined towards the middle distances or is he a 'typical' distance swimmer?

In order to answer this question scientifically and not, as is often the case, leave it to chance, the coach should observe the following aspects:

1 How does the swimmer's performance over long, hard endurance sets (e.g. 10 x 200 m with 20-sec rest intervals) compare with the other members of the training group?
A = above average;
B = average;
C = below average.
2 How does the swimmer react when confronted with such a set?
A = positively (he swims the sets willingly and with enthusiasm);
B = with indifference (swimming the sets out of a sense of duty and without any particular involvement);
C = negatively (he does not enjoy swimming such sets and has to be driven).
3 How should his muscular strength be graded in accordance with TABLE 21, measured from:
– the number of repeats in chin-ups;
– number of repeats of dips (alternatively press-ups);
– height of vertical jumps.

A swimmer who is graded A for all the aspects probably has all the prerequisites for a successful distance swimmer. One who obtains a C classification throughout can be regarded as a 'born' sprinter.

In the sporting world these two extremes are rarely encountered. Most young swimmers will be classed as A in a few aspects, in others as B or even C. In such cases the coach must resort to the additional knowledge of which capabilities predominate in the swimmer: speed or endurance.

	HEIGHT OF VERTICAL JUMP	DIPS
Female sprinters	40 cm or more	At least two more repeats than the average for the training group (♀)
Female non-sprinters	30 cm or less	At least two repeats less than the average for the training group (♀)
Male sprinters	42 cm or more	At least two more repeats than the average for the training group (♂)
Male non-sprinters	40 cm or less	At least two repeats less than the average for the training group (♂)

TABLE 22 Height of vertical jump and max. number of dip repeats (FIG. 166) as supplementary guide in classifying sprinters and non-sprinters

In doubtful cases it would be appropriate to carry out a precise diagnostic investigation at an official sports-medicine research centre. Such a facility is of course at the present time only available to members of a national squad. In any case the decision regarding emphasis on sprinting, middle-distance or distance swimming should only be made after careful consideration.

In connection with the last-named group, it should also be mentioned that there are untold swimmers who could, on the basis of their physical talent, be outstanding distance swimmers but who are put off by the distance training required and who, for this reason, can at best become moderate sprinters or middle-distance swimmers. This illustrates how competitive swimming with its different race distances also calls for different degrees of mental ability, which likewise have to be further developed by training. For the distance swimmer this implies the ability to go on even when fatigue or boredom occur. In this connection, one of the coach's important tasks is to make the long distances more attractive, in order to win over young swimmers with the best physical capabilities to these forms of stress and to the corresponding race distances.

FIG. 209 Vertical jump to establish take-off power. Left: starting position. Right: height reached in jump

19 Organisation of swimming training

Before dealing with the planning of individual training sessions let us turn our attention to the spatial arrangement of practice and training activities: the so-called forms of organisation.

The simplest form of organisation is swimming in line. The swimmers swim side-by-side along or across the pool and walk back to the starting point round the edge of the pool.

Applications of the line include training for basic swimming speed and exercises for a perfect breaststroke or butterfly stroke. In both cases each swimmer needs a reasonable amount of space and a smooth water surface.

If several lines follow one another these are referred to as waves (FIG. 210a). When two lengths are swum in direct succession in wave formation, one wave can start from one side and can be followed on the way back by a wave from the other side.

For practising and training on the spot, e.g. alternate leg-kicks in a vertical position with the arms raised, preference will be given to a free-standing arrangement or a circle.

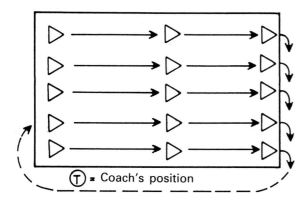

(T) = Coach's position

FIG. 210a

Exercises involving a partner can be performed in pairs. Partner organisation is also suitable for forms of resistance training. One example which could be quoted is towing a partner to improve the propulsive arm muscles.

By varying the types of work a greater overall load can be achieved than would be possible if only one type of exercise was used. For this method of training the organisation of stations is recommended. After the repetition of a fixed number of exercises or lengths, or after a certain load duration without a recovery interval has elapsed, the training is continued with a different stroke on the next length (station) and so on. A typical example of this is circuit training (cf. p. 252), which can be applied in a similar manner to water training. What can also be considered is a combination of swimming stress on one length, followed by a station for press-ups at the edge of the pool, a different swimming load on the next length, and a strength training exercise for the leg extensors at the pool edge, and so on.

If no strokes or drills are to be repeated at the same location or if there is to be no chain or circle swimming in the same lane, we talk of an exercise lane. At every turn, the exercise lane presents a fresh task, but always in a forward direction.

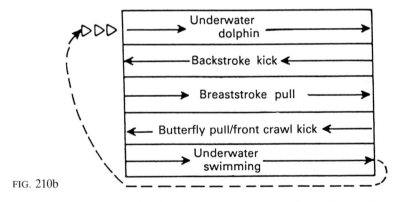

FIG. 210b

One organizational form which has become common throughout the world is the 'conveyor belt' or chain swimming. The swimmers swim on the right-hand side of the lane in one direction and back along the left, when viewed from the starting end (FIG. 210c).

In an extensive interval training set of, say, 30×50 m frontcrawl on 50 seconds, in theory ten swimmers can train in a 25-m lane if each of them starts 5 seconds behind the one in front: $10 \times 5 = 50$ sec, so that there is still a 5-sec gap between the last and first participants, since the first one started at zero on the timescale. This example assumes, however, that all swim at roughly the same speed and that they can at least maintain the 'turn-round' time of 50 seconds. Otherwise the starting intervals would have to be increased to 10 seconds, which would restrict the chain to five swimmers.

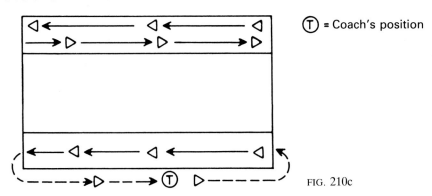

FIG. 210c

In a set of 20 × 100-m crawl on 1:45 min, with 5-sec starting intervals, a maximum of eight swimmers can use a 25-m lane if the average swimming time is 1:20 min or more: 5 × 8 = 40 sec, i.e. the last swimmer starts 35 seconds after the first, so that at 40 seconds the lane is again free for the first swimmer.

If the swimmers are capable of swimming faster, the number of swimmers in the chain is reduced. The following rule-of-thumb can be used to calculate the number of participants:

$$\frac{\text{Average time for two lengths}}{\text{Interval between starts of two swimmers}} = \text{No. of swimmers in chain}$$

With starting intervals of only 5 seconds, there is a danger that the first swimmer, because he is leading, will put more into it physically and be more determined than those behind him who are practically swimming in his wake. For this reason starting intervals of 10 seconds produce a greater independence of the determination applied by each swimmer, but they reduce the number of participants per lane by half.

If several lanes are available for a large training group with swimmers using all four swimming strokes, the organisational problem is that of distributing them over the lanes in such a way that each individual is loaded in the best possible way.

If, for example, two 25-m lanes are available for 16 swimmers, it is recommended that the group be divided on the basis of swimming speed rather than swimming stroke. The chain arrangement can also be organised with a walk back along the poolside (FIG 210c).

20 Examples of training sessions

min	Monday	Tues	Wednesday
0–	TRAINING – running, skipping – obstacle races incl. climbing over bar	Free	TRAINING – running and reaction game 'Fire/Water' – mobility training
10–	– game: ball over rope		and learning a new exercise
20–	– learn and perform flexibility exercises		– in groups of 2 and 3: lift partner, carry partner, 'piggyback', 'wheelbarrow'
30–	– practise: crawl kick		– practise: crawl pull and complete action
40–	– learn: crawl pull and complete crawl action		– learn: crawl breathing 8 × 1 width crawl with 1 × breathing, arbitrary swim- back
50–	– 'Who can do more than 50-m crawl		– running dive from 1-m board with
60–	kick in 2 minutes?'		long glide – plunge from edge
65–	Ball over rope in water		of pool and retrieve rings from bottom

FIG. 211 Example of the most effective distribution of 'training days' over the week, and the content per session during the basic learning period

Thurs	Friday	Sat	Sun
Free	TRAINING – group forms a circle, on a signal one child is chased by another around the circle dodging in and out back to position – shadow running in twos and threes – leg-kicking handstand ('kicking horses')	Free	Free
	– flexibility training with known exercises		
	– learn: diving start and grab start with long glide – practise: crawl breathing		
	– 8-min swim: everyone as far as he can – catching: only in dolphin dive		

EXAMPLE OF A TRAINING SESSION IN THE THIRD TRAINING YEAR

Water training

TRAINING AIMS AND OBJECTIVES	TRAINING METHODS AND FORMS	ORGANISATION: DISTANCE/TIME ALLOCATION
Warm-up: developing feel for water and swimming rhythm	Extensive interval method: 8 × 25 m crawl with 15-sec rest intervals	Chain swimming: 10-sec interval 200 m/6 min
Technique exercises, step-by-step practice of backcrawl arm-movement: alternate pull		
1. Create a mental picture of the action	Re 1: description of action using film, photographs or drawings	Sitting on bench or kickboards
2. Examine movement, perform it without strict attention to detail, not necessarily S-pull but smooth action	Re 2: 'Windmill circling' backwards	Wave formation across shallow end of pool
3. As 2, but in addition feeling water pressure on palms! Not necessarily S-pull but smooth action	Re 3: Ditto in shallow end of pool with partner between legs, holding legs and pushing partner	Same, but in pairs with partner
4. Without assistance: correct position in water; smooth action more important than S-pull	Re 4: Ditto without partner, but with a leg movement	Wave formation across or along pool 300 m/24 min
Improvement of basic swimming endurance; pay attention to 'high elbow'	Continuous method: 400 m crawl, steady medium speed	Chain swimming: 400 m/10 min
Improvement of aerobic endurance and muscular endurance of legs; watch extended body position	Extensive or short-rest interval method: 6 × 25-m alternate leg-kick without kickboard; 3 × in supine, 3 × in prone position; steady medium speed; 15-sec rest interval	Chain swimming 150 m/6 min
Improvement of aerobic endurance and muscular endurance of arms and trunk; watch 'high elbow'	Extensive interval method: 6 × 25-m crawl pull with pull-buoy; 15-sec rest interval	Chain swimming: 150 m/5 min
		Approx. 1200 m/50 min

Land training

TRAINING AIMS AND OBJECTIVES	TRAINING METHODS AND FORMS	ORGANISATION: DISTANCE/TIME ALLOCATION
Warm-up – increase pulse rate – increasing muscle blood flow – protection against risk of injury – warming up muscles – neuromuscular preparation for subsequent stress	Gymnastics and athletics exercise forms: skipping, running on spot, 1 min each	Free-standing in room approx. 3 min
Improve stretch and suppleness:	Flexibility training:	Free-standing around coach
Re 1 and 2: flexibility in hip and lumbar region	1. Standing with trunk bent forwards, bend twice to each foot (knees straight)	15 to 20 repeats per exercise
	2. Legs hip-width apart, hands on hips, head held steady: circle from hips in both directions	
Re 3 and 4: flexibility of shoulder joint	3. Forward circling of arms with left, right and both arms; also reverse circling	
	4. Arms behind head; bend one arm, grasp elbow with other hand and pull it behind the head to the opposite side; ditto with other arm	
Re 5 and 6: improve flexibility in hip joint and and spinal column	5. Sitting with legs outstretched and apart, alternately bend forward to each leg	Between the various exercises, shake out and loosen up the stressed muscles
	6. In hurdling position, bend well forward twice to extended and to bent leg	
Re 7: flexibility of hip joint	7. Adopt 'breaststroke sitting position'	

TRAINING AIMS AND OBJECTIVES	TRAINING METHODS AND FORMS	ORGANISATION: DISTANCE/TIME ALLOCATION
Re 8 and 9: improve flexibility of ankle joints	8. Sitting on heels, support hands alongside knees: raise knees from floor	
	9. Seated balance: hands supported behind body, legs extended, make circles with feet (slow circles as large as possible)	
Re 10: flexibility of spinal column	10. 'Candle': place alternate feet or knees on floor behind head	
		approx. 25 min

EXAMPLE OF A TRAINING SESSION IN THE FOURTH YEAR

(middle of 2nd macro-cycle)

Water training

TRAINING AIMS AND OBJECTIVES	TRAINING METHODS AND FORMS	ORGANISATION: DISTANCE/TIME ALLOCATION
Warm-up: during endurance load as combination exercise	Extensive short-rest interval method: 12 × 50 m alternation of crawl pull + dolphin kick with back-stroke simultaneous pull + alternate kick	Chain swimming: on 1:30 sec 600 m/18 min
Swimming-technique exercises: preparation of a stroke variation	Two-beat crawl: – single-arm pull with one kick of opposite leg (other arm resting on a kick-board); – same exercise other way round – also without board – steady complete action with attention on one leg; – likewise with other leg	One length each in consecutive waves 350 m/10 min

TRAINING AIMS AND OBJECTIVES	TRAINING METHODS AND FORMS	ORGANISATION: DISTANCE/TIME ALLOCATION
Swimming-techniques exercises: contrast exercises	Breaststroke: ¼ length with fists and ¾ length with open hands	One length each in consecutive waves 250 m/8 min
Improving basic endurance	Continuous method: max. distance at steady-speed crawl in 12 min	Chain swimming: 10-sec gaps approx. 700 m/12 min
Team-spirit/game experience; muscular endurance stress on leg muscles; short-term intensive loading in swimming action	2 × 5 min 'push ball' game with large light hollow rubber ball (approx. 80 cm) and flippers: goal is scored by touching opponents' wall of pool	Across any part of pool (approx. 12.5 m × 10 m) 12 min
		Approx. 1900 m/60 min

Land training

TRAINING AIMS AND OBJECTIVES	TRAINING METHODS AND FORMS	ORGANISATION: DISTANCE/TIME ALLOCATION
Warm-up	– gentle running: trotting, running with high knee raising, running on heels, trotting, side-gallop, gallop	Circle
	– Walk, cartwheel, walk, forward roll, walk, swing up into leg-kicking handstand	1 or 2 large waves across pool 5 min
Flexibility	– stretching rear trunk sitting with straight legs: touching toes, head to knee, chest on thigh; backward roll until toes touch floor and knees are against ears	Free-standing
	– stretching front of trunk sitting on heels: supporting at sides with arms, lay upper body back to the floor	

TRAINING AIMS AND OBJECTIVES	TRAINING METHODS AND FORMS	ORGANISATION: DISTANCE/TIME ALLOCATION
	– standing in straddle position, stretching sides of body: springy bending to side with arms held together above head	
	– 3 stretching exercises with partner for arms, shoulders, trunk	In pairs
	– 3 stretching exercises with partner for feet, legs, hips	
	– arm swings in circle forward and contrarotating	Free-standing
	– leg swings forward, back and to sides	/10 min
Muscular endurance with emphasis on arm and shoulder muscles; general endurance	Circuit training at 12 stations (Fig. 212)	30–sec exercise, 30–sec rest interval; as many repeats as poss. at each station 1 circuit/15 min

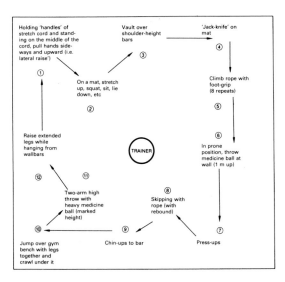

FIG. 212 Circuit training with emphasis on arm and shoulder muscles (example)

EXAMPLE OF A TRAINING SESSION FOR A SPRINTER IN SIXTH YEAR OF TRAINING

(3rd macro-cycle; 1st meso-cycle)

Land training

TRAINING AIMS AND OBJECTIVES	TRAINING METHODS AND FORMS	ORGANISATION: DISTANCE/TIME ALLOCATION
Flexibility	After 20 jumps on the spot: – stretching exercises against a wall – stretching exercises with a towel – stretching exercises for feet by pulling with hands – arm swings in different direction at different speeds – leg swings – trunk circling	Free-standing at edge of pool /10 min

Water training

TRAINING AIMS AND OBJECTIVES	TRAINING METHODS AND FORMS	ORGANISATION: DISTANCE/TIME ALLOCATION
Warm-up as combination exercise and basic-endurance stress	10 × 50 m (25-m butterfly pull with crawl kick plus 25-m crawl)	Chain swimming: on 60 sec, gap 5–10 sec 500 m/10 min
Basic swimming endurance and local endurance of propulsive leg muscles	8 × 50 m backcrawl kick with closed arms held back	Chain swimming on 1:15 min, gap 5–10 sec 400 m/12 min
Local endurance of propulsive arm muscles and basic swimming endurance	6 × 100 m crawl pull with leg kick	Chain swimming: on 2:00 min, gap 5–10 sec 600 m/12 min
Active recovery, variety of stroke	200 m gentle backstroke	Chain swimming: 100 m/2 min
Starting technique, reaction and basic speed	8 × dive start at a signal and 12.5 m sprint in main competitive stroke (swim on easily for 25 m)	In wave formation on 2:00 min 200 m/16 min

TRAINING AIMS AND OBJECTIVES	TRAINING METHODS AND FORMS	ORGANISATION: DISTANCE/TIME ALLOCATION
Turning technique and basic speed	6 × start, turn and 12.5m sprint in main stroke	In wave formation, exercise approx. every 2:00 min approx. 200 m/30 min
Improvement of basic swimming endurance with small proportion of anaerobic energy provision	Extensive/intensive interval method: 16–18 × 50 m in main stroke in 3 sets, progressively from 1st to 6th repeat (6th repeat roughly at full load)	Chain swimming: on 60 sec (for crawl/back-stroke); up to 1:15 min for breast/butterfly; gap 10 sec; 800 or 900 m/18 min
Local endurance of propulsive muscles	200 m crawl action with paddles and leg tube	Chain swimming: 200 m/4 min
Winding down	200 m swum anyhow	Chain swimming: 200 m/4 min
		Approx. 3200 m/approx. 120 min

EXAMPLE OF A TRAINING SESSION FOR A MEDIUM-DISTANCE OR DISTANCE SWIMMER IN SIXTH YEAR OF TRAINING

(3rd macro-cycle, 1st meso-cycle)

Land training

TRAINING AIMS AND OBJECTIVES	TRAINING METHODS AND FORMS	ORGANISATION: DISTANCE/TIME ALLOCATION
Flexibility	After 20 jumps on the spot: – stretching exercises against a wall – stretching exercises with a towel – stretching exercises for feet by pulling with hands – arm swings in different directions and at different speeds – leg swings – trunk circling	Free-standing at edge of pool /10 min

Water training

TRAINING AIMS AND OBJECTIVES	TRAINING METHODS AND FORMS	ORGANISATION: DISTANCE/TIME ALLOCATION
Warm-up with endurance components and different strokes	Extensive interval method: 2 × 200 m medley 2 × 200 m medley leg action 2 × 200 m backstroke	Chain swimming: gap 10 sec, on 4:00 min 1200 m/23 min
Improvement of technique: exercises for feel of water	6 × 25 m: push-off with longest possible glide and an underwater pull to the thighs, then at surface, sculling alongside body with gentle alternate leg-kick	Gap 15 sec, exercise roughly every 2:00 min 150 m/11 min
Technique improvement and improvement of basic speed	6 × 25 m crawl, starting gently and building up to a sprint by feel	In waves, gap 15 sec; on 1:45 min 150 m/10 min
Improvement of basic endurance	Extensive interval method: 20 × 100 m frontcrawl in 4 sets, progressively from 1st to 5th repeat (but still below max.)	Chain swimming: on 1:40 min, gap 10 sec 2000 m/34 min
Local endurance of propulsive arm muscles	6 × 50 m breaststroke pull/double-pulls with crawl kick	Chain swimming: on 1:30 min, gap 10 sec 300 m/approx. 8 min
Basic swimming endurance	400 m brisk backstroke (i.e. rapid pace and tempo)	400 m/6 min
Winding down	300 m swum anyhow	300 m/4 min
		4500 m/approx. 95 min Extra 10 min flexibility training

EXAMPLE OF A TRAINING SESSION FOR A SPRINTER IN EIGHTH TRAINING YEAR

(cf. Fig. 206, Tuesday)
(1st macro-cycle; 2nd meso-cycle; 5th micro-cycle)

Land training

TRAINING AIMS AND OBJECTIVES	TRAINING METHODS AND FORMS	ORGANISATION: DISTANCE/TIME ALLOCATION
Flexibility	Stretching exercises with C, A and B-type exercises	Free-standing at edge of pool /10-12 min
Max. strength/explosive power	– bench presses – standing arm curls with barbell – knee-bends to 90° with barbell (only breaststroke and medley swimmers) – lifting barbell in front of chest up to chin – sit-ups on inclined bench (poss. with weight (e.g. sandbag) behind neck) – from prone position raise trunk (poss. with sandbag behind neck) – arm rotator (inversion) with barbell in supine position – latissimus pull in squat position (on any apparatus) – press from behind neck with barbell (seated, but not for breaststroke swimmer)	In form of stations, each exercise in three sets of 8 repeats with 1–2-min rest interval (2-3 min between stations) /60 min
		Approx. 70 min

Water training

TRAINING AIMS AND OBJECTIVES	TRAINING METHODS AND FORMS	ORGANISATION: DISTANCE/TIME ALLOCATION
Brisk warm-up (intensity equivalent to approx. 2 mmol/l blood lactate)	Continuous method: 600 m, alternation of 50 m back-stroke, 50 m breaststroke, 50 m crawl	Chain swimming 600 m/10 min
Developing local muscle endurance of legs and basic swimming endurance	Extensive interval training 8 × 50 m leg action of main competitive stroke, increasing from 1 to 4	Chain swimming on 1:00 min 400 m/8 min
Developing local muscle endurance of arms and basic swimming endurance	Intensive interval training: 7 (breast) or 8 × 50 m, arm action with pull-buoy, progressive from 1 to 4	Chain swimming on 1:00 min to 1:10 min (breaststroke) 350–400 m/8 min
Limbering up, relaxing	100 m in any manner	Chain swimming 100 m/2 min
Improving basic swimming endurance	Extensive interval training: 12 × 50 m crawl with breathing at every 7th pull, medium speed	Chain swimming on 1:00 min 600 m/12 min
Limbering up, relaxing	100 m in any manner	100 m/2 min
Improvement of swimming speed endurance	Repetition method: 4 × 100 m in main stroke, personally determined max. intensity (approx. 12–16 mmol/l lactate)	In waves, in twos side-by-side in a lane, starting from the top with full competition squad; on 6 min (drying off after each 100 m and limber up on land) 400 m/24 min
Limbering up, relaxing, recovery	100 m in any manner	Chain swimming 100 m/2 min
Improvement of swimming speed endurance	Repetition method: 6 × 50 m in main stroke, at personally determined max. intensity (approx. 12–16 mmol/l lactate)	In waves, in twos side-by-side in one lane; on 3 min 300 m/18 min
Relaxing, recovery (accelerated lactate dissipation)	Continuous method: 900 m, alternating between 50-m backstroke, 50-m breaststroke, 50-m crawl	Chain swimming 900 m/15 min
		3900 m/approx. 170 min

EXAMPLE OF A TRAINING SESSION FOR A MIDDLE-DISTANCE SWIMMER IN EIGHTH YEAR OF TRAINING

(cf. Fig. 207, Monday)
(1st macro-cycle; 2nd meso-cycle; 3rd micro-cycle)

Land training

TRAINING AIMS AND OBJECTIVES	TRAINING METHODS AND FORMS	ORGANISATION: DISTANCE/TIME ALLOCATION
Flexibility	Stretching exercises using type-C, A and B exercises	Free-standing /10 min.
Improving muscular endurance of propulsive muscles	Special strength training: 10 × 90 sec pulling exercises (arm movements of main stroke)	In form of stations: 1. Stretch cord 2 × 90 sec 2. Workhorse or Exergenie 3 × 90 sec 3. Rollerbench 2 × 90 sec 4. Mini-gym 3 × 90 sec with 30-sec rest intervals
	5 × 60 sec as above but with increased resistance	In form of stations: 1. Stretch cord 2 × 60 sec 2. Mini-gym 3 × 60 sec with 60-sec rest intervals /30 min

Water training

TRAINING AIMS AND OBJECTIVES	TRAINING METHODS AND FORMS	ORGANISATION: DISTANCE/TIME ALLOCATION
Warm-up: briskly (intensity equivalent to around 2 mmol/l lactate)	800 m crawl, continuous method	Chain swimming 800 m/11 min
Improvement of local muscle endurance of legs and of basic swimming endurance	Extensive interval training: 6 × 100 m leg-action in main competitive stroke, progressive from 1 to 6	Chain swimming on 2:00 min 600 m/12 min

TRAINING AIMS AND OBJECTIVES	TRAINING METHODS AND FORMS	ORGANISATION: DISTANCE/TIME ALLOCATION
Improvement of basic swimming endurance	Extensive interval training: 4 × 400 m crawl, intensity equivalent to 4 mmol/l lactate	Chain swimming on 5:15 min (girls may be on 5:30 min) 1600 m/21 min
Recovery, loosening up	100 m in any manner	Chain swimming 100 m/2 min
Improvement of basic swimming endurance	Extensive interval training: 16 × 50 m crawl, breathing at every 8th pull, medium speed	Chain swimming on 1:00 min 800 m/16 min
Improvement of local aerobic muscle endurance of propulsive muscles	Extensive interval training: 50, 100, 150, 200, 150, 100, 50-m crawl pull with leg tube, medium speed	Chain swimming on 0:50, 1:40, 2:30, 3:20 min and back 800 m/approx. 15 min
Recovery, limbering up	100 m in any manner	100 m/2 min
Improvement of basic swimming endurance	Extensive interval training: 13 × 100 medley, progressive from 1–4	Chain swimming on 1:45 min (girls may be on 2:00 min with only 11 repeats) 1100–1300 m/ approx. 22 min
Developing speed	8 × 12.5 m sprint, swim on loosely for up to 25 m	In twos, side-by-side, on 1:00 min 200 m/8 min
Recovery, loosening up	100 m in any manner	100 m/2 min 6200–6400 m/ approx. 150 min

EXAMPLE OF A TRAINING SESSION FOR A DISTANCE SWIMMER IN EIGHTH YEAR OF TRAINING

(cf. Fig. 208, Monday)
(1st macro-cycle; 2nd meso-cycle; 5th micro-cycle)

Land training

TRAINING AIMS AND OBJECTIVES	TRAINING METHODS AND FORMS	ORGANISATION: DISTANCE/TIME ALLOCATION
Flexibility	Stretching exercises (type C, A and B)	Free-standing /10 min
Improvement of strength endurance (mainly of propulsive muscles)	– crawl pull with elastic rope – jack-knife – butterfly pull with mini-gym – vertical jumps – crawl pull with Workhorse or Exergenie – raise trunk from prone position – butterfly pull with elastic rope – press-ups – butterfly pull on roller bench – pulling stretch cord with back as attachment point	In form of stations, each exercise being performed every 45 sec at greater intensity, then 15-sec rest; three circuits /30 min

Water training

TRAINING AIMS AND OBJECTIVES	TRAINING METHODS AND FORMS	ORGANISATION: DISTANCE/TIME ALLOCATION
Brisk warm-up (intensity equivalent to about 2 mmol/l lactate)	Continuous method: 1500-m crawl	Chain swimming 1500 m/20 min
Improvement of basic swimming endurance (intensity equivalent to approx. 4 mmol/l lactate)	Extensive interval training: 20 × 50-m crawl 10 × 100-m crawl 5 × 200-m crawl	Chain swimming on 0:45 min, 1:30 min and 2:45 min; (girls may be on 0:50 min, 1:40 min and 3:00 min, with 18, 9 and 4 repeats) 2600–3000 m/ approx. 45 min

TRAINING AIMS AND OBJECTIVES	TRAINING METHODS AND FORMS	ORGANISATION: DISTANCE/TIME ALLOCATION
Recovery, loosening up	100 m in any manner	100 m/2 min
Improvement of local (aerobic) muscular endurance of legs and of basic swimming endurance	Fartlek method: 800-m crawl kick, alternating 75 m at medium speed and 25 m fast	Chain swimming 800 m/15 min
Improvement of local (aerobic) muscular endurance of propulsive arm muscles, and of basic swimming endurance	Extensive interval training: 9 × 150-m crawl pull with leg tube, breathing at every 5th pull, progressive 1–5	Chain swimming on 2:30 min; (girls may be on 8 × every 2:45 min) 1250–1350 m/ approx. 25 min
Acquiring speed	6 × 25 m increasing-speed swims	In twos side-by-side, on 0:45 min 150 m/approx. 4 min
Winding down: recovery, loosening up	100 m in any manner	100 m/2 min 6450-7000 m/ approx. 150 min

21 Methods of determining the level of physical condition – swimming-related tests

Every aspect of training is designed to improve or stabilise the trained condition of the athlete, i.e. in our case to increase and maintain swimming performance.

If the training is to achieve this end it has to conform to the age, the present trained condition, the environment and the time in the annual schedule (cycle), i.e. through training control. It is a well-known fact that the effect of training cannot be simply observed during normal activities.

The coach consequently has to check at regular intervals that the training methods he is using are actually producing the desired effect. In some instances an experienced coach will be able to assess the development of a swimmer's performance over a season from his training results. In the event of an unfavourable development, he will also be able to make appropriate corrections to the training programme in order to achieve the desired improvement. There is, however, a certain element of chance in this procedure.

Instead of relying purely on experience and intuition, the coach should also look for more objective criteria on which to decide with greater certainty whether his swimmer's performance is improving according to plan.

To prevent mistakes not being noticed until a long time has elapsed (weeks or months), he should produce a form of performance diagnosis for each swimmer and keep a written record of his diagnosis. In this way it is possible to detect at an early stage whether a cycle has been too intensively loaded or whether there has been too much training for maximum strength or too little for muscular endurance. It is a matter of regularly checking the actual state of swimming technique and of conditioning which are of greatest importance in swimming.

The actual state can be compared with the current performance of well-known national and international swimmers of appropriate sex, insofar as their values are known. One example is the vertical jump, for which the maximum and average values for world-class swimmers can be found in Counsilman (1980).

Such comparisons provide a reference point of measure for the improvement of those skills or abilities which are furthest below the reference values. The periods of growth and maturation processes (cf. FIGS. 3 and 4) should of course be taken into account when planning such training emphases to compensate for individual 'underdeveloped' or late maturing condition.

For this reason one should not lose sight of the fact that, at the end of the day, it is all the swimming specific conditioning techniques and abilities together that determine competitive performance. It is therefore uneconomical and even counter-productive to improve certain skills to an excessive degree at the expense of others. The neglected skills then become the weakest links in the chain and in their turn reduce overall performance.

Thus, for example, above-average flexibility or maximum strength will not make the anticipated contribution to increased swimming performance if the basic swimming endurance remains under-developed.

The techniques and the physical and mental attributes peculiar to any swimming performance must be improved in a balanced relation-ship. For example, if flexibility has reached a certain trained state, this must just be maintained with a minimal expenditure of time, while other elements of conditioning are improved by a change of emphasis in training.

In order to be able to control this process, both the essential factors in conditioning and also quality of stroke technique must be frequently checked or tested. The next step is therefore regular monitoring of the development of performance, using swimming-related training tests.

The following conditioning factors directly determine competitive swimming performance, as a function of race distance (cf. FIG. 5):

- basic swimming endurance;
- basic swimming speed;
- swimming speed endurance.

At present the most accurate method of determining basic swimming endurance is Mader's (1976) two-distance test, explained on page 134. Because of the apparatus and personnel needed for the test, very few swimmers or club teams are likely to be able to use this method in the foreseeable future.

A simple but nevertheless effective way of determining the state of development of basic swimming endurance related to years of training is the standard continuous load. It consists of swimming 2000 m at as even a speed as possible and in the best possible time. The swimming speed (in m/sec) is then calculated from the time swum and is plotted for each swimmer on a check-chart (FIG. 214).

This test of basic swimming endurance is best introduced in the third year of training. The test distance is initially 800 m, swum in the main competitive stroke (butterfly swimmers do the crawl).

From the fifth year the distance should be increased to 2000 m (cf. TABLE 23). The test should be repeated every two or three weeks. Each swimmer should himself enter the swimming speed he has achieved on the chart (cf. FIG. 214), in order to have a clear and immediate illustration of his development. Besides the distance mentioned, it is recommended that other standard endurance loads also are used at regular intervals, either in the form of over-distances or in the form of interval sets. Interval sets constitute a variation for the swimmer and do not necessarily have to be called tests. By virtue of their comparability, however, they do demonstrate the development of basic swimming endurance in the guise of the average times achieved. Possible pure endurance loads include: 2000 m, 3000 m, 4500 m, 1 hour continuous swimming to cover as many metres as possible.

Examples of interval sets to check basic swimming endurance are:

20 to 50 × 100 m with rest intervals of 10 to 30 sec;
10 to 20 × 200 m with rest intervals of 15 to 30 sec;
6 to 12 × 400 m with rest intervals of 20 to 40 sec;
and so on.

The individual times should be noted for each young swimmer to enable the average times to be calculated.

As an incentive for the swimmers, both the swimming speed in the 2000-m test and the average times for the sets should be plotted and posted by the coach on the club or team noticeboard. In this way the swimmers can accurately follow the course of their development and draw comparisons. The awareness of and the frequent mental confrontation with his own training results ought, of course, to motivate the young swimmer to set himself fresh (achievable) targets and to step up his training.*

From the very first year of training, basic swimming speed can be checked by maximum effort over a short distance of 15 m (cf. TABLE 23). The speed achieved (in m/sec) is a measure of the basic speed. It is calculated by dividing the distance of 15 m by the number of seconds the swimmer takes to cover the distance. If he takes 10 seconds the example gives:

$$\frac{15 \text{ m}}{10 \text{ s}} = 1.5 \text{ m/sec}$$

In order to test swimming speed alone, and not reaction or take-off power, the young swimmer starts from a push-off rather than a dive start. The measured distance should begin 10 m from the start and end at the 25-m mark or at the wall (in the case of a 25-m pool). The stopwatch is started as the swimmer's head passes the 10-m mark. In this way the time can be taken for the last 15 m. The swimmer should endeavour to be accelerating over the first 10 m from the push-off and only swim the last 15 m of the 25 m at maximum speed (TABLE 23).

As they were for basic swimming endurance, so the basic speed results should be regularly plotted and displayed for every member of the team (FIG. 214), so that the individual's development can be followed. The speed test should basically be conducted every three or four weeks, during the last four weeks of each macro-cycle or even once a week (cf. TABLE 23). It is recommended, on the other hand, that swimming speed endurance should not be checked until the seventh training year, using maximum loads lasting about 45 sec.

Taking the basic speed he can achieve over 15 m as his base, the swimmer should swim as far as possible at 90 per cent of this speed (m/sec) after pushing off from the wall. If, for example, a swimmer achieves a basic speed of 1.80 m/sec, he should try to swim as far as possible at a speed of 1.62 m/sec.

In order to measure as accurately as possible the number of metres swum at the speed referred to, there should be marks on the side of the pool at every 5 m. The swimmer himself should work out what intermediate times he needs to achieve at the 20-m, 25-m, 30-m and 35-m marks if he is to maintain the stipulated speed up to those marks.

Using this method, the speed endurance distance can be measured with an accuracy of ± 2 m. If a pace machine is available, its use can

---

* Since this book was first written research has produced a standard test (in principle the same as the 2000-m test), known colloquially as the T.30, which is more accurate.

facilitate speed endurance determination both for coach and swimmer. The calculated speed is set and a note is made of the point in the swim at which the swimmer can no longer keep up with the pace machine.

The distance achieved is plotted as a measure of the swimming speed endurance on the chart (FIG. 214). If training is proceeding properly, this should be increasing as time goes by. The training test described should be employed once a week during the last six weeks of each macro-cycle (cf. TABLE 23). The greatest distance achieved in each year is of course also plotted. It ought to increase from year to year and show a steady improvement.

It is extremely difficult to judge the degree of mastery of swimming technique objectively. One criterion of technique mastery which is reasonably reliable and informative is the number of arm strokes after pushing off from the wall in a 50-m swim.

FIG. 213 Flat-footed squat

There must be a standard speed i.e. standard time for the 50 m which the swimmer should swim. This standard swimming speed should be 85 per cent of his currently achievable best 50-m time. The 50-m time is thus increased by 15 per cent.

The more effective the propulsive phases of each individual swimming cycle are – and this is to serve as a measure of technique mastery – the longer the distance that can be covered per arm pull. In swimming at the speed the coach should ensure that no exaggeratedly long gliding phases are produced, leading to great speed fluctuations, but that the action remains smooth and continuous and is performed in a rhythm close to race rhythm. The number of pulls is likewise entered on the check start (FIG. 214). As mastery of technique increases, this should fall slightly.

Flexibility in the shoulder, hip and ankle joints should be improved until it is certain that any lack of flexibility has no inhibiting influence on swimming technique. For the shoulder joint this means a degree of flexibility permitting double-arm forward circling with extended arms from the buttocks to the stomach, holding a rope or towel at 1½ times shoulder width (cf. FIG. 142). Shoulder width is measured from the outer end of one collar-bone to the outer end of the other. Only for the breaststroke swimmer is this exceptional flexibility of the shoulder joint not absolutely necessary.

On the other hand, for him and for the medley swimmer flexibility of the hip joints is of prime importance. In order to be able to perform an effective 'bent-knee straddle', the breaststroke swimmer should be able to lower his buttocks to the floor between his legs. The legs and feet take up a position like that during press-down in the dynamic straddle (cf. FIG. 120).

The breaststroke swimmer can prove that he has adequate flexibility of his ankle joints by squatting with his hands interlocked behind his neck and with his feet together until his buttocks are touching his heels, without toppling over backwards and without lifting his heels from the floor (cf. FIG. 213).

Specialists in the other three strokes should exhibit the smallest possible gap between toes or balls-of-feet and the floor when sitting with legs, knees and feet outstretched (TABLE 23). From the very first year, such flexibility tests take place regularly every two months. The progress of the development of maximum strength is not tested until the sixth training year, i.e. after maximum strength training has been introduced, when it is checked every three or four weeks. The test relates to the general and special maximum swimming strength.

A good example for determining general strength is the bench press with the greatest possible weight, performed once.

Specific maximum strength can be established in the transitional phase from the pulling to the pushing movement: the swimmer presses with all his might for 2-3 sec with both hands on bathroom scales in front of him at shoulder height on a table or chair. He kneels or stands with trunk erect in front of the scales with his upper arms at right angles to his trunk. The arms are bent at right angles at the elbow joint, as in a butterfly arm-pull.

The final ability to be tested is muscular endurance. It is recom-

TABLE 23

CONDITIONING FACTOR	TRAINING TESTS	TRAINING YEAR IN WHICH FIRST USED	FREQUENCY
1. Basic swimming endurance (BSE)	800-m main stroke in best possible time (speed calculated in m/sec)	3rd	Every 2–3 weeks
	2000 m as above	5th	Every 2–3 weeks
2. Basic swimming speed (BSS)	15 m at greatest possible speed (m/sec) after push off, measured from 10 to 25 m	1st	Every 3–4 weeks (weekly during last 4 weeks of macro-cycle)
3. Swimming speed endurance (SSE)	Swimming at 90% of speed determined in 2, from push-off: distance is measured	7th	Every week (during last 6 weeks of macro-cycle)
4. Technique mastery/ efficiency of propulsive movement	At 85% of basic speed determined in 2, converted to 50 m; swim as few complete cycles as possible in 50 m from push-off	3rd	Every 4 weeks (weekly during last 4 weeks of macro-cycle)
5. Flexibility: Shoulder joint	Forward and backward arm-circling with rope held between hands	1st	Every 2 months
Hip joint	Breaststroke 'sitting position'		
Ankle joint	Breaststroke swimmer: deep squat with feet together and hands behind neck. Otherwise sitting with outstretched legs and extended feet, with minimum gap between balls of feet or toes and floor		

TABLE 23 (continued)

CONDITIONING FACTOR	TRAINING TESTS	TRAINING YEAR IN WHICH FIRST USED	FREQUENCY
6. Maximum strength	General max. strength one-off bench press	6th	Every 3–4 weeks
	Specific max. strength: two-handed press and hold (2–3 sec) (isometric press) against bathroom scales (standing or kneeling; with the elbow and shoulder joints flexed at right angles)		
7. Strength endurance	General: bench presses at 60% of maximum strength determined in 6 until exhausted (number of repeats)	5th	Every 3–4 weeks
	Specific: arm-pull movement with barbell (60% of special max. strength determined in 6) lying on inclined bench until exhausted (number of repeats)		

TABLE 23 Tests to ascertain the state of training of a few important swimming-specific skills

mended that this be measured at regular intervals of three or four weeks, starting in the fifth year of training (cf. TABLE 23).

General muscular endurance can also be tested with the bench press. The swimmer sees how many repeats he can manage at 60 per cent of the weight he achieved once in the maximum strength test.

Swimming specific muscular endurance can be tested with a barbell, for example. Its weight should be 60 per cent of that which was shown on the bathroom scales at maximum pressure for 2-3 seconds. For the specific muscular endurance test the swimmer lies on his stomach with his head down, on a board inclined at an angle of 45 degrees to the floor. Grasping the barbell with both hands, with arms slightly bent, he then performs as many arm movements as he can from the vertical until he touches the board (straight-line butterfly arm-pull). The number of arm movements executed correctly without a rest is taken as a measure of the swimming-specific muscular endurance of the propulsive arm-muscles (cf. TABLE 23).

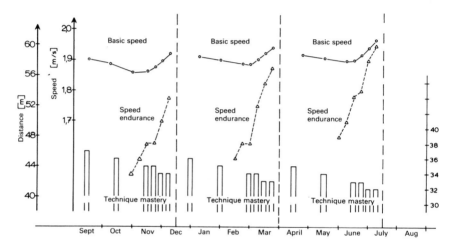

FIG. 214 Example of a completed check-chart for a swimmer, showing the state of training of basic swimming speed, speed endurance and mastery of technique over a training year determined by regular tests

22 Tapering

'Tapering' means controlled peaking and mental-emotional tuning-up for a major competition or competitions. Its effectiveness depends, amongst other things, on having continued to train 'through' less important races or on having omitted only heavy endurance and speed endurance loads during the previous two or three days.

In competitive swimming the tapering period generally extends over 10–18 days before the competition. Its start is arrived at by counting back in days from the date of the swimmer's main race. The first day of a multi-day competitive event can only be selected as the starting point in the calculation if the swimmer is involved in several secondary races on the days before his main race. Otherwise the tapering is shifted and the swimmer continues to train within the framework of tapering. This is particularly applicable to the distance swimmer.

There is a fundamental relationship between the duration of the tapering phase and the length of the complete training period, i.e. with a very short training period, for example, tapering can be limited to just over a week. The duration of the tapering phase is also in inverse ratio to the amount of training: the more a swimmer has trained, the longer he can taper. This means, of course, that a swimmer with a small training load behind him can only allow himself a short taper.

A taper of more than 18 days, on the other hand, is only recommended in cases of obvious drops in performance during full training, e.g. as a result of overtraining. One of the main characteristics of a taper is the clear reduction of the distance used in training to around 80, 60 and 40 per cent of the previous amount for each third of the taper period (see FIG. 215). This rough grading of the distance can be detailed more precisely according to the competitive programme: if the swimmer is faced with a large number of events or several days of competition with a large number of races, he must still swim a lot of distance during the taper. In this case, the last third of the taper period will contain as much as 60 per cent of the original distance, but almost exclusively in the form of aerobic stress.

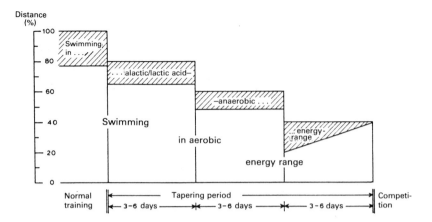

FIG. 215 Reduction in the amount of training and proportions of aerobic and anaerobic swimming during the tapering phase (100% training distance represents normal training)

The training intensity, i.e. the swimming speed, is also reduced as a whole but is interspersed occasionally with periods of maximum intensity: for example, by a test at the race distance, a progressive set loading up to maximum speed, a broken race-distance swim, a test-set at even pace or a length at race speed.

A proportion of the most intensive training loads and one or other of the performance tests should be arranged in the early or mid-morning in order to condition the swimmer to be able to produce a good performance at precisely the time of day at which qualifying races (heats) often take place.

The characteristic feature of these periods of greatest intensity is the race-specific stress. This means that the distance swimmer performs his most intensive programme in the range of basic swimming endurance or aerobic capacity, the sprinter in the basic swimming speed and speed endurance range and the middle-distance swimmer at the overlap between basic endurance and speed endurance. The purpose of the rest of the general training sessions is to maintain the level of all those aspects of conditioning which every competitive swimmer needs, at the state they had teached when the taper began. This is often achieved, despite the reduced distance, by offering a variety of training for basic endurance, basic speed, speed endurance and then technique exercises. Like a précis of a book, all the training aims and methods of the previous cycles occur in a greatly reduced form. The training for maintaining condition between important competitions which follow closely after each other also follows the same principle.

There is a great risk of the tapering phase being almost exclusively sprint training. Over-sprinting occurs particulary in annual or seasonal schedules in which the sprint training is not included until the very end. It must be stressed that such an accumulation of one-sided stresses of the same energy system before a competition (of the creatine phosphate system in the case of sprint training) will result in poor performance in the competition. What is more, the body will not adapt in the short term to changes in stroke technique. Finally, intensive sprint training implies a great neuro-hormonal stress on the swimmer, which does not allow him to recover adequately.

Caution is therefore called for in relation to sprint training in tapering. Not for nothing does Counsilman (1980) recommend: 'Do a fair amount of loosening-up type of swimming. Do some sprinting, but not too much more than you have done over the past month.' This advice for a comparatively large amount of relaxed swimming should be kept in the coach's mind.

The probability of training too hard and too much during a taper is far greater than the likelihood of doing too little. An excessive-stress taper can destroy the success of the training of a whole season. The customary daily training session nevertheless has to be meaningfully filled with swimming in order to prevent idling and a feeling that condition is being lost.

Particularly intensive race-specific loads, be they 4 × 100 m progressive, e.g. in 1:10, 1:08, 1:06, 1:04 min on 6 min for the 100-m backstroke swimmer with a best time of 60 seconds, or a broken 1500 m as 2 × 400 m and 7 × 100 m at race speed with a 10-sec rest interval, are immediately followed by a fairly gentle relaxed swim for up to half an hour.

In addition, the next training session should consist of an endurance programme whose distance has been cut down roughly by half and whose intensity is completely in the aerobic range. Such aerobic swimming limited to 45–60 min is regarded as regeneration or recovery training (cf. Kindermann, 1978).

Sessions of regeneration training are arranged after highly intensive training in the tapering phase, regardless of whether it involves intensive endurance loads for the distance swimmer, speed endurance stresses for the sprinter or training for speed endurance.

The building of those energy reserves which are especially crucial for a race is just as important in the taper, as is the complete recovery of the swimmer from the sum of the preceding training loads. This form of recovery tends to push recharging the energy stores and the mental forces beyond the normal condition (super-compensation). Achieving this aim can be backed up by appropriate reduction of the total training load, by nutritional measures (cf. TABLE 25) and by favourable psychological manipulation.

Satisfactory nutritional measures include electrolytic drinks and high-carbohydrate diet with increased addition of salt (two or three times normal amounts) after intensive endurance training, and a normal diet with preference given to vegetables, non-fizzy mineral water and fruit juices at times of emphasis on speed endurance in training. For basic-speed training it is recommended that the diet be enriched with jellies, rich dishes and jellied meats, as well as fruit juices (cf. TABLE 25).

Psychological manipulation consists in arousing in the young swimmer a realistic expectation of high personal and team performances. This means that the young person should expect a lot from himself and from his fellow-swimmers, but that these expectations should be justified by the training build-up, by the results of training tests and by previous competitive performances. Such optimistic but realistic expectations can only be created on the basis of a sound understanding of the relationships between training and performance, test times and race conditions, and the strengths and weaknesses in the performances of sporting rivals. This calls for a lot of discussion and briefings, both in the form of frequent team-talks and also occasional personal conversations between coach and young swimmer.

Team talks and individual chats occupy a great proportion of the time which has become free as a result of the reduced amount of training. This prevents the unexpectedly large amount of free time leading to enthusiasm-sapping idleness or to excessive indulgence in other activities such as skate-boarding or disco-dancing.

The frequent get-togethers and talks also help to give the young and often not very confident swimmer the feeling that he doesn't have to take on the competition on his own, but can find support and security in the group. This is a sound reason for the recommendation, during the first years of basic learning and basic training that emphasis should be on relay and team competitions rather than individual competitions.

To what extent team meetings can also be used for practising simple methods of self-control or self-regulation, such as deep relaxation of the muscles, or autogenic and mental training, depends on the training age and the maturity of the swimmers, and also on whether the coach has introduced such psychologically-oriented methods in the preceding years of training.

Finally, the team talks also serve swimming purposes. Important technique details are given an airing, before they subsequently become the central point of practical training: fast starts; the rules of starting and turning; breath-holding after start and before touch; energetic touching at finish; and so on.

These technical points of emphasis can be reinforced by the coach showing the swimmer impressive photographs and films. The discussions can also cover tactical considerations, such as relay order, race splits and deliberately saving energy for the most important races.

One must not forget the routine but important briefings about trips: clothing, team behaviour, eating and drinking on the journey, on the significance of competing for the team and for the club.

One essential task for the coach during a taper is to convince his swimmers that they have, through their training up to that point, made the best conceivable preparation for the forthcoming competition and that there is no point in trying just before the competition to catch up on anything which may have been overlooked.

It is inexperienced swimmers in particular who quickly lose confidence because they believe that their performance will have suffered from the reduced training. In such cases the coach must radiate so much calm confidence that such doubts appear groundless. Explanations of the relationship between recovery and performance and including a timed fast set as a test will do the rest. It should be a rule that young swimmers are basically given shorter tapering phases than older swimmers. Besides the psychological reasons cited, this is also justified by different biological adaptation.

The inclusion of strength training in the taper constitutes a difficult problem. While maximum strength and power training do not seem appropriate at such a time (except for sprinters), limited specific and race-specific muscular endurance sets two or three days a week may be recommended when the swimmers have done strength training regularly throughout their preparations.

If a sprinter has done regular strength training over a long period, he should even before muscular endurance training, perform one or two maximum strength and power sets alternating in order to ensure the maintenance of these strength properties during the taper.

This recommendation does not, of course, apply to the last three days prior to the competition. It is a rule that there are three days of recovery between any intensive stress, especially during the last intensive race-specific loads, and the time of the first race in the main competition. This means that during this period there should only be rather relaxed swimming and a few sprints of up to 25 m. Admittedly the energy stores normally top up quickly after the intensive load, but neuro-hormonal regulation needs a longer recovery time (Kindermann 1978).

Naturally there are swimmers who sometimes or even in every taper need this last recovery period (with no training load) to be extended by one or two days. The case may even occur of a swimmer with otherwise average needs having to swim more loosely during the taper as a whole and to swim only a couple of lengths at race speed, because the last macro-cycle or meso-cycle has involved an excessive load. In this context, the following plan (TABLE 24) can only be used as a rough guide to training during the tapering phase. It will certainly need to be modified in the light of the particular conditions of the training group and of the individual swimmer.

The coach will only be capable of arriving at a truly individual taper after several years working with the young swimmer and carefully observing how he reacts to certain aspects of the taper. As the swimmer becomes more experienced and more mature, he will himself be able to feel from the reaction of his body how effective or ineffective the tapering measures are. The coach should therefore frequently use the swimmer's honest answer to the question 'How do you feel in this race speed set?' for a correct estimate of training effect. It may be necessary to have the courage to cut short a set, in spite of the training plan, and replace it by gentle swimming, when the honest

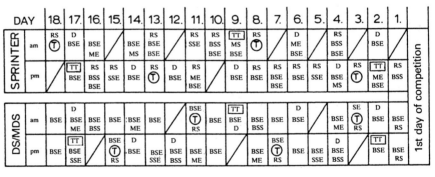

Abbreviations:

BSE = basic swimming endurance	DS = distance swimmer
BSS = basic swimming speed	MDS = middle-distance swimmer
SSE = swimming speed-endurance	D = drills
ME = muscular endurance	T = test
MS = maximum strength	TT = team talk
am = morning	RS = relaxed swimming
pm = afternoon	/ = no training

TABLE 24 Suggested training content and balance during a tapering phase of 18 days in the 7th/8th training year

admission of the swimmer and careful observation by the coach have shown that things aren't just quite right. Such occurrences should not shake the coach's confidence in himself and above all the coach's confidence as seen by the swimmers.

If the training preparation has been systematically drawn up and carefully carried out, what is happening in the majority of such cases is nothing more than fatigue from the preceding training loads. The swimmer simply needs a more active recovery, i.e. a lot of relaxed swimming.

As was mentioned earlier, there is less likelihood of training with insufficient intensity than of doing too much during a taper.

Axioms relating to the duration and extent of a taper

The longer the training build-up has lasted, the longer the tapering period should be made.

The greater the amount of training has been, the longer the taper should last.

The younger the swimmer is, the shorter the tapering phase should be.

The shorter the race distances are, the longer the taper should last.

The more events to be swum or the more competition days with races are in the offing, the greater will be the amount of training during the taper.

The longer the competitive distances are, the more metres have to be swum during the taper.

23 Overtraining

By the term overtraining we mean 'an unplanned reduction or stagnation of performance over a long period in the specific discipline, caused by overstressing the athlete' (Israel 1976).

In rare cases the overstress is the result of excessively extensive or intensive training, but it usually comes about through the combination of training and excessive competitive loads with other physical and mental stresses. Possible physical stresses include:

- lack of sleep (e.g. because of getting to sleep late after evening training);
- minor ailments (e.g. frequent colds);
- local infections (e.g. inflammation of sinuses and gums);
- nutritional deficiencies (e.g. unbalanced diet, mineral shortage);
- stimulants and harmful substances (e.g. alcohol, smoking);
- continuous external stimuli (e.g. light, noise);
- changes in daily routine (e.g. change of school or at school);
- hard physical work (e.g. holiday job);
- free time spent without rest and recovery.

Mental stress factors may be:
- problems at school or work;
- disturbed family environment;
- economic difficulties;
- worry about future and upheavals in life;
- frequent defeats in competition;
- squabbles in squad;
- lack of confidence in coach and training schedule;
- training as a duty without personal conviction;
- monotonous and boring training.

If the overstress is primarily attributable to training, this usually implies errors in training methods, e.g. the omission or neglect of recovery intervals, too rapid an increase in training load, constant high intensity, too many competitions, very one-sided training schedule, etc. (Harre 1977). Overtraining occasionally also occurs as a result of too short a build-up or premature success combined with one of the disturbing factors listed. This is accordingly more likely to occur with an impatient young swimmer than with an older and more experienced swimmer. It is similarly more likely with a distance swimmer and occurs more often after training cycles with repetition or intensive interval training than after extensive continuous stress or overdistance swimming.

An impaired performance resulting from overtraining occurs in most instances after a few other symptoms have manifested themselves. The coach has to be able to differentiate between normal signs of fatigue, which soon disappear, and genuine symptoms of overtraining, which persist for some time. If several of the following symptoms occur, training should immediately be reduced and the sports doctor called in for his advice.

These are symptoms of an excessive state of neuro-autonomic excitation, often called 'staleness', the only ones listed being those which can also be detected by the layman:

- appreciable weight loss;
- loss of appetite, reduced food intake;
- difficulty getting to sleep, disturbed sleep, nocturnal perspiration;
- time-lag in pulse recovery after loading;
- high resting pulse rate;
- pale face, rings round eyes;
- easily excited, tiring quickly;
- moist hands, frequent sweating;
- hands shaking slightly;
- disturbed swimming technique or obvious deterioration of technique;
- frequent false starts in sprint training and in training tests;
- high body temperature.

Israel (1958 and 1976) calls this form of overtraining Basedow overtraining. He considers that the swimmer concerned should be warned that his sporting career is in danger. The following counter-measures are recommended:

- eliminating the physically and mentally stressful factors brought on by the overtraining;
- reducing specific training until it is completely omitted;

- extension of aerobic endurance training (general and basic swimming endurance);
- reduction of all training methods and forms at high intensity (basic swimming speed, speed endurance, intensive interval training);
- light massage, sauna and ultra-violet irradiation;
- relaxing gymnastics and self-control (deep muscle relaxation, autogenic training);
- highly nutritious vitamin-rich mixed diet, not containing too much albumen;
- possibly change of scene to a 'low-mountain climate'.

It is of course so-called Addisonoid overtraining (Israel 1958) that occurs far more frequently than Basedow overtraining because in recent years the amount of water training has considerably increased. There are also excessively numerous periods of energy-sapping intense stresses.

Long-duration identical training of great distances can in itself produce a steady increase in fatigue because the recovery times between the constantly strength-sapping loads become in the long run insufficient to guarantee adequate recovery. Accordingly, Addisonoid overtraining frequently occurs in distance swimmers and middle-distance swimmers who are dedicated in their training.

Addisonoid overtraining is often not recognised as overtraining because in the lower to medium intensity range the swimmer completes training requirements unhesitatingly and without loss of performance. He even continues his daily routine, even if with a certain lack of enthusiasm. Difficulties only start to appear when he tries to swim fast, i.e. in training tests, in simulated competition, e.g. in the broken race distance or in the competition itself.

In such situations the swimmer proves to be incapable of improvement compared with performances achieved previously or even clearly falls short of them. Even then he does not feel exhausted but throughout claims to be in a good enough condition for the races. He maintains, however, that despite his best will and intentions he simply cannot swim any faster.

The danger of undetected Addisonoid overtraining is that the swimmer or coach will, for want of a reasonable explanation, believe that the peak performance has been passed and that there is no point in pressing on. This often leads to disillusionment and a premature end to the swimmer's career.

This failure to recognise an Addisonoid-overtrained swimmer is not helped by the absence of particularly obvious symptoms. All that can actually be detected is the tendency of the body to return quickly to a state of rest. This is manifested in a somewhat greater sleep and rest requirement in the swimmer. A deterioration in swimming technique also sometimes occurs.

All measures against Addisonoid overtraining are aimed at returning the swimmer from the predominantly quiescent condition to a physical and mental preparedness to produce his normal sharpness again. A change of training, however, is essential. If possible there should be a change of environment at the same time. Measures recommended include:

- appreciable reduction of training distances, especially in basic endurance training (little overdistance swimming, hardly any intensive interval training);
- variety of training methods and forms;
- reaction games in water (e.g. black/white) and on land (e.g. volleyball);
- short sessions for basic swimming speed, later also for speed endurance;
- varied gymnastics exercises for skill and agility;
- aggressive sports, 'returning' games, in the open air whenever possible;
- power training with light weights or resistances, later with increasing load intensity;
- participation in games of water polo, fancy diving and scuba diving;
- deep massage (kneading, vibration);
- 'alternate' hot/cold showers or baths, sauna sessions with cold showers;
- possible temporary change of scenery;
- cultural entertainment, music and dancing;
- highly nutritious mixed diet, containing albumen and rich in vitamins;
- occasional luxury of fresh coffee;
- visits to exciting events in other sports.

24 Recovery measures

Measures	Training stress				
	Basic endurance: EXTENSIVE, LONG TOTAL DURATION (AEROBIC)	Speed endurance: INTENSIVE (ANAEROBIC)	Basic speed: INTENSIVE, SHORT DURATION, ALACTIC	Strength: MAXIMUM OR EXPLOSIVE REQUIREMENTS	Muscular endurance: INTENSIVE AND CONTINUOUS
BASIC, APPLICABLE TO EVERY TRAINING STRESS	– Recovery measures, like training measures, eventually lead to over-familiarity effect. They therefore have to be varied continually to prevent them losing their effectiveness. – Extent and intensity of recovery measures depend on age, sex, years of training and trained condition of athlete. – Positive attitude to generate a high emotional condition = making hard training easier to stand. – Employ all means and methods against monotony → music during training, make training environment pleasant → widen interests, encourage hobbies. – Gymnastics and passive flexibility training promote flexibility + strength + recovery. – Plenty of fresh air; brisk walks; sleep with window open. – Autogenic training, breathing exercises: inhale and exhale deeply, hold breath for 3–4 sec, relax muscles slightly → exhale and relax.				
PHYSIOTHERAPY MEASURES	– Hot showers/baths – SAUNA – Whole-body massage by hand	– Hot showers/baths – STEAM BATH (8–10 min duration, 70°C, 100% rel. hum.) – Whole-body massage by hand – Underwater massage: effective only after about 12 hours; take care!	– Hot showers/baths – Vibratory massage	– Hot showers/baths – Partial hand-massage (self-massage) of stressed muscles/ muscle groups – Vibratory massage – Pressure-chamber massage	– Hot showers/baths – Partial hand-massage (self-massage) of stressed muscles/ muscle groups – Vibratory massage – Pressure-chamber massage
Nutrition	– Plenty of carbohydrates – For training session of over 90 min: give drinks rich in carbohydrates during training (glucose concentration not above 15 vol%)	– Vegetables, mineral water	– Rice, icecream, jelly, jellied meats (speed up formation of creatine)	– Albumen supplement (1–1.5 g/kg bodyweight)	
Other	– In hypoxic training: disturbance of albumen conversion → restricted enjoyment of meat and liver → do not perform maximum speed-strength training and hypoxic training simultaneously. – Salt drinking water slightly (lemons, etc), little liquid before meals → gastric juice concentration reduced.				

TABLE 25 Recovery measures after training and competition

25 Technical and training terms

ABDUCTION
Movement of arms or legs laterally outward from mid-line of body.

ACYCLICAL
Not in cycles; composed of different unrepeated movements or techniques, e.g. dive start.

ADDUCTION
Movement of arms or legs laterally inward toward/across mid-line of body.

AEROBIC SWIMMING ENDURANCE
The ability to resist fatigue from long-duration swimming loads with an oxygen supply.

ALACTIC
Energy is provided by the alactic system at the beginning of a load (up to approx. 7-12 seconds), while the ADP is being created from creatine phosphate. This process takes place without oxygen (anaerobically) but causes no lactate accumulation (alactic), provided creatine phosphate is available.

ANAEROBIC CAPACITY
The ability to exhaust the non-oxygen-dependent component of the energy provision process. The greater this capacity is, the greater the lactate accumulations that can be endured while performing. In competitive swimming this is chiefly trained for by 4 or 5 repeats of distances taking about 60 seconds to swim at maximum intensity. Cf. swimming speed endurance.

ANAEROBIC THRESHOLD
The load intensity at which the energy requirement can still be satisfied in the main by aerobic energy provision. The generation and removal of lactate are balanced. This intensity corresponds to a lactate concentration of 4 mmol/l.

ANTEVERSION
Bringing forward an arm or leg.

ATP (ADENOSINE TRIPHOSPHATE)
High-energy chemical substance, representing the only direct energy source for any muscle movement. ATP is present in every muscle cell in a small quantity sufficient for two or three muscle contractions. Reduction to ADP in a muscle contraction is followed by its immediate resynthesis with the help of creatine phosphate (CP), or, in the case of long-duration loads, by means of anaerobic and/or aerobic processes.

BASIC (SWIMMING) ENDURANCE
Type of conditioning which enables any swimming activity lasting longer than 5 minutes to be swum. It is built on a foundation of general (aerobic) endurance but is specific to swimming. Basic swimming endurance is the first part of and the basis of swimming training, both for the training of the swimmer's conditioning and within any of the training cycles. Although the importance of basic swimming endurance in competition increases with race distance, all competitive swimmers have to devote a comparatively large proportion of their training time to increasing basic swimming endurance.

BASIC (SWIMMING) SPEED
The ability to swim a short distance, which must not take more than 7–12 seconds, as quickly as possible.

BASIC TECHNIQUE LEARNING
First period of instruction after learning to swim, in which the four competitive swimming strokes plus starts and turns should be learned, in addition to as many forms as possible of underwater swimming, diving and communal aquatic games. Although learning concerns water activities, this also involves gymnastics instruction, especially maintaining and improving flexibility, as well as general athletic development through gymnastics, athletics and ball games.

BASIC TRAINING
First training stage lasting around two years (following basic technique learning) in which, by frequent swimming technique exercises and regular training the foundation is laid for an increase in average swimming speed and training distance during the developmental training stage. This first stage also includes gradual adjustment to regular training, a sense of responsibility towards the training group and desire to perform well in training and competition. To create the

neuro-coordinative prerequisites for higher and varying swimming speeds, there is an occasional need for practising acceleration at short notice. Besides flexibility, attention is also given to water-related and all-round agility, as well as to balanced strengthening of all the muscle groups.

CIRCUIT TRAINING
Form of training organisation in which different training exercises (movement sequences) are performed at particular stations in a prescribed manner (number, time). The stations are arranged in a circle and are passed through in sequence by those training.

COMBINATION EXERCISE
Swimming technique exercise in which parts of the actions of two different strokes are joined together and performed, e.g. breaststroke arm action combined with crawl kick.

CONDITIONING
The exercise properties which can be changed (by training) and whose force effect permits improved performance. In competitive swimming this conditioning consists of basic endurance, basic speed, speed endurance and muscular endurance, general endurance, maximum strength and explosive power.

CONTRAST EXERCISE
Swimming technique exercise in which the swimmer consecutively performs incorrect and correct movements in order to sharpen up his perception of water pressure, body position and (muscle) power being applied and to use this to advantage in his swimming.

COORDINATION
Collaboration between central nervous system and skeletal muscles within a controlled movement sequence; also the coordination of component movements such as the arm and leg movements in swimming.

COORDINATIVE SKILLS
The motor properties which can be changed (by learning and practice), whose control, coupling and adaptation components permit the improvement and economisation of movement sequences or actions. For swimming, these are water-related spatial awareness, sensitivity to pressure, ability to relax, flexibility, speed of movement and general coordination.

CREATINE PHOSPHATE (CP)
High-energy chemical substance stored in the muscle cells. The amount stored is some four times greater than that of the ATP and collectively covers the energy demand of a maximum load lasting 7–12 sec. The ADP produced by the reduction of ATP is restored to ATP again by CP, thereby ensuring the presence of sufficient ATP at the start of every muscle load.

CYCLE
'Circle'; circular or identical repetition of movement patterns or training aims and methods in periods of equal duration.

CYCLICAL
In a cycle, repeating in a similar manner in the form of a 'circle', e.g. the multiple consecutive arrangement of movement patterns in the butterfly.

DEVELOPMENTAL (BUILD-UP) TRAINING
Second training stage of two to three years (following basic training), in which all the swimming-specific and general endurances, with the exception of maximum strength and high-level speed endurance, are 'built-up' and trained for. Accordingly, participation in competitions, the distance and intensity of training, also increase considerably, especially for the non-sprinter.

ELITE TRAINING
Third training stage of arbitrary duration (following developmental training). Intended to raise the swimmer to a national level and keep him there. This stage of training involves all the swimming-specific and general motor skills at a greater intensity and distance. It includes training for swimming speed endurance and maximum strength, with emphasis dependent upon the swimmer's age, naturally with a clear differentiation between distance swimmers, middle-distance swimmers and sprinters.

ENDURANCE TRAINING
Training to increase either general endurance by repeated movement patterns (e.g. running, cycling, rowing) or basic swimming endurance by swimming using the continuous, fartlek (speed-play), extensive and intensive interval methods.

EXPLOSIVE POWER
The aspect of conditioning of a swimmer which provides the ability to overcome great resistances by rapid contraction of his muscles, e.g. to

accelerate the stationary mass of his body as quickly as possible in the swimming direction in a dive start.

FLEXIBILITY (MOBILITY)

The range of movement at the joints. It depends on the elasticity of muscles, tendons, ligaments and on the structure of the joint. The neuromuscular 'relaxability' also plays an important role. Flexibility therefore occupies a position between conditioning and technique exercises.

GLYCOLISIS

The breakdown of glycogen/glucose into lactate/lactic acid: the anaerobic component of energy provision. The aerobic and anaerobic reduction routes are identical as far as breakdown into pyruvic acid/pyruvate. Depending on the load intensity, the pyruvate is fed into the citric-acid cycle and is reduced with the help of oxygen (aerobically) into CO_2 and water or, at high load intensities (a lot of pyruvate), is reduced to lactate.

HYPOXIC TRAINING

Training with a restricted supply of oxygen. In swimming this is achieved by a reduced breathing frequency. The freestyler, for example, will breathe only on every fourth, fifth or eighth pull. The swimming speed and rest interval for hypoxic training should correspond to those for extensive interval training. Hypoxic training does not – as has often been assumed – produce an improvement in anaerobic performance, but increases aerobic performance. Such training also probably reduces breathing requirements (breathing frequency). It thus has an indirect effect on improving a stroke under competitive conditions, e.g. at the end of a race.

INTERVAL TRAINING, EXTENSIVE

A training method used to improve basic endurance (aerobic capacity): the load norms for swimming should be set as follows:

A = improvement of basic swimming endurance
N = 10–100, depending on distance of repeat
D = 25–400 m
F = in all strokes, even pace and progressive
I = medium intensity, i.e. 77–87% of currently possible race time, equivalent to 4 mmol/l lactate
R = 5–60 sec, depending on distance.

INTERVAL TRAINING, INTENSIVE
A training method for improving both basic endurance and also speed endurance (anaerobic capacity). The load norms for swimming should be set as follows:

A = improvement of basic swimming endurance and speed endurance
N = 10–30, possibly in several sets
D = 50–150 m
F = in all strokes, even pace and progressive
I = high intensity, i.e. 85–90% of the currently possible race time (equivalent to 6–8 mmol/l blood-lactate)
R = 1 to 2 times load-duration, up to max. of 90 sec.

LACTATE
Salt of lactic acid, often used synonymously with lactic acid. Lactate is the end product of the anaerobic conversion process. It is mainly produced with loads lasting longer than 12 seconds and less than 2 minutes, executed at maximum intensity. The unit of lactate (or blood lactate) is mmol/l. Values at rest are approx. 1.5 mmol/l, the highest values of 25 mmol/l being recorded after 400-m races in athletics.

LACTIC ACID
Usually regarded as synonymous with lactate (q.v.).

LACTIC ACID SYSTEM
Energy provision takes place through the lactic acid system with very intensive muscle loads after the majority of the creatine phosphate has been consumed, i.e. after the end of the alactic phase, and the reconstitution of the ADP has to be ensured via glycolisis. This process is likewise anaerobic and reaches its peak after about 45 sec.

LOAD NORM
Quantity for controlling the training load in the form of an indication of the nature or duration or intensity or frequency or break in the training load. Each of the load norms quoted is interrelated to the others; only if all the norms are established is an effective guide to training obtained.

MACRO-CYCLE
The longest identically repeated period in a training year with certain development emphases and training aims/methods.

MAXIMUM STRENGTH
The aspect of conditioning producing the ability to apply the greatest possible muscle tension (static maximum strength) or to overcome the greatest possible resistance (dynamic maximum strength). Maximum strength governs explosive power and, in the case of stresses in excess of 50 per cent of the maximum strength, also determines muscular endurance.

MESO-CYCLE
One of several medium-sized periods within a macro-cycle. It repeats the training aims and methods of the preceding meso-cycles in similar fashion but is intended as a whole to improve performance.

MICRO-CYCLE
Shortest training division within a training year, which is repeated within the meso-cycle in identical fashion with regard to its training aims/methods and its load dynamics.

OVERTRAINING
Unplanned stagnation or deterioration of performance as a result of the coincidence of training stress with other physical and/or mental loads.

OVERTRAINING, ADDISONOID
Stagnation or drop in performance in conjunction with forms of listless sleepy behaviour. It is most likely to occur as a result of protracted periods of extensive middle-distance and distance training.

OVERTRAINING, BASEDOW
Stagnation or drop in performance with attendant phenomena indicating an excessive state of neuro-autonomic excitation, e.g. weight loss, sleep problems, loss of appetite, heavy sweating.

OXIDATION
(Biological) oxidation means the 'combustion' of foodstuffs using oxygen. If there is a sufficient quantity of oxygen, the pyruvate broken down from glucose enters the citric-acid cycle and is reduced with the help of oxygen in stages to CO_2 and water. This produces the ATP required for muscular contraction.

PERIODISATION
Division of a long training period (e.g. training year) into periods – mostly cycles – which have specific functions in producing a high performance.

pH-VALUE
The pH-value is an abbreviation for the value of the hydrogen-ion concentration of an acid or a base. Human blood at rest and at 37°C has a pH-value of 7.38. With intensive physical loads, by virtue of the anaerobic energy supply, a great amount of lactate accumulates and is transmitted by the working muscles to the blood. This lowers the pH-value. At the highest lactate values measured, the blood still only has a pH-value of 6.85.

PRONATION
Inward rotation of the forearm.

REACTION TIME
The time between the occurrence of a signal stimulus (e.g. starting gun) and the appearance of the first visible reaction (e.g. swinging movement).

RECOVERY MEASURES
Systematic speeding up of recovery (regeneration) after hard training. It should ensure that the consequences of the training loads do not lead to overtraining. Recovery measures are divided into active measures (e.g. relaxed swimming) and passive measures (e.g. hot showers, massage, sauna, etc.). The diet matching the training also counts as a recovery measure.

REPETITION TRAINING
Training method for increasing swimming speed endurance (staying power) in which distances of 50 m to 150 m are repeated between 2 and 5 times at the maximum steady (or slightly increasing) speed. Repetition training leads to acidosis (high lactate accumulation) and calls for great willpower from the swimmer. It is therefore appropriate to have comparatively long rest intervals of 2–10 minutes between the individual repeats, and also to carry out repetition training at the most on every second or third day.

RETROVERSION
The taking back or swinging back of an arm or leg. The underwater phase of the crawl pull, for example, constitutes retroversion.

ROTATION
Turning the body or part of the body about its longitudinal axis.

SCULLING
Forward propulsion of a boat or body by helical movements of propellor-like parts, e.g. the blade of an oar or hand/forearm combination, working on the principle of hydrodynamic lift.

SCULLING EXERCISE
Swimming technique exercise in every possible body position and attitude in the water, in which the swimmer moves forward exclusively by helical reciprocating movements of hands and forearms. In order to advance in the water, the hand/forearm movement has to be quick and at right angles to the swimming direction. The pressure surfaces must form an acute angle to their own direction of movement.

SKILLS, MENTAL
The ability to think, feel and want. Insofar as they relate to swimming, they are influenced by the learning and training processes, by success and failure in competition, as well as by failed expectations; they affect the swimmer's attitude.

SPEED
The ability to execute any movements in the shortest possible times.

STRENGTH; MUSCULAR STRENGTH (POWER; FORCE)
Strength as a factor of conditioning is the ability of the muscles (using metabolic processes and cooperation with the nervous system) to overcome an external resistance or to act against it. Muscles can develop strength or power without changing their length (static or isometric behaviour), by shortening (dynamic concentric behaviour) or by lengthening (dynamic eccentric behaviour).

STRENGTH TRAINING, AUXOTONIC
Training to strengthen muscles by exercises in the course of which the muscle tension is increased or varied. The state of tension of the muscles involved is being increased, for example, when a swimmer performs an exercise against the increasing resistance of a stretch cord or expander. Phases of greater and lesser muscle tension also occur, however, during a movement sequence with a barbell.

STRENGTH TRAINING, CONCENTRIC
Strengthening training in which, in overcoming a resistance, the insertions (attachments) of the contracting muscles are moved towards their origins (in the direction of the centre of the body), e.g. in arm curls with a barbell.

STRENGTH TRAINING, ECCENTRIC
Strengthening training in which an external force against the resistance of the contra-acting but capitulating muscles increases the distance between their origin and insertion (attachment). An example of this is the slow lowering of a heavy weight to the floor.

STRENGTH TRAINING, ISOKINETIC
Training to strengthen the muscles in which an exercise is done at a constant speed (but also with constant effort). This is in most cases done against the resistance of an (isokinetic) apparatus, which reacts to an increase or reduction of the speed of movement by increasing or reducing the resistance. Isokinetic strength training originates from physical therapy and in the field of competitive sport is used mainly in swimming, because the swimmer can employ his maximum possible strength by virtue of the speed in each phase.

STRENGTH TRAINING, ISOMETRIC
Strengthening training by muscle contraction without the insertion (attachment) moving closer to the origin of the muscle, i.e. without the muscle length changing. It is best performed against immovable resistances or a resisting partner of similar strength.

STRENGTH TRAINING, ISOTONIC
Strengthening training by muscular contractions with parts of the body moving, keeping the muscle tension as even as possible (but hardly possible). It can be performed using steady movements when inertia has been overcome. In most cases, so-called isotonic strength training is really synonymous with auxotonic strength training.

STYLE
The individual execution of a swimming stroke as a function of conditioning, coordinative and psycho-cognitive skills, as well as of the physical characteristics of the swimmer.

SUPINATION
Turning the forearms outwards.

SWIMMING MUSCULAR ENDURANCE
A specific capability of the muscles as a whole to apply the requisite muscle tension for a certain swimming speed for a particular duration or swimming distance.

SWIMMING SPEED ENDURANCE
The ability to make great use of the non-oxygen-dependent component of the energy provision process, i.e. to incur a high oxygen debt and to endure a high lactate accumulation while swimming. Synonymous with staying power and anaerobic capacity.

SWIMMING TECHNIQUE EXERCISES (DRILLS)
Multiple simple and compound swimming movement sequences, which are executed frequently and under varied conditions in training

in order to refine and implant (consolidate) the swimming technique. The aim is to improve the relationship between energy expenditure and swimming effect (economisation of movement), and to adapt to changes caused by growth, trained condition, state of knowledge, the swimmer's water-related movement sensitivity, as well as by external conditions, e.g. wave formation (movement adaptability).

TAPERING
Systematic 'peaking' and tuning up of the mental and emotional attitude for a competition. Its start is calculated in days counted backwards from the day of a swimmer's main competition (main race).

TECHNIQUE
The currently accepted most favourable solution for a movement pattern or action, e.g. butterfly stroke.

TRAINING
Training is a systematically controlled process, in which, in accordance with an objective, condition changes are produced in sports-motor performances, activity and sporting behaviour by measures relating to content, method and organisation.

TRAINING AIDS
All technical aids for the performance of training: sports equipment such as kickboards or leg tubes, instructional and demonstration aids, marking and measuring equipment, partitions, additional loads in the form of tee-shirts or life-jacket, observational instruments.

TRAINING EXERCISE
A form of training in which, instead of complete or partial movements from swimming strokes, a special movement sequence is used, e.g. crawl arm-pull towing a partner.

TRAINING FORM
The movements or movement sequences with which a training method is applied. In interval training of 20 × 100 m crawl, for example, the form of training is the crawl.

TRAINING PLAN
Training plan or schedule for improving, recovering and maintaining sporting performance. It should start with an analysis of existing sporting ability and individual capabilities (actual condition) and with realistic long-term objectives (desired condition) and should be designed systematically to convert the actual state to the desired state by means of training measures. It is directed primarily at the motor

and mental skills involved in competitive sport, but it has to take account of the necessary extension of sporting savoir faire and attitude changes to become an independent self-assured sportsman. The plan must likewise include existing external training possibilities, as well as the personal talent and state of development of swimmers. A proper plan will provide for regular checks on the trained condition reached as well as on sporting performance; it will be modified on the basis of the results of the checks. The amendments will be directed in particular towards improving the skills or abilities that are less well developed.

VERTICAL JUMP

A standing high-jump to increase explosive power for the swimmer's push-off and start, on the one hand, and on the other to establish his potential sprinting ability or explosive power (of his legs). The difference in height is measured between the points reached when standing and when at the top of the jump.

References

ABSALJAMOW, B., et al: Krafttrainingsapparate in der Vorbereitung von Spitzenschwimmern. Der Schwimmtrainer (1980) 15/16, 24—28.

ATTERBOOM, H.: Sprint Training Programs. Swimming Technique 17 (1980) 4, 26—30.

BARNES, W.S.: The Relationship Between Maximum Isokinetic Strength and Isokinetic Endurance. Research Quarterly 51 (1980) 4, 714—717.

BAUERSFELD, K.-H./SCHRÖTER, G.: Grundlagen der Leichtathletik. East Berlin 1979.

BERGER, P.: Erholung und Regeneration im Schwimmtraining. Jugend und Sport 38, (1981) 8, 236—273.

BERGER, J./LOTZ, I.: Zu einigen Fragen des Krafttrainings im Kindes- und Jugendalter. Theorie und Praxis der Körperkultur 28, (1979) 8, 672—677.

BLASER, P.: Die Entwicklung der konditionellen Fähigkeiten Schnelligkeit und Schnelligkeitsausdauer im Sportschwimmen bei Schülern der 6. Klasse. Theorie und Praxis der Körperkultur 27 (1978) 6, 445—447.

BLEY, W.: Schwimmtraining mit Kindern und Jugendlichen — Zur Problematik der Periodisierung. Munich 1977.

BÜHRLE, M./SCHMIDTBLEICHER, D.: Der Einfluß von Maximalkrafttraining auf die Bewegungsschnelligkeit. Leistungssport 7 (1977) 1, 3—10.

BULGAKOVA, N. SH./VANKOV, A. A.: Die methodischen Prinzipien der Planung des mehrjährigen Trainings von Freistilschwimmen. Der Schwimmtrainer (1980) 15/16, 33—38.

BULGAKOVA, N./VANKOV, SH.: Lebensalter und Schwimmen. SOVIETSKII SPORT 19.4. 1973.

CARL, K.: Talentförderung — Leistungsentwicklung. Probleme einer frühzeitigen Spezialisierung im Training. In: HAHN, E./KALB, G./PEIFFER, L. (Ed.): Kind und Bewegung. Schorndorf, 1978, 173—180.

CLARYS, J.P.: An Experimental Investigation of the Application of Fundamental Hydrodynamics to the Human Body. In: ERIKSSON, B./FURBERG, B. (Ed.): Swimming Medicine IV. Baltimore 1978. International Series on Sport Sciences, Volume 6.

COUNSILMAN, J. E.: Variations in Sprinting Workouts. The International Swimmer 16 (1980) 10, 15—16.

CURRAN, CH. T.: Isometric, Isotonic and Isokinetic Training Programmes and Swimming Performance. The International Swimmer 16 (1980) 6, 11/12.

DALAND, P.: Tapering. Swimming World, 15 (1975) 5, 48—49.

DEMETER, A.: Sport im Wachstums- und Entwicklungsalter — Anatomische, physiologische und psychologische Aspekte. Sportmedizinische Schriftenreihe der Deutschen Hochschule für Körperkultur Leipzig, Bd. 17. Leipzig 1981.

DRAKIC, B./PARANOSIC, V.: Neurophysiologische Aspekte der Angst bei Sportlern.

In: Vanek, Miroslav: Svetovy Kongres ISSP Prague, 3.—9. 10. 1977. Prague 1978, 129—132.

ERIKSSON, B. O.: Physical training, oxygen supply and muscle metabolism in 11—13-year old boys. Acta Physiologica Scandinavia. Supplement 384 (1972), 1—48.

FEIGE, K.: Determinierende Tendenzen in der Leistungsentwicklung von Spitzensportlern — ein Beltrag zum Training und zur Betreuung von Jugendlichen. In: FEIGE, K. u.a. (Ed.): Report on the Third European Congress on Sports Psychology. Schorndorf 1973.

FILIPPOVICH, V.I./TUREVSKII I.M.: Über die Prinzipien der sportlichen Orientierung von Kindern und Jugendlichen im Zusammenhang mit der altersspezifischen Veränderung in der Struktur der Bewegungsfähigkeiten. Leistungssport 7 (1977) 6, 503—508.

FOMIN, N.A./FILIN, W. P.: Altersspezifische Grundlagen der körperlichen Erziehung. Schorndorf 1975.

GAISL, G./BUCHBERGER, J.: Der aerobe Übergang bei 10- bis 11jährigen Sportschülern. Leistungssport 9 (1979) 3, 202—205.

GAISL, G./BUCHBENDER, J.: Veränderungen des aerob-anaeroben Übergangs bei 13- bis 14jährigen Sportschülern nach 3 Jahren Training. Leistungssport 12 (1982) 1, 62—66.

GALBREATH, R.: Sprinters Need More Sprinting. Swimming Technique 16 (1979) 2, 37—39.

GERHARDUS, H.: Über den Einfluß eines Leistungs-Ausdauertrainings im Kindesalter auf kardio-pulmonare Parameter. Dissertation DSHS Cologne 1980.

GÜRTLER, H./BUHL, H./ISRAEL, S.: Neuere Aspekte der Trainierbarkeit des anaeroben Stoffwechsels bei Kindern im jüngeren Schulalter. Theorie und Praxis der Körperkultur 28 (1979) Suppl. 1, 69—70.

HARTLEY-O'BRIEN, S. J.: Six Mobilization Exercises for Active Range of Hip Flexion. Research Quarterly 51 (1980) 4, 625—635.

HIRTZ, P.: Koordinativ-motorische Vervollkommnung der Kinder und Jugendlichen. Körpererziehung 29 (1979) 1, 11—16.

HIRTZ, P.: Koordinative Fähigkeiten — Kennzeichnung, Alternsgang und Beeinflussungsmöglichkeiten. Medizin und Sport 21 (1981) 11, 348—351.

HOFFBAUER, R.: Zum Einfluß von frühzeitiger Spezialisierung und vielseitiger schwimmotorischer Ausbildung auf die wettkampfsportliche Leistung. Thesis, German Sports High School, Cologne, 1980.

HOGG, J.: Beweglichkeitstraining und seine Bedeutung für den Wettkampfschwimmer. Suppl. to Leistungssport (1978) 14, 113—126.

HOLLMANN, W./HETTINGER, TH.: Sportmedizin-Arbeits- und Trainingsgrundlagen. Stuttgart/New York 1976.

HOLMER, I./GULLSTRAND, L.: Physiological response to swimming with controlled frequency of breathing. Scandinavian Journal of Sports Sciences 2 (1980) 1, 1—6.

HOLT, L. E.: Scientific Stretching for Sport. Halifax 1973^2.

ISRAEL, S./BUHL, B.: Die sportliche Trainierbarkeit in der Pubeszenz. Körpererziehung 30 (1980) 5, 193—199.

JOCH, W.: Die Entwicklung der Motorik in der Pubeszenz. Jugend und Sport 33 (1976) 11, 401—405.

JOCH, W.: Motorische Entwicklung und die Probleme der Talent- und einer frühzeitigen Leistungsförderung. Sportpraxis in Schule und Verein 21 (1980) 9, 183—184.

JOCH, W./KRAUSE, J.: Altersabhängige Veränderungen motorischer Schnelligkeitsfaktoren bei Kindern und Jugendlichen von 6 bis 18 Jahren. Sportunterricht 27 (1978) 11, 405—413.

JOCH, W./SCHMIOL, G.: Zu einigen Aspekten der Altersproblematik im Schwimmen. Leistungssport 12 (1982) 2, 107—113.

JOHN, H. G.: Verwirklichung eines kind- und jugendgerechten Weges zum Leistungstraining aus der Sicht des Pädagogen. Der Schwimmtrainer (1980) 13—14, 32—37.

KALGANOV, N. E.: Konsultationen: Besonderheiten der Trockenarbeit in den verschiedenen Altersgruppen (Jugend). Der Schwimmtrainer (1980) 15/16, 22—24.

KASCH, F. W.: Maximal Oxygen Uptake in Older Male Swimmers During Free Swimming and Stationary Cycling. Swimming Medical (1979) 4, 143—146.

KEUL, J., et al.: Biomechanische Grundlagen des Kinderleistungssports. In: DSB (Hrsg.): Belastbarkeit der Kinder und Jugendlichen im Leistungssport. Suppl. to Leistungssport (1982) 28, 28—46.

KIEPER, CH./SCHMIOL, G.: Leistungszuwachs von Schwimmern bei unterschiedlicher Trainingsquantität und Trainingsintensität. Leistungssport 12 (1982) 2, 126—133.

KINDERMANN, W./KEUL, J.: Anaerobe Energiebereitstellung im Hochleistungssport. Schorndorf 1977.

KINDERMANN, W.: Regeneration und Trainingsprozeß in den Ausdauersportarten aus medizinischer Sicht. Leistungssport 8 (1978) 4, 348—357.

KOINZER, K.: Die Berücksichtigung der geschlechtsdifferenzierten Entwicklung im Sportunterict (1). Körpererziehung 29 (1979) 1, 11—18; 2/3, 83—88.

KOMADELI, L.: Sportmedizinische Probleme beim Training mit Jugendlichen. Leistungssport 5 (1975) 1, 74—84.

KÖNNEKER, J.: Zum Problem von Trainingsumfang und -gestaltung im internationalen Schwimmsport — eine Untersuchung an Teilnehmern der Weltmeisterschaften 1979 in Berlin. Thesis, German Sports High School, Cologne, 1980.

MADER, A., et al: Zur Beurteilung der sportartspezifischen Ausdauerleistungsfähigkeit im Labor. Sportarzt u. Sportmed. 4 (1976) 5, 109—112.

MARTIN, D.: Grundlagen der Trainingslehre. Part I Schorndorf 1979[2]; Part II Schorndorf 1980.

MARTIN, D.: Die Ausdauerleistungsfähigkeit im Kindes- und Jugendalter aus trainingswissenschaftlicher Sicht. Leistungssport 10 (1980) 6, 456—463.

MARTIN, D.: Konzeption eines Modells für das Kinder- und Jugendtraining. Leistungssport 11 (1981) 3, 165—176.

MARTIN, D.: Die Leistungsfähigkeit und Entwicklung der Kinder als Grundlage für den sportlichen Leistungsaufbau. In: DSB (Publ.): Belastbarkeit der Kinder und Jugendlichen im Leistungssport. Suppl. to Leistungssport (1982) 28, 47—64.

MARTIN, D.: Leistungsentwicklung und Trainierbarkeit konditioneller und koordinativer Komponenten im Kindesalter. Leistungssport 12 (1982) 1, 14—25.

MATVEYEV, L. P.: Allgemeine und spezielle Grundsätze, die im sportlichen Training zu realisieren sind. Theorie und Praxis der Körperkultur 28 (1979) 9, 737—740.

MATVEYEV, L.P./MOLTSINIKOLOV, K. G.: Über Gesetzmäßigkeiten der beginnenden Spezialisierung im Sport. Theorie und Praxis der Körperkultur 28 (1979) 11, 907—912.

MEINEL, K.: Bewegungslehre. East Berlin 1976.

NEMESSURI, M.: Funktionelle Sportanatomie. East Berlin 1963.

NÖCKER, J.: Belastungsfähigkeit des jugendlichen Organismus in den verschiedenen Entwicklungsstufen. Mat. Med. Nordmark 32 (1980) 4, 177—186.

PLATONOV, W. N.: Concerning the Use of Large Work-Loads in Modern Swimming. Plavanie (1977) 1, 15—18. (translated from the Russian by the USA Swimming Coaches Association).

PLATONOV, V. N./SACHNOVSKII, K. P./YUDIN, V. G.: Wege der Optimierung im

Aufbau der langjährigen Vorbereitung von hochqualifizierten Schwimmern. Der Schwimmtrainer (1980) 15/16, 29—33.

RAHN, S./RÄSCH, W.: Zu Problemen der Gestaltung der Wettkämpfe im Grundlagentraining. Theorie und Praxis der Körperkultur 27 (1978) 10, 684—690.

RAHN, S.: Belastungsgestaltung im Anfängertraining. Theorie und Praxis der Körperkultur 28 (1979) 8, 677—683.

REISCHLE, K.: Chronofotographische Zulängenregistrierung bei Delphin, Rücken und Kraul. Suppl. to Leistungssport (1978) 14, 31—49.

SCHNABEL, G.: Zur Wirkung bewegungs- und Leistungsverwandter Sportarten im Training des Schwimmers. Theorie und Praxis der Körperkultur 22 (1973) 5, 419—427.

SCHROEDER, CH.: Anwendung allgemeiner und spezieller Trainingsmittel im SSG-Training. Körpererziehung 28 (1978) 4, 173—175.

SCHLEIHAUF, R. D.: A Biomechanical Analysis of Freestyle. Swimming Technique II (1974) 4, 89—96.

SHARP, R. L./COSTILL, D. L.: Force, Work and Power: What They Mean to the Competitive Swimmer. Swimming World 23 (1982) 2, 41—43.

SIEGEL, D./DAVIS, CH.: Transfer effects of learning at specific speeds on Performance over a range of speeds. Perceptual Motor Skills 50 (1980) 1, 83—89.

SMIT, P. J./DAEHNE, H. O./VAN WYK, G./STEYN, E.S.: Interval Training and the Progressive Load Principle in Novice Child Swimmers. In: TERAUDS, J./BEDINGFIELD, E. W. (Ed.): Swimming III. Baltimore 1979, 240—249.

STALLMAN, R. K.: Causes of high attrition in competitive swimming. Swimming Technique 13 (1976) 2, 34—40.

STEINER, H.: Auswirkungen des Leistungstrainings auf die psychische Entwicklung. In: DSB (Publ.): Belastbarkeit der Kinder und Jugendlichen im Leistungssport. Suppl. to Leistungssport (1982) 28, 65—73.

STEMMLER, R.: Entwicklungsschübe in der körperlichen Leistungsfähigkeit. Theorie und Praxis der Körperkultur 26 (1977) 4, 278—284.

STIEHLER, G. et al: Methodik des Sportunterrichts. East Berlin 1974.

SWEETENHAM, B.: Micro Cycles. International Swimmer 17 (1980) 4/5, 7—9.

TERAUDS, J./BEDINGFIELD, E. W. (Ed.): Swimming III. Baltimore 1979. International Series on Sport Sciences, Volume 8.

THIESS, G./GROPLER, H.: Die Ausbildung der sportlichen Technik im Anfängertraining mit Kindern. Theorie und Praxis der Körperkultur 27 (1978) 3, 199—201.

TROUP, J./PLYLEY, M./SHARP, R./COSTILL, D.: Development of Peak Performance: Strength Training and Tapering. Swimming World 22 (1981) 8, 25—28.

TSCHIENE, P.: Einige neue Aspekte zur Periodisierung des Hochleistungstrainings. Leistungssport 7 (1977) 5, 379—382.

TSCHIENE, P.: Kritische Überlegungen zur Talentsuche und -förderung. Leistungssport 9 (1979) 3, 158—166.

VAITSEKOVSKI, S. M.: Die allgemeine Konditionsschulung im modernen Training jugendlicher Schwimmer. Der Deutsche Schwimmsport 20 (1970) 46. Suppl.: Für die Mappe des Technikers 3/4.

VILKNER, H.-J.: Zur Vervollkommnung der motorischen Reaktionsfähigkeit in den Klassen 2 bis 6. Körpererziehung 28 (1978) 8/9, 397—402.

VOLKOV, V.M./LUGOVTSEV, W. P.: Zur Begründung des spezifischen Einflusses von Trainingsbelastungen auf die Wiederherstellungsprozesse. Leistungssport 9 (1979) 2, 122—127.

WEICKER, H./SCHUBNELL, M. (Ed.): Sportmedizin im sportwissenschaftlichen Studium. Schorndorf 1979.

WEINBERG, R./BARTHOLD, R. P.: Anxiety, quality of movement and performance. In: VANÉK, M. (Ed.): IV. Svetový Kongres ISSP Prague 3.—9. Oct. 1977. Prague, 1978, 795—797.

WEISS, U.: Belastbarkeit und Trainierbarkeit des Bewegungsapparates bei Kindern und Jugendlichen. Jugend und Sport 37 (1980) 8, 254—258.

WEISS, U.: Belastbarkeit und Trainierbarkeit der aeroben und anaeroben Leistungsfähigkeit bei Kindern und Jugendlichen. Jugend und Sport 38 (1981) 8, 243—247.

WINTER, R.: Zur Beachtung und Nutzung von Altersspezifika der Kindheit im Übungs-, Trainings- und Wettkampfbetrieb der Sportgemeinschaften. Theorie und Praxis der Körperkultur 27 (1978) 10, 772—775.

WINTER, R.: Zum Problem der sensiblen kritischen Phasen der Kindheit und Jugend. Theorie und Praxis der Körperkultur 28 (1979) Supplement 2, 91—92.

WINTER, R.: Grundlegende Orientierungen zur entwicklungsmäßigen Vervollkommnung der Bewegungskoordination im Kindes- und Jugendalter. Medizin und Sport 21 (1981) 9, 282—285.

YAKOVLEV, N. N.: Die biochemische Grundlage der Ermüdung und ihre Bedeutung in der sportlichen Praxis. Leistungssport 8 (1978) 6, 513—516.

Anon: Land Conditioning in the GDR. International Swimmer 14 (1978) 7, 5—6.

Index

abduction, 283
acidosis, 121
action economization, 48
acyclical, definition, 283
Addisonoid overtraining,
    280–1, 289
adduction, 283
adenosine diphosphate
    (ADP), 118
adenosine triphosphate
    (ATP), 118
aerobic capacity, 126
age, starting, 14
alternate starting dives, 84
alternating back starts, 87
anaerobic capacity, 283
anaerobic-lactic acid energy
    provision, 118
anaerobic threshold, 283
ANDFIR, 123–4, 168, 192
anteversion, 284
arm rotator, 180
assessment, 233
    competitive strokes,
        239–40
    physical condition, 262–70
    race distance, 240–2

backstroke, 37–8
    arm action exercises, 61–3
    combination exercises,
        102–3
    contrast exercises, 100–2
    coordination exercises,
        63–4
    leg action exercises, 59–61
    starts, 44–5
    swimming technique
        exercises, 59–64
backward dolphin dive, 82
backward starting dive, 85
Basedow overtraining,
    279–80, 289

basic speed training, 9
basic swimming endurance,
    125–37
    constant-speed sets,
        129–31
    definition, 284
    descending sets, 127–8,
        131
    and general endurance
        training, 126
    intensity, 132–3
    speed, 126–37
    testing, 263–4, 268
    two-distance test, 134–5
basic swimming speed,
    138–48
    definition, 284
    group training, 146–7
    irregular spurts, 146
    sensitising sprints, 146
    sprints, 146
    spurt, quick turn, spurt,
        146
    spurts in middle of pool,
        145
    testing, 265, 268
basic training, 284
basketball, 159
boxing dives, 84
breaststroke, 41–2
    arm action exercises, 77–8
    combination exercises,
        102–3
    contrast exercises, 100–2
    coordination exercises,
        79–82
    leg action exercises, 73–7
    swimming technique
        exercises, 73–82
    turns, 45–7
breathing, 121–2
broken swims, 189, 192, 193
build-up training, 14

bumping race, 148
butterfly, 39–40
    arm action exercises,
        68–70
    combination exercises,
        102–3
    contrast exercises, 100–2
    coordination exercises,
        70–3
    leg action exercises, 65–8
    swimming technique
        exercises, 65–73
    turns, 45–7

canoeing, 163
chain swimming, 244
chinning, 178
circuit training, 104, 244,
    285
classification into training
    groups, 237–42
clothing, maximum strength
    training, 154
combination exercises,
    102–3, 285
competition:
    team, 221
    in the training schedule,
        195–9
competitions, tapering for,
    271–7
competitiveness, mental, 30
composition of training
    programmes, 23–6
conditioning exercises, 30,
    285
contrast exercises, 99–102,
    285
conveyor belt, 244
coordination, definition, 285
coordinative skills, 27, 28,
    30, 285
crawl, 35

combination exercises, 102–3
contrast exercises, 100–2
creatine phosphate (CP), 118, 286
cross country running, 217
cross country skiing, 163
cycles:
definition, 286
the training year, 200–10
cyclical, definition, 286

determination, 30
development psychology, 19–22
development-related training programmes, 8–12
dips, 177
distance, assessment of race, 240–2
dive starts, 43, 44
exercises, 82–7
diving, 214, 220
doctors, 212
dolphin dives, 82
dolphin glide, 87
drag, 149–50

early developers, 16
eighth training year, 232–6, 256–61
elasticity of muscles, 11
elbows, strength training, 169
elite training, 286
transition to, 18
endurance training, 118–22, 234
basic swimming, 30
definition, 286
muscular, 160–7, 168–74
energy supply, 118–22
race reserves, 273
essential skills, 27–32
evaluation, 32
explosive, power training, 159–60, 168–74
explosive power, 286–7

fartlek, 128, 193, 214
feel for the water, 28, 222
exercises to improve, 93–9
gliding exercises, 94–6
sculling exercises, 94, 97–9
feeling for pace, 128
feet, strength training, 172

fifth training year, 222–5
first year of training, 211–13
flexibility, 28, 287
joints, 28
muscles, 11
flexibility training, 104–17, 216, 234
partners, 104
passive 3–S stretching exercises, 105–6
static stretching, 105
type-A exercises, 106–8
type-B exercises, 110–12
type-C exercises, 113–16
warming up, 104
fourth training year, 219–22, 250–2
frog-dive start, 43, 44
frontcrawl:
exercises for arm action, 53–6
exercises for coordination, 56–8
exercises for leg action, 50–3
swimming technique exercises, 50–8

general training methods, 3–4
gliding exercises, 94–6
glycolysis, 118, 120–1, 287
grab start, 43, 44
groups, classification into, 237–42

handstand bends, 177
head, strength training, 169
high-arc dives, 85
high jumps, 159
hips, strength training, 171–2
holidays, 207, 211, 229
hygiene, 19, 212
hypoxic training, 233–4, 287

illness, variety in training and, 4
injuries, training and, 7
intellectual training, 1
interval training, 287–8
isometric training, 156, 157, 181–2

jack-knife, 175
joints, flexibility, 28

jumping, explosive power training, 159
jumping-in, tuck position, 83

knee-bends, 175, 176
knees, strength training, 172

lactate, 288
lactate accumulation, 130, 131, 134–7
lactic acid, 118, 120–1, 288
late starters, 14, 16
latissimus pull, 183
lifestyle, 217
load intensities:
muscular endurance training, 165–6
training cycles, 203, 209
load norm, 288
training, 123–4
long-term training programmes:
composition, 23–6
emphasis, 23–6
planning, 13–22

macro-cycle, definition, 288
maximum strength, 289
testing, 267, 269
training, 150, 153–9, 168–74, 229
medical checks, 212
medicine ball exercises, 160, 179
mental competitiveness, 30
mental condition, pre-race, 274
mental development, 19–22
mental skills, 291
mental stresses, 278
mental training, 19–22, 233
meso-cycle, 289
mobility training, 104–17
monitoring, 32, 226–7
motivation, 231
motor skills, 27
movement pattern, 7, 48
muscles:
alternating tension and relaxation of, 141, 144
elasticity, 11
endurance training, 118–37
explosive power training, 159–60, 168–74
flexibility, 11

maximum strength
    training, 150, 153–9
strength training, 149–50
and swimming speed, 138,
    141
weight lifting, 156–7
muscular endurance, 219,
    222, 226
definition, 292
testing, 267–70, 269
training, 160–7, 168–74

nervous system, speed
    training and, 139
nutrition, 212, 229
pre-race, 274

organisation of training,
    243–6
overtraining, 278–81, 289

partners, organising, 244
pattern learning theory, 7
performance, attitudes to, 30
periodisation, 289
pH-value, 290
physical condition,
    swimming-related
    tests, 262–70
piked start, 43, 44
plunging, 84, 214
press-ups, 175, 176, 177, 179
progressive training, 12, 14
pronation, 290
pull length, 143–4
pulse rate, basic swimming
    endurance, 133
push-offs, 215

race-specific stress, 272
reaction time, 140, 217, 290
recovery measures, 212, 229,
    282, 290
regeneration training, 273
regularity of training, 12
relax, ability to, 28–9
relaxation and tension
    alternation, 141, 144
relays, basic swimming speed
    training, 147
repetition training, 188–9,
    290
retroversion, 290
rotation, 290
running dive, 83

safety rules, 231
schema learning theory, 7
school holidays, 211
sculling, 290
    exercises, 94, 97–9, 291
second year of training,
    214–16
self-awareness, 21
self-control, 274
self-massage, 220
sense of pace, 128
sensitising sprints, 146
seventh training year, 228–32
short-long back starts, 87
short-long starting dives, 85
shoulders, strength training,
    170
sixth training year, 223–8,
    253–5
skills, essential, 27–32
skiing, 163
sleeplessness, 217
speed:
    basic swimming
        endurance, 126–37
    basic swimming speed, 9,
        138–48
    definition, 291
    endurance training, 188–94
speed-play, 128, 193, 214
spinal column, strength
    training, 171
sprint training, 273
staleness, 279
starting age, 14
starts, 43, 44–5
    emotional condition, 233
    exercises, 82–7
    reaction time, 140
static strength training, 155–6
static stretching, 104
strains, training and, 7
strength:
    definition, 291
    and swimming speed, 141
strength training, 104, 149–
    87, 234, 291–2
    for maximum strength,
        150, 153–9, 168–74
    taper, 275
strokes, 42
    assessment of competitive,
        239–40
    backstroke, 37–8
    breaststroke, 41–2
    butterfly, 39–40

consolidation, 48
crawl, 35–6
frequency, 143–4
testing, 266–7, 268
style, 292
supination, 292
swimming speed endurance,
    188–94, 228
definition, 292
testing, 265–6, 268
swimming technique
    exercises, 48–103,
        102–3, 292–3
    backcrawl, 59–64
    breaststroke, 73–82
    butterfly, 65–73
    contrast exercises, 99–102
    feel for the water, 94–9
    frontcrawl, 50–8
    starts, 82–7
    turns, 97–93

tapering, 226, 271–7, 293
team competitions, 221
team meetings, 274
team spirit, 217, 229
team talks, 274–5
technical knowledge, 30
technique training, 7
tension and relaxation
    alternation, 141, 144
tests see assessment
tethered swimming, 55
third training year, 216–19,
    248–50
3–S stretching exercises,
    105
training camps, 229
training control, 32
training cycles, 200–10
training groups, 237–42
training methods, 211–36
training programmes,
    development-related,
    8–12
training schedules,
    theoretical basis, 1–12
training sessions:
    examples, 247–61
    organisation of, 243–6
    variety in, 2–5
training year, dividing up,
    200–10
turns, 45–7, 215
    swimming technique
        exercises, 87–93

underwater rugby, 227
underwater swimming, 223

variety in training, 2–5
vertical jump, 294
volleyball, 159

water polo, 223
water resistance, 149–50
water sensitivity, 28–9, 222
    exercises to improve, 93–9
    gliding exercises, 94–6
    sculling exercises, 94, 97–9

weight lifting, 156–7, 180, 181
wrestler's bridge, 175
written records, 227
wrong/right exercises, 99–102

year, dividing up, 200–10